BEYOND
THE GUNSIGHTS

BEYOND THE GUNSIGHTS

One Arab Family
in the Promised Land

YOELLA HAR-SHEFI

HOUGHTON MIFFLIN COMPANY BOSTON 1980

Library of Congress Cataloging in Publication Data

Har-Shefi, Yoella.
  Beyond the gunsights.

  1. Palestinian Arabs — Israel — Social conditions.
2. Israel — Ethnic relations.   I. Title.
DS113.7.H33713   301.45′19′2705694   79–24407
ISBN 0-395-27614-4

Printed in the United States of America

V 10 9 8 7 6 5 4 3 2 1

ACKNOWLEDGMENTS

THIS BOOK would be burdened by more blunders and inadequacies, and certainly would have reached the shelves much later, had it not been for the generous help and warm encouragement of my many mentors, collaborators, and friends, all of whom gave unstintingly of their counsel, their time, their labor, and their sympathy.

I am honored to express my gratitude to Shoshana Hasson, Naomi Balak, Ruth Kornblit, Lilian Servier, and Heather Kennedy, in Israel; to Maxa Saltiel, Dr. Arnold Soloway, Peggy Myers, Dr. John Wettersten, Joanne Klotz, Dr. Jancis Long, Judith Kipper, Ceil Sutherland, and Terry O'Neal, in the United States.

I am proud to acknowledge my debt to Dr. Judith Buber Agassi, who actively followed the progress of this book from its conception. I have been greatly assisted by the clear, concise, and illuminating research and exposition of the situation of the Israeli Arabs in *Israel et ses population* by Doris Ben-Simon and Eglal Errera, published by Presse Universitaires de France.

I wrote the original manuscript in Hebrew and translated it into English with the help of Charles M. Sawyer from a rough translation kindly prepared for me by Richard Flantz of the English Department of Tel Aviv University. I am grateful to both of them. Charles Sawyer showed his usual mastery of style and structure and thereby saved me from many pitfalls in our joint effort to present esoteric material for the American general reader. Nevertheless, the story still retained many obscurities, which Ellen Joseph, my editor at Houghton Mifflin, was quick to point out to me. I then expanded those chapters and brought the book to its final form. Frances L. Apt, the copy editor, had the complex task of checking consistency, not only of style, but also of story. I am obligated to her for performing this task with humor, insight, and uncompromising accuracy.

Last and most cherished are the two godparents of my book, my literary agent, Jacques de Spoelberch, and Ellen Joseph, my editor at Houghton Mifflin, whose enthusiasm and infinite patience, combined with understanding and loving guidance, nurtured this book into existence.

To all my friends, Jews and Arabs, whose lives, actions, and convictions have inspired this book: I could not hope to do you justice. I will be well content if I succeed in shedding light on you and your struggle.

PREFACE

IT WOULD ALL seem like a joke in poor taste were it not true. World problems hinge on Middle East problems. These problems hinge on the Middle East war. This war, it is often said, is rooted in the presence of the Zionist State of Israel: an area covering 7992 square miles, only 156 more square miles than the State of New Jersey, with a population half that of New Jersey. With the limelight directed so strongly on Israel, the media and the public in general managed somehow to gloss over the intriguing fact that more than half a million Israelis are non-Jews, chiefly Arabs, chiefly Muslims. The difficulties of Israeli Arabs, with ties of blood and tradition to Israel's declared enemies, have been ignored.

Israeli Arabs are centered in three rural areas. Hardly any Arabs live in dominantly Jewish neighborhoods, and few Israeli Jews know any Arabs, have Arab friends, or have regular contact or intimate relations with them; there are almost no intermarriages.

The exceptions are Arab politicians, who are fairly widely known, Arab students who attend Jewish universities and even stay in Jewish dormitories, and a very few free professionals known to their Jewish colleagues. Arab workers in predominantly Jewish neighborhoods are faceless. Even as a community, Israeli Arabs are all too often confused, even by other Israelis, with the so-called Palestinians; that is, Jordanian citizens in territories occupied by Israel since the Six Day War of 1967, or refugees in camps known to be housing Palestinians. More often, the very existence of this community is ignored altogether.

Perhaps the joke is even more bitter; perhaps peace in the Middle East is impossible in such a situation.

This book describes the Israeli Arabs.

The account is offered as an accurate portrayal of real events. That such things actually happened, and in the sequence which they appear here, is well known, though seldom discussed by most Israelis, Jew and Arab alike. Only the names given here are wholly fictitious. The fictional Arab village is a near parallel to a real Arab Israeli village, and the career of its mayor follows closely the career of a good friend of mine, a young Arab Israeli. However, all the characters in this book, including the central character, Mayor Walid Abu-Hana, are composites of real-life characters. The views, emotions, and motives they display should not be assumed to represent those of any specific persons. These views, emotions, and motives are real enough, but none of the characters in this book is a carbon copy of any of the real characters on whom the following account is based. The main reason for these composite portraits is to respect the strong reticence common among Moslem farmers over having their personal life made public. Since these characters are composites, I naturally found it awkward and artificial to preserve my own identity as the narrator.

YOELLA HAR-SHEFI

New York, June 1979

PROLOGUE

"IF THE PEACE TALKS fizzle and another war starts be-tween Israel and the Arabs, the Egyptians will have to re-place their defense minister, General Gamassi," thought Maya, as she drove, keeping just within the speed limit, along the Tel Aviv–Haifa expressway.

Gamassi won't be able to go to war this time the way he did in the Yom Kippur War: with cold calculation, a burn-ing hatred, and a clear goal of destroying the enemy. This time he'll hesitate. He cannot disregard his recent friendship with Ezer Weizman, his Israeli counterpart. There is a bond now between the suave, dignified Egyptian general and Ezer with the crafty grin, a bond forged through tough contests in negotiation. There are other things he'll keep in mind — like the little children who waved flags and threw flowers at him when he accompanied Sadat on his historic visit to Israel. Could he forget the little children, and if not, could he steel himself to send bombers, Maya wondered.

She chuckled. Maybe in this fact was to be found an ex-planation of Begin's curious retrenchment in the days fol-lowing the euphoria of Sadat's visit to Jerusalem. It was back to square one on the board. Maybe Begin had panicked after the face-to-face meeting. Maybe he was afraid of losing the military option. When war must be waged, there can be no room for hesitation, no consideration of the humanity of the enemy, no time for compassion. And perhaps it was this worry — that once the Egyptians were seen as human beings, as persons, Israel would lose the will to wage war — that had caused Begin to grow cautious.

Speeding along the expressway, Maya pondered about why

her attitude toward Arabs was so different from that of many Israeli Jews. Was it merely because she was such close friends with Walid Abu-Hana, the young Arab politician? When she thought of Arabs in the abstract, she was unable to block out Walid's candid, friendly face. She argued stridently with her friends who were determined to preserve the image of "the Arabs of Israel" as an amorphous mass, faceless and threatening. They dismissed Walid as a "nice guy but not exactly the typical Arab." He became "your Walid," and in that phrase Maya heard an echo of the contemptuous old European reference, "your Jew."

When reason failed, they lost patience with her. "You think they love us, do you?" they taunted her. No one needed to remind her that there was precious little reason why *they* should love *us*.

The most pointed arguments she had were with Walid. Once, after the terrorist action at Ma'alot, they almost parted enemies. Fedayeen from the PLO had surprised a class of high school students from Safed on their annual outing, as they were spending the night in the school building. When the Israeli army began its operation to free the hostages, the terrorists massacred twenty-one boys and girls and wounded many more. Maya, covering the event for her newspaper, returned to her office shocked and shattered, like the girl she had helped place on a stretcher, drenched in blood, a look of cold terror in her eyes, screaming.

The next day Walid came to Tel Aviv and suggested they meet for lunch. Maya, in her anguished state, met him as if she were the representative of the Jews meeting the representative of . . . yes, Al Fatah, the despised PLO. Walid immediately felt the barrier between them, and he didn't understand.

"I was there yesterday," Maya burst out.

Walid paled a little. "The village council of Kafr-Hama sent a cable to the minister for the interior, condemning the terrorist action," he began, with some hesitancy in his voice.

"You know what you and your damned village can do

with your cable of condemnation," Maya exploded. "That isn't going to bring one little girl back to life. It won't even give any of them another hour of life."

"You're crazy," said Walid. "You're talking as if I were there..."

"That's exactly it. You weren't there!" yelled Maya.

"They didn't attack Jews; they attacked Israelis," said Walid, invoking their agreed-upon premise that, though they were of different nationalities, Jew and Arab according to their identity cards, they were citizens of the same state, Israel. "They found a class of Jewish pupils from Safed at Ma'alot, but they could just as easily have found a class of Arab pupils from Kafr-Hama. We're all in the same boat..."

"Really? Really? Then why weren't you there? If you're such a conscientious citizen, why didn't you come to offer yourself as a substitute hostage in place of one of the children inside?"

There was a silence.

"They weren't even considering an exchange of hostages. Everyone knows Al Fatah wouldn't have agreed to that."

"All the same, dozens offered themselves — Dayan for one. Politicians, too; even foreign ambassadors. Where were you when the others stood up?"

"They would have plastered my face with spit. They would have said that I'm sucking up to the Jews, that I'm a worm, crawling to the rulers; and your people would have said that the chairman of the Hama Council is an opportunist, trying to make political capital out of the blood of children and the tears of bereaved parents." Walid spoke in a low voice, not looking at Maya.

"And that was enough to soothe your conscience? To think I have to hear this from you, my best friend ... Well, it looks as if we don't stand a chance. Either of us. It looks as if the winners will be the butchers who massacred the children at Ma'alot, as well as those of our teachers who jumped out the windows, abandoning the children inside. They can celebrate their victory together, and people like

you and I, who believe that Jews and Arabs can live together in this land, can stay home and lock ourselves in for
fear of 'what people will say.' "

They finished their steaks in silence, avoiding each other's
glance. Maya continued thinking that Walid had lied to
himself. It was true that the terrorists might have found a
class of Arab pupils from Kafr-Hama in that school building.
But it wasn't true that the story would have ended the same
way. They wouldn't have massacred Arab girls from Hama.
They wouldn't have been capable of that, and anyway, what
good would it have done them? They wanted revenge on
Jews; they wanted to break the Jews' spirit. They had no
blood-reckoning with the Arabs of Israel. Certainly there
were scores to be settled among the Arabs. Those who fled
in 1948 were bound to resent those who stayed, and once
the Jews were thrown into the sea, there would be time for
reckoning. But in the meantime, there was no blood lust
against "our brother Arabs" in Israel.

At the same time Walid reached a different conclusion,
as he later confessed to her: It's easy for her to talk. I'd like
to see her in my position. If I'd offered myself as a hostage,
even the Jews would have been contemptuous of me. They
would have said I'm a hypocrite, and a self-righteous one at
that. But she's right about my not even considering it. The
thought never occurred to me. I probably would have behaved differently had an Arab class been kidnaped. I hate
this whole situation. I wish they'd leave us alone, let us live.

BEYOND
THE GUNSIGHTS

He was part of my dream,
— I was part of his dream.

LEWIS CARROLL

1

MAYA GILEAD had met Walid Abu-Hana in 1969.

It all began when a minor news item from a field reporter reached the night editor's desk. The editor was in his routine mood of despair, swamped with reports he considered superfluous, and sat reading aloud in a tragic voice the feeble articles of the lower echelons, arousing commiserating laughter among his colleagues. Maya absent-mindedly picked up a page lying on his desk, headlined: COUNCIL CHAIRMAN WILL GO ON PLAYING SOCCER. And below it: "Walid Abu-Hana, a second-year student at Bar Ilan University, has been elected chairman of the Kafr-Hama local council. Twenty-three-year-old Abu-Hana, elected at the head of a non-clan list, has promised his supporters that he will go on playing soccer even while he is in office."

"Throw it straight into the basket," the night editor said.

"Don't be in such a hurry." Maya smiled. "You might be throwing the revolution into the basket."

"I told you she was crazy," he said to his colleagues, bemoaning once more the unpredictability of this special correspondent. "An Arab plays soccer, and she sees a revolution."

Maya Gilead was a special correspondent for a big Israeli daily. She was known for tough, sometimes ruthless reporting, an x-ray quality of investigation, and inimitable style, with a tendency toward pronouncing cutting judgments. People introduced to her were invariably taken by surprise. One army officer, who was outraged at a scalding criticism of the most sacred of Israeli cows, the army, exclaimed in total disbelief, "But you're so little!" She was slim and agile, with short, unruly hair. Perpetually dressed in jeans, when seen from afar she was frequently mistaken for a schoolboy. All in all, Maya was a maverick in her profession. She had an exasperating contempt for routine, a nose for trouble, and a marked tendency to pick quarrels over matters that seemed trivial to most of her colleagues.

She shied away from glamourous subjects like fashion or entertainment, but when tackling difficult topics in the political, social, or economic arena, she imbued her coverage with a sense of drama and a human touch. Often she flew in the face of popular opinion but managed to do so with aplomb. She lampooned the most revered institutions of the country but was dedicated to certain things: human dignity and equality of man, freedom of thought and expression. To her they were not clichés; rather, they were the cornerstones of her value system. If she had one fault that deserves mention, it was that, in her single-minded devotion to her profession, she sometimes ran roughshod over those around her — her editor, her friends, even her own family on occasion. When Maya sensed a major story shaping up, there was no way of deterring her from penetrating to the heart of it. The moment she spied the item on the Arab mayor, her eyes gleamed in the way which foretold that nobody and nothing could stand in her way. The night editor said to Maya appeasingly, "Suit yourself. I'll bet when you're done with this young man, he'll find himself becoming a national figure." Maya threw a friendly if somewhat absent-minded grin in his direction. She was already planning her project.

The next day Maya set out for Kafr-Hama to interview Walid.

She was very curious about this fellow. Even among the Jewish population there were hardly any outstanding young people in politics. A council chairman, or mayor, aged twenty-three was quite unknown among the Jews. Among the Arabs it was unbelievable. Maya wondered at the abysmal ignorance of the Jewish and the Arab populations, about each other, reflected even in the behavior of an experienced journalist, so unaware of how extraordinary the election of such a person was that he had wanted to throw a report about it into the wastebasket. A young man of twenty-three chairing discussions in which the elders of the Arab village participated! In a culture where the word "elder" was synonymous with "revered"!

And if that were not enough, this youngster had been elected on a non-clan ticket. It was like the Ku Klux Klan electing a black president. What had happened there, she wondered. How had it happened? Was it an accidental combination of circumstances that had given birth to a two-headed sheep with a very brief life expectancy, or was this indeed the beginning of a change? Maya's antennae suggested the second possibility. She was good at learning important things from symptoms that at first seemed completely marginal. Like the casual mention that the new chairman played soccer. What was so special about soccer? Nothing, if the fellow was from a *kibbutz*, a *moshav* (collective), or a city — Jewish, of course. But an Arab soccer player was quite another story. She thought that it would be interesting one day to research and write about the lack of sports activity among young Arabs in Israel. Yes, and a student too. That in itself was nothing special. But the fact that this fellow had chosen to study at Bar Ilan, which was a Jewish religious university, certainly did arouse curiosity.

Just don't build great expectations around him so that there'll be no disappointment, she cautioned herself gravely, and went on looking out at the road.

*　*　*

Much later, when this road had become routine, she tried to reconstruct that first journey, that conscious sense of transition from one sphere to another. That morning she had deliberately left Tel Aviv after the wave of traffic entering the city in the morning had been absorbed deep in the city's arteries. She sped along the coastal road, so familiar that she drove without seeing until she reached the Netanya intersection, where she turned right, to the Beit Lid junction. She glanced casually at the British police building, a relic of Mandate times, now a prison inhabited of late mainly by

Fatah members, and continued east. She was traveling through the landscape of old Eretz Israel. A moshav that had not yet dandified its appearance, its old houses not yet disguised as luxurious villas; a road that grew narrower and narrower, with distances that increased between vehicles. On in a straight line until you see close up, in front, as if it were on the palm of your hand, the town of Tulkarm, no longer on the other side of the border, forbidden and threatening, but now accessible and open to all, though still alien and uninviting. A sharp turn to the left, past a kibbutz or two, a moshav or two, and then, without signs or markers, or even boundaries — "green" or otherwise — the landscape suddenly changes, with the colors and the smells that surround you, and you know that, though you feel at home, you have actually entered your neighbor's yard. Even the road itself does not greet you, does not spread itself out passively under your wheels, but, rather, seems to test your right to use it. Curving, climbing, dropping, and changing direction without the customary warnings, the road seems to declare that it is not accustomed to visitors from the outside and serves only those who know what to expect after every curve or turn.

It's not alien, thought Maya; it's just different. And the difference cannot be defined in terms of the black dresses of the women squatting in the fields or the few white *kaffiyehs* on the heads of the men, who generally dress in Western style. Arab men and women work also in the fields of the Jewish villages. Even the architectural characteristics of the Arab village are not enough to explain it. The whole contains all these, but is far greater than the sum of its parts. How else to explain the sense of change in landscape when it is the very same landscape, or in the colors of the sky when the same sky is spread above your head during the whole journey, or in the smells when you've been breathing the expanses of the same delightful freshness from the moment you left behind the stifling air of the city?

Maya was a blind patriot, head over heels in love with this country, which she had adopted as her own at the age of ten. Once, when a visiting colleague from abroad had asked her what was so special about it, she confessed that sometimes she felt that before God created the world He produced a pocket edition of the universe just to try out how it would work. And that was Eretz Israel. A miniature with no element missing. Sea and desert, the lush green of the Jordan Valley and the arid yellow of Sinai, the blazing basin of Jericho and the snowy peak of Mount Hermon, the soft hills of the Lower Galilee and knifelike sharpness of the Negev craters. And in this entire spectrum of hues, all of which were inseparable parts of the concept called "home," she knew how to make a clear and unartificial distinction whenever she entered the Arab sphere.

While concentrating on the unfamiliar road, trying to take in something of the villages that were no more than names, because she had no friend or acquaintance in them and had neither slept nor dined there, Maya thought of the black and abandoned signs she had passed on her right. DANGER! FRONTIER AHEAD! And until the Six Day War they had represented a real warning that beyond spread several hundred meters of demilitarized land and beyond that enemy territory. The mosque of Tulkarm on the horizon. Enemy land. The sign had remained there after the war, stuck in its place, void of its force, forgotten.

Soon the road entered a large plain, then led right into the center of a sizable village, which spread out around it and climbed up the surrounding hills. On the left was a soccer field and on the right a large building, apparently the school. Behind the soccer field stood a service station, where she stopped. A number of young men kicking a ball around stopped playing and approached her. They gazed inquisitively at her, at her car, at the press sticker on her windshield, and made way for one of their party. She opened the door and, without thinking, reached a hand out to the young man smiling at her.

"You're Walid," she said.

"And you're Maya," he said. "I'll show you the way to our home."

He got into the car beside her.

Maya was suddenly elated. She was happy that this was Walid. She felt completely at ease. One of the qualities that helped her in her work was her ability to be at ease with everybody. She felt now as if she had known Walid for a long time. She couldn't look at him, because driving along the paths teeming with two- and four-legged beings demanded all her attention. Nevertheless, from time to time she stole a glance at him. He was exactly as she'd expected. She tried to pinpoint what it was that pleased her about him. Maybe the fact that all his fingernails were trimmed. She was always put off by the sight of one long fingernail, which so many Arab young men allowed to grow on the little finger of one hand. Maya had tried a couple of times to discover the purpose of this fingernail. Once someone had told her that it was useful as a substitute for a screwdriver, and she didn't know if he was pulling her leg or trying to find a logical explanation for a not very rational fashion. Once someone else had offered a more reasonable explanation: the long fingernail was an indicator that its owner was a man of means and did not need to break his nails in manual labor. Had she been asked to sum up her first impressions of Walid, she would have expressed her feelings in a very embarrassing sentence. She would have said, "He looks like one of us."

Since she prided herself on not discriminating between people and was indeed very strict with herself about this, Maya immediately wondered about her sentiment. Have I really caught myself out, she asked herself. Do I like him because he doesn't look like an Arab? She held an on-the-spot self-trial and found herself innocent. Had Walid been wearing a kaffiyeh and a robe, her impression of him would have been exactly the same: he could be one of us. What she meant to say was, What I like about him is that he is himself and is not trying to be anyone else. Young Arabs often attempted to look like Jews, the criterion being what the Arab thought that the Jew thought was fashionable. Maya continued thinking, or rather sensing, for her thoughts would become crystallized only after years of friendship with Walid.

Walid was obviously delighted by the attention aroused by her driving him through the village in her car. To Maya, this was one more point in his favor. A woman driving, yet he didn't show a shadow of embarrassment. A woman at the wheel of a car in an Arab village was, in those days, something like a camel with three humps. The steering wheel was a distinct status symbol, so the place behind the wheel belonged to the man. But Walid felt perfectly at home. He guided her expertly through the alleys into the center, which was already too small for a village the size of Kafr-Hama, already far too narrow to contain carts and donkeys, the private cars, the pickups, the trucks, each of which was doing its best to draw attention by prolonged and sporadic blasts of the horn. Maya felt as if they were all running around in a haphazard manner, oblivious of their immediate surroundings and almost heading right into the two restaurants, the coffee houses, and the grocery shops around the center. Among this apparent bedlam, pedestrians calmly wended their way and children ran about.

Maya was not familiar with Kafr-Hama. But this village was not different from other Arab villages within the Green Line, the internationally recognized de facto borders of Israel as they existed in 1967, on the eve of the Six Day War. Mentally, Maya checked her surroundings against the legacy of the hemmed-in Arab communities that she knew all too well, albeit as an outsider.

In 1948, when the dust of the Israeli War of Independence settled, it was found that most of the Arab population either had fled or had been driven from the territory of the new Jewish state. The Arab exodus included most of the upper class and virtually all of the leaders. Those who stayed on the land remained largely in the Galilee to the north, in the heartland of the country in a grouping of villages referred to as "the triangle," and in the Negev Desert, to the south. The last were the nomads, the Bedouins, many of whom served voluntarily in the Israeli army, as scouts mainly, and therefore were looked on by the Jews more favorably than were the other Arabs. Several of the northern villages had a mixed population of Arab Christians, Arab Muslims, and Druses, a separate ethnic group observing a mysterious religion. The Druses were reputed to be excellent fighters, and because of a long history of blood baths between the Muslims and the Druses, there was a natural alliance between the Jews and the Druses, who became the only non-Jewish Israelis subject to compulsory military service.

Maya's straying thoughts returned to Kafr-Hama, the biggest village in the triangle, the hard core of the Muslim *fellaheen*, or peasant Arab farmers, within Israel.

Although Israel's Declaration of Independence promised equal rights and representation to all minorities — mused Maya — events had not turned out exactly that way. During the very first years, when the memory of the bitter fighting was indelibly stamped on the national consciousness, it seemed almost natural to impose military rule in the areas inhabited by Arabs. The legal basis for these measures rested ironically on the "Defence Regulations" — the antidemocratic laws enacted by the British in the time of their Mandate to crush the Jewish struggle for independence. Military governors, administrative bodies, and military courts were established by the state after 1948. Anyone wishing to leave the governed areas, for whatever reason and for however short a time, was required to obtain a written permit. Curfews were routinely imposed. It was peacetime martial law.

These regulations came to pass without any apparent opposition. The dazed Arab population took stock of their new situation. Before the War of Independence they had been the indigenous, well-rooted majority, highly skeptical of the Jewish adventurers, who were mostly European intellectuals trying to transplant a Western vision of Jewish national survival, social equality, and economic revolution onto the Levantine soil. Estimates vary as to how many Arabs stayed and how many fled when war broke out, but it can be safely said that before the War of Independence there were about 800,000 Arabs in the area that constituted the new State of

Israel. Afterward, only about 160,000 remained. The entire Jewish population of Israel at independence equaled the number of Arabs who fled. Painfully conscious of their new minority status, of their lack of leadership, the remaining Arabs submitted apprehensively to whatever their future might bring, falling back on religion, tradition, and each other.

Maya shook off her historical reverie to observe the bustling village. Taking in the sight of so much conspicuous growth and prosperity — the utility poles along the streets, the upper stories added onto old structures, the traffic that choked the thoroughfares — Maya reflected that despite the years of military rule, important progressive social changes had taken place in the Arab communities. When the military administration was abolished in 1966, new winds started to blow among the Israeli Arabs. She sensed, intuitively, that this young man whom she was about to interview embodied many of these new trends. She felt a surge of excitement as it occurred to her that he might become one of those who would determine the direction of his people's future.

Within a few minutes they had stopped outside a house. Walid opened a heavy iron door, and they climbed some stairs to the second floor. Maya had the sense of lots of space and many rooms. They entered a reception room, a very large room draped with heavy curtains, containing several armchairs and a contemporary bookshelf, of the type to be found in almost every modern Jewish house, full of current literature in Hebrew. On the wall were hung pictures of a high school class and of a group at the teachers' college. And a tapestry portraying a bride in a sedan chair on a camel's back with an oasis in the background. A white telephone in the corner. Maya smiled inwardly. This proves to all that the young mayor is with it. Even in Jewish houses the white and colored telephones had just started replacing the old black ones. On the table, a tray holding packs of cigarettes of all kinds and brands so that each guest could have his choice. Everything clean, sparklingly clean, not a speck of dust. Where are all the members of the household,

Maya wondered, and before she could restrain herself she said, "I hope I haven't frightened everybody out of the house."

"There's no one to frighten off," said Walid. "This is my house, and I'm a bachelor."

Maya felt a touch of envy. How does a young fellow get such a spacious house all to himself, she wondered. Most Israelis lived in very compact, even crowded, apartments. Indeed, the prime concern of the young Jewish Israeli, second only to the threat of war, was how to afford a place to live in.

In the doorway of the kitchen, which was equipped with all up-to-date appliances that showed no signs of use, appeared a young woman in traditional peasant dress. She smiled. There could be no mistake. It was the same smile.

"I'd like you to meet my sister Leila."

Leila shook Maya's hand affably, without a trace of self-consciousness. She exchanged a few words with Walid and left the room. Several minutes later she came back with a tray and placed on the table a bowl of watermelon cut into cubes, soft drinks, honey cakes, and other refreshments. Now the sound of many footsteps was heard coming up the stairs, and Leila disappeared. Soon the room filled up with the same young men they had left not long ago at the soccer field. They all took their places, with Walid sitting in the place of honor, next to the white telephone. Maya sat beside him. They were all men, but this was to be expected. Although Maya had intended to stay for about two hours, she found herself deep in a conversation that had no end, listening enthusiastically to the story of their struggle against the old system, against the establishment, against the elders, against tradition, against the whole world, in fact. She stayed for lunch and then was invited for coffee in the rooms of Salah Abu-Hana, Walid's father.

The spacious room in which the older Abu-Hana received his guests was in a building apart, opposite Walid's, with a big enclosed yard between the houses, guarded by a heavy iron gate. The guest room was scrupulously clean, its walls blue-tinted plaster, the most popular color in Arab villages. A low bed in the corner opposite the door served as a couch; a big table stood in the middle. Next to the bed was a heavy iron brazier containing the ever-burning coals to keep the coffee fresh and ready for any caller. Salah Abu-Hana was a man of solid build, dressed in traditional garb, with a generous, warm, and open countenance. He spoke in a very low, quiet voice, to which everyone present listened attentively.

Maya was struck by the cordiality of his welcome. There was no trace of the effusiveness she encountered so often when meeting Arab notables, intended, she presumed, to mask their uneasiness at meeting a woman obviously not subservient and perhaps even socially superior. The old man appraised her keenly, though kindly, and she deeply regretted not being able to communicate with him in his own language.

Salah Abu-Hana said something in a bantering tone, and the young men doubled over in laughter, clapping Walid affectionately on the back.

"What did your father say?" asked Maya.

Walid hedged a little and finally translated. "He said that he can tell at once that you are very discerning, and that if I want to win your sympathy, I will have to use more than my abundant charm."

Maya grinned mischievously at the patriarch, and he returned the glance. Already she felt as though she had a special relationship with the venerable family head.

"What is your opinion of your son's political venture?" she asked through Walid.

"You cannot win a race when you pick a docile colt," Walid translated, "but Allah be praised for blessing my stable with more than one colt."

"How many siblings have you?" Maya asked Walid.

"Six," said Walid.

"How many brothers and how many sisters?"

"I meant six brothers," Walid replied, reddening slightly. "We are twelve children, seven brothers and five sisters," he said, correcting his former count, which — in accordance with the Arab custom — ignored the unimportant women-folk.

"All from the same parents?"

"Yes," said Walid. "Of course."

Salah Abu-Hana smiled broadly and asked something.

Walid translated with a hint of apology in his voice for asking so personal a question. "My father asks if you have children."

"Yes," Maya answered, "I have a son."

Salah Abu-Hana did not need an interpreter for that. He spoke rapidly.

Walid translated. "My father says that it is lonely to be an only child. He says you should bring your son with you when you come next time so that he can enjoy the feeling of a big family."

This was an opening for a more intimate introduction to her hosts, and she inquired about the other brothers.

Walid smiled expansively. "It is a long list. Each one is different. One, an older brother, has just graduated in economics from Hebrew University in Jerusalem; another is tending the sheep. Allah willing, you will meet them all in due time."

Maya was aware that there was not the slightest change of tone when Walid mentioned the second brother. Indeed, he showed equal pride in both.

Salah Abu-Hana interjected something with an air of mock scorn, and all present enjoyed Walid's embarrassment as he translated. "Father says that all his children are busy putting in a decent day's work, and I am the only one that is free as a lark. But don't believe him," he volunteered in self-defense; "I was up this morning at one o'clock to load trucks for market."

Maya noted again how strong was the empathy between father and son.

She was fascinated by the seeming ease with which the Abu-Hana family combined the old and the new, the traditional and the modern. Leila wore the traditional dress, and her prompt disappearance from the room, when she had heard male guests' voices approaching, showed that she followed the behavior dictated for an Arab woman. But two younger chattering sisters, glimpsed passing in the yard beyond, wore shirts and slacks, like teen-agers from a Jewish town. One of the young people in the room, a giant of a man whose eyes followed Walid with a fond if not quite idolizing expression, whispered to Maya conspiratorially, "It is lucky for all concerned that the older of the two girls we just saw outside was not born a boy. If she were a man, she would revolutionize the country in the time it takes Walid to bring some minor changes into the village."

Maya learned that this Goliath was Taufik, Walid's best friend and lieutenant.

Time flew; more refreshments were brought. At last she could stay no longer. Regretfully, she rose to leave, extending her hand to the patriarch.

Salah Abu-Hana clasped her hand through the thick cloth of his robe.

Walid hurried to explain. "My father washed and purified himself for the fifth prayer, the last of the daily rituals, and he cannot touch a woman till after the prayer."

He was relieved that she was not offended, but it was equally evident that he saw no need to be embarrassed by his father's piety.

Searching her way carefully out of the maze of the narrow dirt roads toward the highway and then driving unhurriedly in the direction of Tel Aviv, she reviewed in detail the last few hours. The political story that had unfolded during her interview with Walid and his young supporters fulfilled all her expectations. She now had just the sort of story that would enable her to introduce the Jewish public to the intricacies of local Arab politics. It was clear that she was going to have difficulty confining the rich material on the Abu-Hana family into a single article. It would, at the very least, have to be a big feature story.

"I already miss them," she admitted to herself, thinking both of the young mayor and his father, and feeling slightly foolish about her sentimentality.

2

MAYA'S FIRST ENCOUNTER with Arabs in the Promised
Land had been very frightening indeed. It was just before
the Partition Resolution, and she was ten years old, a refugee
from the Holocaust sent by the Youth Aliyah program to the
youth village of Ben Shemen.

At her first meal in the dining hall, the children had
wanted to find out if she knew Hebrew. They stuck a spoon
in front of her nose and asked, "What's this?" She just stared
at them; she didn't even understand what they were asking
her. Three months later, Maya — who had only recently received her Hebrew name in place of the Polish one she had
been given at birth — had learned enough Hebrew to get a
part in a play that was being put on one Friday evening,
Sabbath eve. Her adoptive parents wanted her to visit with
them over the weekend, but because of her part in the play,
she couldn't leave until the next morning, and there were
no regular buses on the Sabbath.

Saturday morning an instructor took her to the road that
cut through the village and told her, "Wait for a service cab.
If the driver has room, he'll stop and take you. Don't hitch
a ride; it isn't safe."

The day before, they had talked in class about Arab rioting and about the need to take care and not leave the village
after nightfall. The newspapers had reported bloody incidents all over the country. Maya remembered the warnings
as she raised her hand to stop the approaching cab. In those
few seconds, as she flagged the cab and got in, she realized
she'd made a dreadful mistake. It was an Arab cab, full of
Arabs. She was panic-stricken to the roots of her hair, and
so intent on not revealing her confusion that she almost

forgot all the Hebrew words she was so proud of knowing. "To Tel Aviv? I need to go to Tel Aviv."

The driver answered something, laughed, and drove on. She tried to shrink in her seat and to look at the other passengers without having them notice. Then she decided to pray. But she didn't know to whom. She's been raised in a home where no one prayed. And during the war — the "war" for her was always the Second World War — she'd been hidden in an orphange affiliated with a Catholic convent. Her parents had been killed at Treblinka, a Nazi extermination camp. At the end of the war her aunt had found her and taken her in. Gradually, she stopped attending church. And now she didn't know whom to pray to.

She concentrated hard and began a silent soliloquy: "Look, God, I'm just a little girl. I don't know how to talk to you, as God of the Christians or God of the Jews, or maybe Allah . . . But if you're God, you know that a little girl can't know the answer. I'm asking you to help me. Don't let them do anything to me. You know how hard it was for a Jewish child to remain alive during the war. I want so much to live. Please, God, I can't promise you that I'll always pray to you. And I won't know how to address you. But I promise to try always to do the right thing. I really will try. If you're God, then you don't care how I address you. And whatever kind of God you are, Christian or Jewish or Arab, you surely can't want something to happen to a little girl like me . . ."

She was so immersed in prayer and in being prepared for the unexpected and awful that she was astonished when she heard someone say, "Tel Aviv? That way Tel Aviv, bus." She saw that they were in the center of Lydda, the Arab city she used to see only through the bus window on her way home for a visit. Now it was an enemy city. Her heart stopped beating. But the cab pulled up, everyone got out, and the driver said to her, pointing, "There's the bus to Tel Aviv. Stand there." Her legs shaking, she tried to walk erect and unconcernedly toward the bus stop. She may or may not have been imagining: everyone, but everyone, was looking at her, scrutinizing her and exchanging remarks in guttural

Arabic, which for some reason sounded highly threatening.

The bus was in no rush. No one was in a rush. A ride on this bus, which belonged to the Arab bus line, was always an adventure, the beginning and end of which were never fixed in time. Arab women — carrying sacks, chickens screaming with their legs tied, clusters of children, large flat round baskets of vegetables on their heads or empty under their arms — pitched their camp in the space that was supposed to be a bus station, and prepared for an indefinite wait.

The bus stood there. The driver had disappeared, apparently for a meal, and no one was upset. No one apart from Maya, of course. Maya's blood pounded in her temples, and she felt as if her heart were about to burst through her mouth. She had even forgotten about praying, and just kept repeating like a spinning top, "God, please help me. I'm really only ten."

Finally, the driver arrived and everyone spilled comfortably into the bus, with the children and the sacks and the vegetables and the chickens, until the aisle was full. Maya had managed to slip herself into one of the front seats not far from the driver so that she could have eye contact with him through the large mirror above the steering wheel. It made her feel a little more secure. This was one of the longest journeys of her life. True, there'd been longer and more terrifying journeys in the trains crossing Poland during the Nazi occupation. But then it seemed almost natural, for the whole world was one big dread, and life was one long journey from one station of terrors to a place of even greater terror.

But this was something else. Here was a world of blue sky and sea and sun. A lot of sun, and white shirts and short pants and oranges and dancing the *hora*. A world of festive Sabbath meals and talks and friends; of long discussions into the night — to which Maya listened intently — about the meaning of life and about good and evil and about the rebirth of nation and homeland. And no need to fear, and going to sleep contentedly tired, and getting up full of curiosity for the new day. In this new world, to fall back suddenly into fear is a terrible thing. It's as if the old terror is still pursuing you. This was why it was so important to Maya not to get carried away by this fear. To control it. She started looking at the other passengers, and each time she imagined that they were consulting among themselves on what terrible fate to administer to her, she would scold herself and find a more innocent, reasonable explanation for the expressions and whisperings that had so terrified her seconds earlier.

The bus continued on the journey. No rush, stopping frequently, progressing a little; a long argument between the driver and the passengers; driving off again. Finally it reached its last station. Everyone got off.

"Tel Aviv?" she asked the driver.

"Yes, Tel Aviv."

But it wasn't Tel Aviv. It was the terminus of the Arab bus line in Jaffa.

In later years, recalling this terrifying journey, she wondered if people casually saying "Tel Aviv, Jaffa" remembered what an abyss used to separate the Arab Jaffa from the Jewish Tel Aviv.

In 1947 the ten-year-old Maya did not attempt to confront the Arab Jaffa by herself. She knew that her adoptive parents were *"ma'apilim,"* as in those days people referred to the Jewish refugees, the survivors of the Holocaust who had reached the shores of Eretz Israel, with no possessions except an abundance of dreams, despite the British Mandate and the sealed borders. Her folk were practically penniless. In their "apartment" of one room, a corridor, and a kitchenette of two square meters, and conveniences shared with two other families, they had nothing but the two iron beds they'd received from the Jewish Agency, and some orange crates that served as temporary furniture. She closed her fist tight around the money in her embroidered purse and hailed a cab to take her from the heart of Jaffa to the door of her parents' flat in Tel Aviv.

Years later, when she had become a highly reputed journalist who often traveled alone in areas considered dangerous during times of war or unrest, refusing to carry any personal weapon and turning a deaf ear to all warnings, she asked herself more than once whether the self-confidence she felt in the midst of an Arab population did not stem from that journey in the Arab bus from Lydda to Jaffa in the year the state was born. It was as if she felt that a woman in her prime, as she now was, must not shame the courage of a girl of ten.

She believed that as long as people could move in this country without fear, it would be possible to overcome all the other problems. This was why it was important to fight fear and fear-mongers, and to root out any pretext for inciting fear.

3

WHEN MAYA SAT DOWN to organize the material for the feature article on Walid, she found that she had undertaken a difficult task indeed. Her paper would not be inclined to publish a learned dissertation on the political and social changes in the Arab community. She would have to convey this between the lines of a Horatio Alger story: young upstart climbing to the top. She realized how removed the Jewish public is from the life of the Arabs in their midst. The relations between the two communities were so very one-sided. Most Arabs speak some Hebrew and virtually all the younger generation speak it fluently, owing to the compulsory-education laws and the Hebrew-language requirements in the schools. Hebrew national newspapers are widely read in the Arab communities, and many Israeli Arabs follow the events of national politics as avidly as Israeli Jews do. By comparison, precious few Jews speak more than a few phrases of Arabic. The prevailing disregard of the Arabs and their culture discouraged the Jews who came from Arab countries from passing on their knowledge of Arabic to their children. Hardly any Jews are informed on events in the Arab communities.

Ever since the abolition of the military government, Arab men have been streaming into the Jewish farms and towns, supplying most of the unskilled labor and trying hard to assimilate themselves as much as possible into the ways and customs of the Jewish majority, at least during the working day. All this was one-way traffic, with the result that to the average Jew, his Arab fellow citizens lost all individual identity and disappeared into a uniform, undifferentiated mass, referred to simply as "the Arabs." In many cases, the Jew was hard put to cite a single Arab acquaintance by name when asked if he knew any Arabs personally. He probably was not aware that the friendly "Uri" in his garage, or "Dani" at his favorite lunch counter became Abed or Muhammad at night. If asked specifically, the Israeli Jew would affirm emphatically the complete equality of civil rights in the State of Israel, and would mention the Arab Knesset members to prove his point. The knowledgeable never failed to point out the abolition of the military administration.

Maya sighed dejectedly. Although it was a fact, and a very happy one, that the military administration was no longer in force, there was no doubt that its duration, from the War of Independence until 1966, served as the incubation period of many of the ills that plagued relations between Arabs and Jews in Israel. The security of the state had been the prima facie reason for the initial establishment of military rule, yet it became entrenched because the Israeli government had a vested interest in preserving the semi-feudal order in Arab society and hence was loath to replace it with genuine democracy. Israeli leaders were quite content to leave the Arabs alone. At the time hardly a single voice was raised to warn that in the long run we would have to pay dearly for this policy of "benign neglect."

Indeed, the years of military rule, combined with the neglect by the government and the indifference of the Jewish public, produced an insidious system of patronage that thrived in all the Arab rural areas. Corrupt lower- and middle-echelon Jewish officials lorded it over the fellaheen with the help of ever-ready parasitic Arab middlemen. These officials relied on the ignorance of their charges, all of whom, illiterate farmer and literate merchant alike, had no way of knowing that petty corruption was not official policy. For the average Arab citizen, the state was synonymous with the stuffy official who withheld the desired license to travel until his palm was properly greased. To many who endured it, the corrupt era of peacetime martial law seemed to be the natural order, especially with the legacy of the

Ottoman Empire so fresh in collective memory of the native population.

The termination of military rule — after a protracted struggle — created the mistaken notion that all wrongs had been righted. But the Arab citizen was a long way from being treated as an individual enjoying direct access to the various governmental agencies. Arbitrarily, a new intermediary interceded between the Arabs and the state: Departments for Arab Affairs grew like weeds. Every political party acquired one; every branch of government introduced them; the prime minister had his, too; and even the Histadrut, the organization of trade unions (the Israeli equivalent of the AFL–CIO), channeled its dealings with Arab workers through its "Arab department."

All these Arab departments were manned with "experts in Arab affairs," probably the new incarnation of the men who had previously run the military administration. Nobody could say wherein lay their expertise. One thing was clear, though: once again the Arab citizen was not an individual; he or she was just a particle of some amorphous entity characterized as the "Arab sector," which only "the experts" were smart enough to handle.

Maya had to admit there was some logic to this apparent absurdity. The experts were familiar with the old order of the Arab society and as such had a stake in preserving it. They were natural brokers in an unholy transaction by which the ruling Jewish Labor Party backed the patriarchal Muslim social structure and aided its leaders in preserving their rule within the Arab sector in exchange for their sizable bloc of votes in national elections.

The systematic corruption was sustained in part by the Israeli electoral scheme. In national elections the Israeli voter votes once. There is no such thing as a split ticket; every voter must vote a straight ticket. Each party publishes a slate of candidates, called the party list. The number of seats allocated to a given party is proportional to its percentage of the popular vote. Candidates are seated in the same order in which they appear on the party list. Individuals who aspire to public office must concern themselves more with currying favor with the party bosses who are responsible for compiling the list than with winning the support of their constituents. Among the Jewish population, the voting pattern was the same in both national and local elections. But among Arab voters, local elections were another realm entirely from elections to the Knesset. The reason for this was a de facto trade-off between the Jewish political establishment and the ruling clans from the Arab sector. The establishment supported the biggest, most firmly entrenched clans in the local elections campaigns in exchange for their votes in national elections. Thus was preserved the absolute loyalty to the *chamoula,* or clan, the supremacy of the elders, and the complete subjugation of women. Under such a system it was an easy proposition for the heads of the chamoulas to retain their power in local elections and to deliver votes to the ruling party in national elections.

All things considered, the very fact of Walid's election was astounding. Here he was, hardly more than a boy and a junior member of a tiny clan, to boot, daring to throw his gauntlet at the feet of all the ruling chiefs. Maya's thoughts brought her back to the Abu-Hana homestead. The father loomed again in her memory, and she suspected that he was the hidden strength behind the son. Suddenly she knew what else had drawn her into Abu-Hana's world, something that had eluded her when she first tried to articulate it. Now she realized what it was: an atmosphere of harmony. Yes, that was it! Walid's harmonious and closely knit family shielded him from the poisonous feelings of frustration and bitterness that dominated the atmosphere in the Arab enclaves. As luck would have it, just when he became an adult, the lid was lifted, the military administration came to an end. Walid was aware that this had been made possible by the persistent pressure of a Jewish popular movement that had protested vehemently the injustice done to Arabs. The irony was that twice the motion to abolish military rule had been defeated with the aid of Arab Knesset members from the Labor ticket, who docilely voted the party line to retain the repressive military regime.

Walid's manhood blossomed in that period of renaissance of interracial relations following the burial of military rule and the heady optimism after the victory of the Six Day War.

For years, the Israeli Arabs had been inundated by a torrent of boasts and threats broadcast from Egypt and Syria, Jordan and Iraq. On the verge of the Six Day War — as in all the previous wars — their dilemma was clearly spelled out. Their country was at war with their people. No one can be sure what was in their hearts. But Israeli Arabs did not rise against the state. After the war was over, they looked with disbelief at the other side of the border. They found a backward society, a backward economy, and a backward administration.

But most distressing of all were the refugee camps of the Palestinians. Their education, medical care, and food rations were provided by United Nations agencies. The Arab countries, the very ones that had declared their readiness to die for the Palestinians, were not ready to welcome them and to allow them to live in their midst as equals. As a result, many of the Israeli Arabs felt vicarious pride in the Israeli military victory and in the state's civilian accomplishments. They were eager to increase their participation in all major activities.

Walid Abu-Hana, like many others of his generation, took stock of his life and his society. Compared to the rapid and kaleidoscopic changes in the Jewish settlements, the Arab villages were stagnating despite their prosperity. Walid did not waste energy in blaming the elders or the government for the disparity. He directed all his resources to the application of contemporary techniques and attitudes to life in his home village. Declaring himself a candidate for town council, he and other like-minded young men from different clans put together a slate of candidates loyal to no clan.

They campaigned on a reform platform. No more voting for a corrupt councilman just because he is the candidate of one's own clan. No more voting for a candidate because his clan could supposedly extract more largess from the central government. Votes should be given to the most competent and trustworthy candidates, the ones who will serve the village best. Better schools, better roads, more electricity, just taxation, careful budgeting of public funds. One of Walid's most ambitious ventures was local industrialization. Maya remembered the enthusiastic nods of agreement from his followers when he explained to her the problem: traditionally, most of his people were farmers, and many of them farmed not their own land but that of the landlords, as sharecroppers. When the landlords sold their land to the Jews, the fellaheen were left empty-handed.

In 1948, when many landowners fled, the state took so-called custody over the land of absent owners, and more and more fellaheen were left with nothing. When, in 1953, the state made some reallocation of the lands in the Arab sector, the Arab farmer found himself with roughly 10 percent of the farmland he had worked before the inauguration of the state. Maya remembered that she blushed at this point, but Walid was not interested in tearing open old wounds. His sights were set on the future. He continued, telling her there was no way his people could survive on these meager lands, and certainly not if they continued to farm the land in primitive ways, like their forefathers. So they introduced new technology to their farming, with the aid of the Ministry of Agriculture. But intensive farming meant that fewer farmhands were needed. The surplus labor force thus produced did not remain unemployed; they supplied the unskilled labor to the Jewish economy. The men brought home good wages; certainly they were better off than ever before.

"But this is not good enough," Walid declared. "I don't want our youth simply to fuel the rapid progress of the Jewish economy while their own village stagnates. If, instead of selling our labor in Tel Aviv, we invest our industry in Kafr-Hama, we'll reap better financial benefits and we'll breathe new life into our society."

"But if they earn good salaries," objected Maya, "what's wrong with their working in Tel Aviv?"

"Ah, but they cannot compete on equal terms; they simply don't have equal opportunities. The Jews occupy all positions of importance."

"Well, it takes time," said Maya, fumbling slightly. "They can progress slowly. What will be the good of establishing an industrial plant in Kafr-Hama if you then put it under unskilled management?"

"Wait a minute." Walid smiled. "I have no intention of exchanging discrimination against Arabs for discrimination against Jews. You can bet that if I have a plant here, I'll get the best experts, undoubtedly Jews in most cases. But they'll be here only as long as it takes them to train our people to the point where they can take over and take their destiny in their hands.

"You see, Maya, there are so many issues involved. Your people say, 'Look how the Arabs prosper; what more do they want?' Well, we want a hell of a lot more than that: we want better elementary and secondary schools so that we have a better chance to compete for the universities, and we want some chance of employment for those who graduate and who at this moment can do nothing with their diplomas but hang them on the wall. And last but not least, I don't want the village to become a sort of overnight motel — the place where the men come back to sleep and visit their subservient wives and stranded families while they work and play somewhere else. You see, there's no point in putting all the blame on the elders, on the heads of the mighty clans, or on the government. I think time has come to put ourselves to work and see what we ourselves can do."

Maya reflected that if one judged by his output during the few months that he wielded power as mayor, Walid was as good as his word. Given half the chance, he might change positively the fabric of Arab life in Israel, channel frustration and bitterness into challenging cooperation. Maya enumerated in her article all the goals that the young mayor set for himself, his achievements to date, and the dangers that loomed ahead. She alerted her readers to the fact that, though on the surface there is complete accord between the declared policy of the Israeli government and Walid's goals, in reality he is perceived as a threat. Israeli leaders are wary of him because he is the new generation of Israeli Arab; he takes his citizenship for granted. When told that he deserves equal treatment, he hears just that and does not absorb the hidden messages, which are broadcast to him simultaneously in many ways: (a) you deserve it if you prove yourself trustworthy; (b) without our magnanimity, you would not be so well treated; (c) therefore, we expect you to show proper gratitude and remember always how indebted you are to us.

Maya pointed out that Walid's straightforward, egalitarian approach scared both the so-called experts on Arab affairs and the pillars of the traditional Arab patronage system because it made them superfluous. This young man had worked a miracle, Maya wrote, when he formed a coalition of young men dedicated to bringing about meaningful political, social economic, and cultural reform in their society. Instead of being passive drifters in the stream of events, they were determined to shape events. More important, they decided to give priority to these common goals over the existing order of absolute, binding loyalty to the clan.

To raise the slogan of the non-clan ticket in municipal election in the Arab sector took courage; to call on the young generation to take the reins from the elders took vision; to succeed in inspiring enough young people with this message to get elected to the local council proved that Walid Abu-Hana has what it takes to make a true leader. The fact that he skillfully exploited the animosity between councilmen of rival clans to get elected chairman of the council of Kafr-Hama proved that he might become in the future a shrewd politician. Walid Abu-Hana is a figure to watch. Young Arabs all over the country follow his fortunes anxiously, hoping for his success while predicting his downfall. He is watched by the power brokers of the traditional regime no less closely; if he succeeds, others will follow. Therefore, he must be stopped.

Maya recalled to her readers that the Arab sector was frequently referred to as "the bridge" in the future peace between Israel and its neighbors. She expressed her belief that only if people like Walid were allowed to assume leadership would this hope have any chance of becoming reality. Describing in detail the awe-inspiring job that Walid and his men had already accomplished, and the impenetrable obstacles he faced whenever he approached any branch of government essential to fulfilling his promises, Maya called for the government to abandon its patronizing and contemptuous attitude toward the Arab sector and meet Walid on equal terms.

The full-page article was published under the headline AN ARAB VILLAGE CRIES FOR HELP AND NOBODY LISTENS. It ensured the entry of the young mayor of Kafr-Hama into the pitifully short list of names mentioned whenever the Arab sector was in the limelight. Maya wondered if she had helped to establish him in national politics or had hastened the demise of his career. If he stayed longer in the shadows, he might have more time to shore up his defenses. She wondered whether the article precipitated an inevitable showdown, and worried about its consequences.

4

THE TROUBLE WITH WALID was that from the time he knew his own mind, he had had no respect for sacred cows.

Old men in the village claimed to recognize this trait in him when he was still an infant at his mother's breast. Other neighbors disputed this, blaming Walid's parents for pampering him and not disciplining him properly. Both groups agreed that his independent streak had shown itself early.

He had never had regard for his elders, they said. Never. Even when he was very little, no higher than the grass.

This was not precisely so.

Walid had full confidence in the world of adults, and in the world of the elders even more. But the adults soon taught him the important rule of "respect but suspect." Once, when he was very small, in the first or second grade, his mother sent him with a gift — a white cloth bag full of slices of goat's cheese — to her mother's home. Walid's grandmother had a lovely vegetable garden, one of the largest and best maintained in the village. Everything grew there, all the good things of the land. Walid walked barefoot among the rows of lentils, reaching out left and right and cracking green lentils between his teeth with great delight, as if they were pistachios. Farther off, on the patio in front of the house on the hill, his grandmother and his younger uncles watched him approach while they sat enjoying coffee and idle conversation of an early afternoon.

When Walid reached them and his grandmother left to put the cheese in the larder, the scowling uncles asked, "Did you really eat green lentils?"

"A few," Walid answered. "I only tasted them. To see if they're ripe."

"Oh, woe!" moaned an uncle. "Woe, woe! Those lentils belong to the snake, and he won't forgive you."

Walid did not understand how his grandmother's lentils belonged to the snake, but he didn't want to make matters worse with silly questions.

"I'll return them," he offered. "I'll bring some from home and return them."

"That won't help. If someone picks green lentils, the snake will come and bite him at night while he's sleeping."

Walid didn't cry, though his lower lip trembled.

"There's only one way," said the uncle. "Sometimes it helps."

"What? What?" asked Walid.

The uncles consulted among themselves, then explained to him gravely: "If you run forty times from here to that rock and back, and piss on the stone a little each time, the snake may forgive you."

It didn't occur to Walid to doubt them. How could one question the word of one's uncles? He ran and pissed and ran and pissed and arrived home exhausted, to fall asleep within minutes, without even washing his hands.

In the middle of the night his parents awoke to terrible cries. "Snake! Snake!..." Walid was sitting up in bed with hazy eyes. Twice, Salah Abu-Hana roused all his children out of bed, raising the mattresses and shaking out the blankets to check that no snake was hiding there. Only the third time did one of Walid's big brothers confess that his uncles had told him about the hoax they'd played on the boy. From that time on, he learned to question the wisdom of his elders and not to accept it as absolute truth.

When Walid was ten, something extraordinary happened. Everything in the village was disrupted. The adults gave one explanation for all the strange things that were happening: war. Afterward, they called it the Sinai War because all the fighting occurred in the Sinai Desert, to the south. When

Walid was old enough to understand, he learned that the Sinai War of 1956 was a clash between Israel, France, and Great Britain against Egypt, occasioned by the seizure of the Suez Canal by Egyptian forces.

For the Jews of Israel it meant war, with its attendant stepped-up activity and avid interest in the latest news of the fighting, but for the Arabs of Israel it was quite another matter. Sealed off by the military administration, most villages had to rely on the propaganda of the Arab radio stations across the borders for their information about the war. Because they were Arabs, Walid's uncles, his father, and his older brothers did not serve in the army. Yet Kafr-Hama saw more of the military activity associated with the war than other Arab villages because it offered a good vantage point from which Israeli troops could observe the Jordanian forces, just across the nearby border. Israeli troops commandeered the schoolhouse, setting up an observation post there.

The village children were never so attracted to the school building as during those days. They gazed, wide-eyed with excitement, at the men in uniform, and were fascinated by the officers who uttered short, authoritative commands into walkie-talkies.

Very soon, right under the noses of the soldiers in the school, the village children developed a military organization. Each neighborhood had a regiment of its own, with a regiment commander. The trademark of a regiment commander was a walkie-talkie — a matchbox with strings trailing off into nowhere. Walid was the regiment commander in his neighborhood, and his soldiers were children from kindergarten age to the fourth grade. The supreme commander, the general, was a boy in the fifth grade; he sat in the olive grove and issued commands.

Regiment Commander Walid, together with the other regiment commanders, kept close watch on the army drills and training in the schoolyard. As soon as the soldiers dispersed, the little regiment commanders would run off to their own neighborhoods to start drilling and marching their own soldiers. Barefooted, armed with sticks, and terribly serious.

The commanders were aware that these drills represented a preparatory stage before a battle, with real weapons, between the neighborhoods. Walid wanted to make sure that his troops would be at the peak of fitness, so he didn't spare them. He ordered them to cover a six-foot-high clump of *sabras*, cactus plants, with a layer of thick grass. Then he lined up his men, rucksacks on their backs. Standing on top of the clump so that he could spot evaders, he ordered his soldiers to run up to the top beside him and then jump down. The earth was wet, for it had rained a short while before. The boys' bare feet slithered on the grass and stones, but the army is the army, and they ran and jumped without complaint.

Until the last man. He was the Benjamin of the group. A little boy in kindergarten, a spoiled only son. Walid didn't hesitate. He had had no Israeli army education, but he sensed instinctively that a leader must set an example. He jumped down, lifted the five-year-old soldier onto his shoulders, ran up to the top again, and, holding the child's hands and ankles, jumped.

The soldiers cheered, and the little boy cried. In landing, Walid had fallen on the boy's leg, spraining his ankle.

Walid's seconds-in-command took the wailing child home to his mother. The commander himself hid underground in his grandmother's home.

Relatively speaking, the incident was passed over quietly enough. The boy's mother couldn't punish Walid, and she was unable to vent her wrath on his father, because it was he who healed her son's leg. Salah Abu-Hana was known in the entire region as a gifted bone doctor. Anyone suffering from a broken arm or leg would hurry or be carried to him. Even if a lamb fell into a pit and broke its legs, its owner would bring it to old Abu-Hana.

When Walid decided that the storm had died down enough for him to return home, his father acted as if nothing had happened. Walid would have preferred a punishment. Not being punished now set him the challenge of exemplary behavior. But fate intervened. For just when he had firmly resolved to justify his father's faith in him, war was declared between his neighborhood and the adjacent one.

No ordinary war. From house to house, with live ammunition, with mortars. Adults, who didn't understand weapons very well, called these mortars slingshots. Strips of leather wound around sticks, from which the soldiers slung pebbles at the enemy. To Walid's credit it must be said that it was not his men who fired the first shot. The other neighborhood had issued the call to battle. Walid simply returned fire. He had no choice. His soldiers fought bravely.

The enemy fled in retreat, Walid and his men rushing after them, like the Israeli soldiers chasing the Egyptians in the Sinai. Walid spotted the enemy commander fleeing, seeking shelter in one of the houses. He aimed his mortar carefully at the door of the house and waited. Suddenly the door creaked. The shell flew. Right into the eye of a baby in the arms of its mother, who was just about to leave her house.

The fighting stopped at once. Both sides understood that the situation was grave for all concerned.

The soldiers vanished as if the earth had swallowed them. Walid sneaked back to his home and quickly changed his clothes, hoping that the baby's mother might not have recognized him.

Everyone realized that it had been an accident, that Walid was very sorry and had meant no harm. But the gravity of the incident made it necessary to hold a *sulha* ceremony between the two families, and Walid's father atoned for his son's misdemeanor with money and cattle and a plea for forgiveness.

The children in the village waited to see what would happen to Walid. He needed no one to tell him that had he had a different father, he would barely have got out of it alive. As it was, Salah Abu-Hana landed his son a resounding slap on the face. And yet, it was this miserable incident which changed Walid's status inside the family — and to the good. Abu-Hana sat his son down for a man-to-man talk. He didn't shout or curse at the boy but spoke quietly, as he always did. "If you can command others," he said to Walid, "and if you can take responsibility for what others do, that means it's time you were responsible for your own deeds. We have a large farm and lots of work, and we're short of hands. Instead of running around with a slingshot, you can herd the sheep."

From that day on, Walid started taking the sheep out to pasture. Like an adult. It was a bit hard, but if you work like an adult, you get treated like one. He began to get a man's rights at home. Even more important was the other task his father gave him after the slingshot disaster. These were still the times of military administration, and anyone who had work or business outside the village needed a permit from the military governor to leave the administered area. Only children under thirteen were exempt from this requirement. The large herd of the Abu-Hana family grazed regularly on lands close to the nearby Jewish city. Since only the father had a permit, he would remain with the herd all week long, returning home for Fridays, the holy day of rest in Islam.

Now that he had decided to give Walid some responsible tasks, Abu-Hana got Walid to come to the Jewish city almost every day, to bring him fresh clothes, food, and news from home. The boys in the village were green with envy. In those days even grownups and elders regarded a visit to the city with awe. They would prepare for the event, making lists well in advance of what to buy and what to do, and on their return they related their tales to an eager audience.

And here was this brat, whose beard had not yet started to grow, traveling every day in Jewish buses as if it were the most natural thing in the world. Boys much older than he, who had never traveled farther than the nearest village, listened avidly as he recounted the wonders of the world outside, telling them about the bread of the Jews, quite different from the Arab *pita*, the fishponds of the kibbutzim, the train, the fascinating shops in the Jewish city.

As early as this he consolidated his position as a kind of

emissary of his society to the Jewish society outside. His frequent trips to the city elevated him in the family as his father's deputy, for he was the only one who could travel freely, bringing his father's word back to the family.

Many elders tugged at their beards, remarking that exposing the boy to so many outside influences would be unhealthful. And then there came the confrontation between Walid and the religious-instruction teacher, to prove them right.

The religion instructor at elementary school was a heavily built man, with a large paunch, who was always equipped with a long, thick wooden ruler. Many grown men in the village still grab their buttocks reflexively at the sight of a ruler whenever a child pulls one from his schoolbag. Nor was this man only a teacher, although in those days that was no small thing. He was also a son of the Antar family, a family of landowners with large estates in the village, in Jaffa and Hebron, and — so it was rumored — in Lebanon, too. Because of the prestige and power of his family, the teacher could tear a boy apart without fearing that the boy's father would even dream of complaining.

Walid didn't appreciate being hit with a ruler. The first couple of times he said nothing. To show he was a man. The third time he grabbed the ruler from the teacher's hand, dived under the desk, slipped between the amazed teacher's legs, and ran away.

The teacher didn't hurry after him. He figured it'd be best if the little brat got what was coming to him from his own father. When the teacher arrived at the Abu-Hana house that evening, Salah Abu-Hana himself was waiting for him, with a smile of welcome.

The teacher informed him of his son's behavior: he had run away from class.

"From what class?" asked Salah Abu-Hana.

"From the religious-instruction class," answered the corpulent teacher, with a sanctimonious expression.

"I'm surprised that the Holy Koran frightens him so,"

Abu-Hana said, innocently. "I thought this was what made him run away —" and handed the embarrassed teacher the heavy ruler.

What they said to each other at this point is not known. Years later Walid told Maya that he was hiding behind the cupboard all the while, to be ready for any storm that might erupt. But he was so terrified that his ears rang, too loudly for him to hear a single word.

Walid returned to school and the teacher to his ruler, though he did not appear to notice Walid anymore. But that didn't help. After one of the pupils received some especially hard raps with the ruler, Walid decided that something had to be done, and organized the first protest strike in the village, though how such an idea occurred to him he does not remember.

Somehow he managed to convince the other pupils in his class that if they all declared that they weren't prepared to be taught by the religious-instruction teacher, the teacher would be replaced.

The children marched behind him to the council building, where they stopped. Their courage had deserted them. But Walid was resolute: they must choose delegates to appear before the head of the council and demand that the teacher be replaced.

However, the head of the council was also the head of the teacher's clan. The famous Sharif Antar, member of the Knesset. The man whom even the Jewish chief of the district police would not speak back to.

The children halted in the space outside the council building, elbowing each other, fidgeting, shifting their weight from foot to foot. Walid and two of his good friends confronted the secretary.

"What do you want?"

"To see the head of the council."

"What for?" the secretary asked, with an amused smile. "Have you brought him a present? Did your teacher send you?"

"We're demanding that our religious-instruction teacher be replaced."

"What?"

"The fat one. We don't want him. We've decided to demand another teacher."

The people in the building gathered around, not sure how to treat this situation. They looked as if they'd just seen a genie come out of a bottle.

"*Yalla, yalla,* get out of here, scram," snapped the secretary, waving his arms at the three boys.

Walid didn't move. "We won't leave until we speak with the head of the council. We speak on behalf of our class."

The secretary went to the door and rubbed his eyes. The children were standing there, like a flock of frightened sparrows. The noise brought Sharif Antar out of his office. "What's going on, here?" he asked, fuming. The janitor started explaining, because he hadn't registered the secretary's signal. "These boys want to speak with you. They don't want their religious-instruction teacher."

The roar that emanated from Sharif Antar's throat sent the children outside flying in all directions. Walid's two friends shrank against the wall. But Walid stood firm. He later admitted to Maya that in all likelihood he had been rooted to the spot in terror. But his stubbornness drove Sharif Antar into a frenzy. He charged wildly at the boy, and only the secretary's strong arm, it appears, saved Walid from a direct confrontation with the head of the council. The secretary grabbed the delegate by the scruff of the neck and swung him out the window into the back street, a short run away from his home. "Run," he shouted after him. "And don't let us see you here again."

* * *

As soon as he finished the elementary grades, Walid transferred schools. His older brother Rasem was already studying at the Hebrew agricultural high school in Pardes Hanna. Walid followed in his footsteps. Salah Abu-Hana believed that his sons should begin their independent lives from a position of equality. He wanted to provide them with an education that would assure them equal opportunities and a sense of self-confidence not only within the Muslim populace, but anywhere in the State of Israel.

Walid adapted to the new school without difficulty and soon won friends. But after a while Pardes Hanna lost its special magic for him. It was no fault of the school. The reason lay elsewhere.

Two of Sharif Antar's sons had been sent to study at the high school in Nazareth, the largest Arab city in the state. Walid feared that his status among his peers was in danger.

In Pardes Hanna the pupils wore short pants, blue shirts, and sandals. At the high school in Nazareth the pupils wore long trousers, starched shirts, and jackets, like the actors in Egyptian movies. The Antar boys told their friends in the village about the holy water in the Spring of the Virgin, about the church bells, the soccer field and the government building. And they had stories about visits to the Diana and the Ambar cinemas, about movies starring Farid El-Atrash and Abd-el Halim Hafez. There was no television in Israel yet, no movie house in Kafr-Hama; and in Pardes Hanna Arab films were not screened. Walid understood that he wasn't really living unless he, too, got to Nazareth.

Two years after beginning his studies at Pardes Hanna, Walid received a permit from the military administration allowing him to study at the high school in Nazareth. Clothes were sewn for him, his suitcase packed, and he set out.

Suddenly, in his fifteenth year, he felt, for the first time in his life, a sense of dread, a lack of confidence. He was a villager among city people, a Muslim among Christians. He felt suffocated by the jacket; he wasn't comfortable in the long trousers. His classmates looked as if they'd been born with the crease in their trousers. He sat stunned by the absolute silence in the classroom and the authority emanating from the old pedantic teacher. After the friendly relations at Pardes Hanna, where pupils addressed teachers by their first names, the strict discipline in the Nazareth school terrified him. As he sat there, trying to listen to the content of the teacher's words, not merely to his threatening tone, Walid suddenly felt a pain in his ear. He was afraid to turn his head. Before the pain had passed he felt another blow. In precisely the same spot.

The boy sitting behind him was amusing himself by flicking Walid's ear lobe with the traditional long nail. He was confident that the young greenhorn would not dare to complain or make a sound. Walid's ear turned red and swelled up. The rhythmic pain made him dizzy. He gritted his teeth.

When the redeeming bell rang, Walid hurried out to recess, with hard questions seething inside him. Apparently it had been a mistake to transfer. He had to work things out: perhaps this was not for him; perhaps it was not too late to go back.

At the end of the recess, the assistant headmaster, a copper bell in his hand, lined up the classes in columns. The students all stood at attention in absolute silence, and each time he rang his bell another class filed into its room. The boy with the long fingernail positioned himself behind Walid. As soon as the assistant headmaster turned his head, Walid felt a sharp pain pierce the swollen ear.

He didn't stop to think. He forgot his dread of the place, his dread of the headmaster, his dread of the assistant headmaster with the bell. He swung around, grabbed the redheaded sadist, and charged at him like a wild beast. Three teachers struggled with Walid until they managed to separate the two boys. But not before Walid's tormentor had received a solid thrashing. Walid became something of a hero since, not so surprisingly, it turned out that the other boy was a notorious bully.

While he was being questioned in the headmaster's office, the father of the boy he'd beaten burst in. He bent over Walid and said through his teeth, "I'll finish you right away!" Walid shrank. The man wore the uniform of a police officer. Among the villagers a police officer was considered terribly important. Even more important than a headmaster or an official.

To Walid's surprise the headmaster was not impressed. "Leave this pupil alone," he said. "We'll take care of him."

"You're going to let this mad dog bite my son?" the officer roared.

"We will punish whoever needs to be punished," the headmaster responded drily.

The officer's son was expelled from the school after a thorough investigation showed that he had tormented all the village boys and had even bullied many of his Nazareth schoolmates, who endured his violence for fear of his father.

From then on Walid was known at the school as "the tiger from Kafr-Hama." This incident shortened the period of his acclimatization, and very soon he became the first village boy to be invited to join the school soccer team.

Soccer became his great love. When, after high school, he completed his studies at the Arab Teachers' College in Haifa, his friends were sure that now at last he would settle down, forget the nonsense of soccer, and become a respectable and solid teacher. Instead, he managed to surprise even his father when, while continuing at his job, he enrolled in a course for soccer coaches at the Wingate Institute for Physical Culture.

Allah have mercy on him. A teacher, and still kicking around a soccer ball, like any ordinary young brat!

5

AFTER GRADUATING from the Arab Teachers' College in Haifa, Walid received a teaching post and had to face the realization that he did not enjoy teaching.

He found it hard to understand how it had happened that, after being accepted as a student in the sociology department at the Hebrew University, he had started studying at the Teachers' College. He himself didn't know what he was looking for there. He had simply given in to all the smart ones, those who always poke their noses into somebody else's affairs, who'd asked, "What're you running to the university for? Have you any idea how difficult university studies are? And anyway, what'll you get out of going to the university? What can an Arab do with a degree in sociology?"

Walid was ashamed to admit that his ambition was to be a social worker. Yet he ended up in the college. Two years later, when he graduated, he was sent to teach at a distant village, whereas other young men who had toadied to certain officials received jobs in their own villages, though they had no qualifications.

He was too busy to be bitter. Besides, it was a good period for the Arabs in Israel. The long-awaited end of the military administration of Arab-populated areas had arrived. Now the young men of the village could come and go as they pleased. The land lay open before them. The word "citizen" finally had reality, and it seemed that everything was possible. Many of the young men, and some of the older ones, left their villages every day to work in Tel Aviv, or in cities nearer the village, and returned home in the evenings or for weekends. The men of Kafr-Hama, who had been tillers of the soil in previous generations, sought different sources of livelihood. Much of the Arab land had been appropriated by the state, and the remaining areas were being worked by new methods learned from the Jews. Now they could produce more from each *dunam*, with far less manual labor. But there was no unemployment. In the Jewish cities and towns there was always a shortage of working hands.

The problem was what to do after work if you weren't going home. When there is no one to visit and nowhere to go. Many frequented the sidewalk cafés and watched the city stream past them. They were dazzled by the suntanned thighs and breasts that paraded by, painfully jealous of the young men in uniform or jeans lighting cigarettes for these dazzling beauties, embracing a waist, patting a shoulder. It hurt to see this easy camaraderie, the free and casual intimacy that excluded them, unintentionally but decisively.

And then they returned to Kafr-Hama. In Kafr-Hama they felt at home, but at home there was nothing to do. Nothing but discuss politics. To talk with swagger among one's friends of imagined conquests in the Jewish cities, and to gaze surreptitiously at the village girls. Very cautiously, so as not to start gossip.

Walid couldn't waste a moment on such idleness. His spare time was dedicated to his great passion — soccer. From the time he was chosen to play on the school's team in Nazareth, he had channeled all his energies onto the soccer field. He was a competent teacher, not because of any special talent, it seemed, but because he came out well in comparison with his colleagues. The pupils worshiped him, and all of them knew that their teacher was studying at the Mecca for soccer coaches, at the Wingate Institute for Physical Culture.

His ex-schoolmates also admired him.

"Ah, ah," his childhood friends sighed when they gathered around him like bodyguards at weekends. "*Wallah*, if only we could do that too."

"Why not?" asked Walid. "Kibbutz Gan Shoshanim is much smaller than our village, and see what a marvelous soccer team it has."

"Rubbish," they said. "How can you compare?"

"Why can't we compare?" Walid asked. "If you wanted it, we could build a soccer team here in Kafr-Hama. Have you forgotten what Herzl said — 'If you will it, it is no dream.' "

They laughed. *Wallah,* he's making fun, this clown. But Walid could tell they imagined themselves running about the soccer field.

At the Wingate Institute he was advised that to organize a soccer team in his village he should apply to Hapoel, the sports association of the Histadrut. Everyone was aware that the Histadrut and the government were the same thing, because the same party ran both. At Hapoel he understood that if he wanted to organize a sports club in Kafr-Hama, he would have to make up, in a very unsporting way, to a great many people who had nothing to do with sports. A team required money. Money required a budget. And for a budget one had to pay.

Walid didn't grumble about the system. Someone who has grown up in an Arab village during the days of the military administration takes a lot for granted. It was clear to him, though, that any activity which created an opening in the national arena, where Jews and Arabs could meet, socialize, and compete, was a prize worth striving for.

So he didn't protest. But he figured he had other options. He returned home, assembled his friends, and advised them that if they were to secure a budget from Tel Aviv, they'd have to eat a lot of crow. He had a different suggestion: they should hire themselves out for a day to one of the kibbutzim.

"We'll offer our services to Gan Shoshanim for a mobilization day," he said.

They looked stupefied. "They don't mobilize Arabs. What's got into you?"

Walid doubled up with laughter. "It has nothing to do with the army," he explained when he caught his breath. "For example, if they have fruit-picking to do, and there aren't enough people working in the orchards, they mobilize the whole kibbutz — teachers, dairymen, schoolchildren, even the aged. Each works according to his ability. I suggest we check out which kibbutzim in the area have such a burning need for labor, and then we can offer ourselves for a mobilization day. The money we earn will go into a common fund from which we can buy equipment, and then we'll be our own masters."

The suggestion was enthusiastically accepted.

Walid had no difficulty finding a kibbutz that would cooperate. Most of the kibbutzim still objected to employing hired laborers, but a mobilization day was a different matter. Especially since what was involved was a revolutionary idea — an Arab youth group attempting to set up and finance a sports club through their own labor. And last but not least, the people in the neighboring kibbutzim knew and liked Walid, since they all had business and social contacts with his family.

Walid's mobilization day was a hit. The other young men urged him to arrange more days like it. They worked like devils, picking oranges and cleaning the stalls in the cow sheds to prove the efficiency of Arab labor. In those days the term "Arab labor" was synonymous with negligent, shoddy work. Later, the Six Day War changed many concepts and attitudes, including this one — as most of the manual tasks and almost all the domestic services were taken over by workers from the occupied territories, who worked as cheap labor — Arab labor became a synonym for labor, pure and simple.

Working in the kibbutzim proved a fantastic experience for Walid's friends. Working, then resting and eating in the dining hall, sitting at the table ogling the kibbutz girls walking around in short pants and partly open shirts, through which one could see so much that one's eyes glazed.

They tried hard to behave as if this was the most ordinary of experiences. Some were afraid to light a cigarette lest anyone notice how their hands were shaking. The women were oblivious of their discomfort. The fellows braced their knees, placed their hands over their groins, and were afraid even to glance at each other. Only Walid felt quite at home.

He joked with the girls he knew by name. The other men were impressed. "*Wallah,* this stud really knows how to keep his cool. What a man!"

Walid was proud of his friends. After the first mobilization day, the work coordinators of the kibbutzim in the area began to besiege him. "Don't you need money anymore?" they asked.

In the village the cafés were now empty during the evenings and weekends, because Walid and his friends were playing soccer every spare hour. The Kafr-Hama team became a magnet. Soccer grew into a central issue among the local young people. It was more than just a game; it was exciting, filled space and time, provided shared experiences, set attainable goals. It taught them to compete with their Jewish peers on equal terms. It created a new order of priorities. In place of the all-encompassing loyalty and obedience to their respective clans, there was the self-esteem that stems from mutual challenge and commitment.

Walid became the village's Mr. Soccer. He had no need to travel to Tel Aviv to court the functionaries. The Hapoel people now started appealing to him to ensure that the Kafr-Hama soccer team wore the Hapoel emblem on its uniforms.

From its first appearance in local competitions, it was clear that an extraordinary team had been formed. The players didn't swear or fight or threaten the referee. They played to win, but they also knew how to lose. This kind of civilized behavior upset their opponents, who tried the time-worn trick of insulting the other players. If you curse someone, his honor requires him to reply, especially if you curse his sister or his mother. Then a brawl ensues, the game's disrupted, and everything's fine.

Walid was afraid that all the rules of fair play he had worked to instill in his players would vanish in the face of the hostility of the opposing teams. He decided he wouldn't let games be disrupted. He didn't want newspaper reports of riots at the Kafr-Hama soccer field. With bitter experiences behind him, he developed a strategy. He started spreading some of his friends among the crowd to prevent outbursts before they began. And any opponent who tried to provoke the Kafr-Hama players on the field received a whispered threat in his ear that if he didn't respect the rules of the game, they'd crack his nuts for him personally, but off the field, after the game.

"Learn from the Israeli army," Walid taught the members of his team. "We'll select the time and place of the attack. But on the field we keep our mouths shut and don't answer."

"Even if they insult my mother?"

"Especially if they insult your mother. We'll pay them back for both your mother and your father, but later."

After two or three rounds of games, the Kafr-Hama team proved that referees could referee in an Arab village without having to fear unruly fans.

The sports columns of some newspapers praised the team, though only briefly. Still, there was enough attention for the team to sense the rise of its status.

Very soon it dawned on the Kafr-Hama young men that, together, they were a force to be reckoned with. The knowledge that they could work effectively as a team, could rely on each other, changed their values and priorities.

During the period of tension that preceded the Six Day War — and during the war itself — when all the men in the surrounding kibbutzim were mobilized into the army, leaving many of their enterprises in danger of collapse, the young men of Kafr-Hama organized assistance operations for these kibbutzim. They manned key positions, brought in the harvests, took care of the livestock. When the war ended, they felt they'd contributed an integral part of the victory. In the period immediately after the war, when the borders were opened and the land began stretching its muscles — as if re-created in an expanded edition during these six days — the young men of Kafr-Hama cherished the notion that they also held a share in this moment of opportunity, the chance to mold their world anew.

While young fellows in other villages gave up whatever feeble attempts they had made to influence their own society and consoled themselves by discussing world problems, the young men of Kafr-Hama had a better grasp on reality. They asked themselves why their village was not more like the neighboring moshav, the Jewish village. "It's a pity we can't adopt their methods, enjoy the same facilities," they said. Walid challenged them: "Who says we can't? What's to stop us? Let's take matters into our own hands." And that was how the "Young Men's List" was born — the first Arab political non-clan ticket in the municipal elections.

When news got around about the formation of the Young Men's List for the council elections at Kafr-Hama, the political functionaries who were involved in any way with the Arab sector came sniffing around to find out what kind of person this Walid was. They soon decided that they had nothing to fear from him; he was so boyish and innocent. They recommended to their respective bosses that he be given token support, if only to frighten the traditional possessors of office. Let him do that for us; then it'll always be easy enough to get rid of him, they concluded.

The quantity of attention he received flattered Walid. Every visit of a cabinet minister, a government representative, a senior official, or a Knesset member in the Abu-Hana house raised his prestige among the young men of the village. Walid accepted every gesture of friendship at face value. In his mind's eye he could already see his dreams acquiring flesh and sinew, becoming reality.

He was not aware of the expressions of envy and resentment within the village, and his seeming indifference poured oil on the flames. A whispering campaign began against the local wonder boy. They gossiped that Walid was endangering the future of the girls of the village. Others went further, claiming that all the traditional values would be jeopardized. A leader of one of the opposing lists, claiming to represent progress, started visiting the homes of village notables and warning them, "If this fellow isn't stopped, you'll have to find bridegrooms from outside the village for your daughters."

"Why on earth ... ?" his interlocutors asked.

"It's like this," Walid's rival explained hastily. "Before the soccer craze, all our young men had their minds set on one thing only: to get married. And there's nothing surprising about that — until they set up a home, there's nothing for them to do. At the most they could go to Netanya or Hadera to see a movie. What did they do at the movie? They watched other couples smooching. They themselves had nothing to do, because we don't allow our daughters to be in male company out of their parents' supervision before their marriage. Even in the city they could only waste their money on whores, or fantasize and play with themselves. So they had to get married.

"Marriage isn't just a woman; it's also status. A married man can invite his friends home. He doesn't have to wander about in the streets. Even when he's in Tel Aviv, he's not under stress. If he gets horny over Jewish females, he can hurry home and plow his wife. But what's happened now? Now they have nothing on their minds except soccer."

The elders listened, and their wives eavesdropped.

"And that isn't all," Walid's opponent explained. "Men who don't hurry and get married start scoffing at tradition and ignoring the respect due their fathers. Why?" he continued, rhetorically. "Because if one wants to get married, one must respect one's father so that he'll pay the *mohar*, the bride-money, willingly. And more important still, marriage means home and home means land. So a young man who wants a home respects his parents, to be worthy to be given a plot for a house. No one'll give his daughter to a man who has no home."

The elders nodded, and their wives gazed at Walid with hostility. Some of them broached the subject with Walid's mother. Maybe if Walid himself got married, his pals would also stop their foolishness.

She tried to test his attitude. Cautiously mentioned the virtues of one of the budding beauties. Walid laughed. "I've got no time, Mother," he said.

"It's all because of the soccer," the elders said, nodding sagely.

6

EVEN AFTER WALID'S ELECTION as chairman of the village council, many of the villagers refused to take him seriously. They were certainly not pleased about his having dared to run for an election on a non-clan list, and were even less happy to witness his success in getting onto the council. Yet they had no doubt that his career would be short and end in a decisive failure. Meanwhile, they'd let the wonder boy learn for himself that administration is no child's game. Nor soccer, either.

They were right. No sooner did he occupy the mayor's chair when an immediate problem demanded his attention: water. Kafr-Hama suffered from a water shortage. Its water system had been designed when the village had fewer inhabitants, carried out less extensive farming, and followed sanitary practices that demanded much less of the precious liquid. But since the establishment of the State of Israel, the village had developed at a dizzying rate. The standard of living had risen; life expectancy had risen; the mortality rate had dropped; agriculture had become based on intensive irrigation; and every home had a faucet in the kitchen and a shower in the bathroom. The result: a serious water shortage.

Those who suffered most were the less well-off young families who had built their homes on the outskirts of the village, on the hillsides. Even when a couple did manage to get a water pipe extended to their home, they found that during most of the day there was not enough pressure to pump the water up the hill.

The leaders of the village, in traditional fashion, had shed their responsibility by declaring that the government should install a new water system.

But the authorities replied that water systems are the responsibility of the local councils. To improve the water supply, the village must first do its share and then apply to the government.

The water continued to flow sluggishly.

Walid viewed the problem from a different angle. The village couldn't wait for a new system to be installed; everyone needed water now. So until the situation improved, there had to be a just distribution of available water.

Walid divided the village into several zones and fixed "water hours" for each of them. This would assure that every zone, every home, even the most elevated and distant, would enjoy a regular supply of water during the appointed hours.

This scheme was implemented for a few days, but nothing changed. The chairman called his followers to an emergency meeting, appointed them council inspectors, and sent them out to the various areas.

It soon appeared that all the villagers were in favor of the new arrangement — for everyone other than themselves. The young inspectors issued several warnings and then started closing taps.

The village seethed.

Everyone understands that when a man is running for election he tosses out promises like confetti. But after being elected, one should act moderately and not disrupt tradition and people's lives.

They said that they'd predicted trouble with this young upstart.

Let him go and play soccer, and leave the running of the village to adults.

Walid and his young followers were unruffled by all the commotion.

Walid intended to proceed with his reforms — paving the roads, updating the sewage system, building a community center with a library and recreational facilities — but he needed money. Unfortunately, the council's treasury was empty.

Walid knew that the council's budget — as in all municipalities — consisted of local taxes and the financing allotted by the Ministry of the Interior from the national budget. The amount of government money was proportional to the number of residents and to the local taxes. Walid decided to find out who owed money to the council in back taxes and how much; and if the village had received from the government all the money that was coming to it. He sat down to examine the ledgers, and after he'd managed to decipher them, he discovered that the council's activities up to his election were all financed with government money, and that the moment the money ran out, the council continued its financing "on paper." In other words, the council would give work to contractors and not pay them. The contractors would stop work halfway through the job and then besiege the council offices. Whoever shouted loudest was the first to receive some partial payment. Because there was never enough to pay even one contractor all that was owed him, huge sums were expended on projects that were never completed, so nothing actually got done.

Roads, for example. The roads in the village had never been designed to accommodate the heavy traffic that had been rolling over them since the rapid economic expansion after the Six Day War. They were no more than alleys. There were no road signs, and everybody drove as he pleased. A villager might climb behind the wheel of a heavy Mack truck and race through the alleys as if they were superhighways and he was driving a Mercedes.

This kind of traffic took a heavy toll in lives. Walid went to a ministry official in Jerusalem and requested that the government put up money to build at least one central road. His request was turned down. He was advised that the Ministry for the Interior participates in the budgets of local councils according to specific criteria. For example, it gave a fixed sum for every *lira* of local taxes paid by the residents.

Walid was prepared. He pulled out his surprise card. "I checked the municipality ledgers and I discovered something strange — Jewish municipalities obtain a lot more per capita than we do."

The official was surprised. In his experience, an Arab council chairman shouted, but he had not yet met one who prepared his homework. He said, "Listen, Walid, you're right, but we're not so wrong either. We'll shell out some money so that you can start your road — but I want you to know something: the Jewish residents get more per capita, but they finance their local services from their own pockets. They pay their local taxes. The Arab municipalities impose local taxes, but they never bother to collect. I am well aware that the local services in Arab villages are inferior to the services in Jewish places. But I want you to know that whatever is being done in the Arab villages is being done with government money."

Walid went back and rechecked the books. The guy was right. At the next council meeting the mayor spoke fervently, declaring that an effort had to be made to collect the back taxes. "Otherwise we won't get a penny from the government," he said.

Older members of the council tried to calm him with words of wisdom acquired from experience. "Don't worry," they said. "They won't give anything now, but when it gets close to the elections to the Knesset, they'll come running to bring you the money."

But Walid was adamant about doing things his own way. A close examination of the list of debtors to the council revealed that the poorer the resident, the better his tax performance. The rich almost never paid up.

When he recounted all this to Maya, she asked: "Aren't the rich ashamed not to pay? Isn't it a matter of pride?"

Walid explained fellaheen psychology. The poor are ashamed not to pay — they don't want anyone to know they aren't paying because they don't have the money. But the rich are sure that no one would think they're short of money. So if they don't pay, it's just proof that they're rich enough to laugh at it all.

Neglecting the warnings not to rush too much, not to push local traditions too hard, Walid announced that the council would stop supplying water and other services to all those who did not pay off their tax debts to the council.

Let's see him do it, the village elders retorted.

He showed them.

The villagers were furious. Tempers ran high.

Elders and notables walked through the streets flushed and fuming like cocks before a fight. Everything about Walid infuriated them, but what infuriated them most was not the matter of the money, but the injury to their dignity and to the foundations of their society. Had Walid been alone, the whole affair could have been finished quickly. They could have pronounced him *majnun*, crazy. But many young men supported him. They actually possessed the nerve, the gall, the Jewish *chutzpa*, to carry out inspections in the homes of others' clans, and even in those of their own families. *Allah yerachmo* — God take pity on us. What will the world come to if their sons obey this freak of a chairman and consider him more important than the dignity and authority of one's own clan, of the elders and parents. Woe and disaster!

Notables, property owners, and clergy began to haunt the doorstep of Salah Abu-Hana. The expressions on their faces boded no good.

Although Salah Abu-Hana was a head of a very tiny clan, a one-family chamoula, his status in Kafr-Hama and indeed in the whole Arab triangle exceeded by far his quantitative significance. Several circumstances contributed to make people pronounce his name with the respect and reverence usually reserved for the very rich, the very mighty, or the very holy. Salah Abu-Hana did not stake a claim to any of the three. He was a man of deep faith, but his piety was devoid of any trace of self-righteousness. He was firm and unrelenting with the powerful, and gentle with the helpless. He was hardworking, almost Spartan in his habits. Allah favored him, and he prospered and found happiness in his family and in his toil. Or maybe so it seemed to the outsider, because even when misfortune befell him, Salah Abu-Hana did not despair or lose his good humor.

Many a man in Kafr-Hama had sired as many sons as he, but none was blessed with seven sons who, to the last one, were intelligent, industrious, genial, and extremely devoted to each other. There was a time when it had seemed that Allah resolved to test Salah's fiber. Shortly after independence, the State of Israel decided to appropriate all Arab lands whose owners did not physically reside within its borders. Not content with that, the government ruled that any Arab lands whose owners could not prove clean and valid title would also be confiscated. This was a hard blow for Salah Abu-Hana. He was the only son and heir of his father, but because he had been an infant when his father died, his uncle was named guardian and technically held title to the lands. When Salah achieved manhood, his uncle gave him the lands, but all the legal formalities were postponed from one year to the next because they did not attach any importance to them. The uncle was among those who fled during the war. Thus it came about that, though Salah Abu-Hana never moved from his village, most of his lands were taken from him.

He did not give up without a fight. He refused to take this blow lying down, and he had fought the state in the courts. He lost, though the Supreme Court commiserated with him, mentioning the regrettable gap in his case between law and justice. The state offered him compensation as a gesture of good will. He proudly declined. "I don't consider myself a loser," he told the government representative. "You won, but the decision in your favor is based on legalistic regulations. I am well content to be left with nothing but justice; justice will prevail." Since his lands were placed under the Administration of Estates of the Absentees, Salah Abu-Hana often referred to himself as a "present absentee."

Sages, landowners, and workers alike admired his courage and were prepared to pity his financial misfortune. Too soon. Salah Abu-Hana, with the diligent help of his wife and children, prospered rapidly. His second son, Hassan, who assumed the responsibility of the firstborn because of Omar's absence, demonstrated a real genius for business.

Even before the War of Independence, Salah Abu-Hana developed cordial relations with the kibbutzim and settlements in the neighborhood. When several Muslim fanatics started to incite the village against Jews, and his opinion was called for, he firmly vetoed such notions. "These are our neighbors," he said. "People who get up before dawn to till the land and who raise such beautiful cattle cannot be so evil as you claim." Thus, he and his children became frequent visitors in Ein Ganim and other collectives.

Little Hassan did not fear the Jews, and at the age of twelve, he discovered ways to cooperate with them that were as remunerative as they were ingenious. Hassan was the acknowledged "finance minister" of the Abu-Hanas; he became responsible for their diverse interests: farms, cattle, olive oil, tobacco, trucking, a gas station, among others. With all the brothers working together, and with absolute mutual trust, pooling all their resources and withdrawing money only when necessary, the Abu-Hanas acquired a fortune that was something to marvel at. Many envied Salah's happiness more than his riches. Some of his sons acquired academic titles, other were farmers — but all treated each other with equal respect and consideration, and honored and loved their parents.

Yes, no doubt about it, Salah Abu-Hana was a man of great wisdom and integrity, somebody to reckon with. This was the consensus of the self-appointed delegation of elders and notables who filed into his guest room that sun-drenched afternoon. His only failure was that no-good son of his, Walid. Well, maybe Salah was not aware of his son's policies. They would unburden their hearts to him — and he would call his son to order.

Old Abu-Hana received them graciously, with his customary hospitality, his pleasure reflecting clearly his conviction that good will had brought them hither.

They sat on the wicker stools and the leather armchairs placed around the large room. In its corner near the bed, the brazier held its glowing embers. No one had ever entered Salah Abu-Hana's room without being offered coffee in tiny *finjans*, which were repeatedly filled from the small, one-handled brass coffee pot emitting its fragrant aroma. The walls were covered with certificates, diplomas, and class photographs of his sons. Prominent among them was the impressive, clearly foreign photograph of the eldest, Omar, receiving his degree at the American University in Beirut. Omar had five children, but his father had never set eyes on the grandchildren, for his first-born had grown to adulthood in exile in the Jordanian kingdom and had gone to work in Saudi Arabia. There were times, before the Six Day War, when old Abu-Hana almost gave up hope of seeing his son again and rejoicing in his grandchildren. Now, since Israel declared the Open Bridges policy and allowed tens of thousands of Palestinians living in Arab countries to visit their relatives in Israel and in the West Bank, plans were being made for Omar's long-awaited homecoming.

The visitors came in, sat down, sipped the excellent coffee, and exchanged words about the weather, the crops, the price of sheep. Very slowly and delicately they began guiding the conversation toward the subject of their concern. They spoke about the difficulties of raising children, which wasn't as easy today as it once had been. They expressed sympathy toward a father who found himself today with a rebellious son.

Cautiously, they moved from the general to the particular and turned their focus on the grief of Salah Abu-Hana, whose son was causing him such trouble. Can such a thing be? they asked. This son of his, who's playing at being council chairman, had sent them the son of So-and-So, a miserable creature with no lands of his own, who had never dared to sit in the presence of notables. And here, the son of this nobody had been sent to them, and he had come into their houses and made notes. Once, when there had been order, he would not even have dared to step into the doorway of the guest room. And now? Now that he knows how to write, he comes in and makes notes. Like an emissary of the sultan in the old days. And what for? Because they, or, more precisely, the wife, had filled the laundry vat with water. Can one launder without water? Who had ever heard of a thing like that?

Will the son of this nobody, who doesn't even own a vegetable plot, come to tell them when to turn on the faucet inside their own homes? Does the water belong to his father?

Oh, woe to the eyes that see such things. This is what happens when the young are permitted to play at administration.

At first they spoke moderately, glancing all the time at Abu-Hana to gauge how far they could go. What they saw encouraged them. Abu-Hana sat listening in concentration, nodding his head while they spoke, with rapt attention. They fell silent and waited for him to speak.

"It is God's truth you speak," said Abu-Hana. "Each word is a precious stone. The Prophet himself could not have expressed it better. Administration is a difficult and responsible business, and a person should have learned from his own experience before he tells others how to behave. Had you asked my advice, I would have told you not to elect Walid. I told my son that I was not pleased about his running for office, but I said I would not stand in his way. I have great faith, I said to him, in the wisdom and intelligence of the people of our village. Who and what are you compared to them? Dust at their feet. You can be quite sure that they'll find better, wiser, and more respected people to lead them than my young and inexperienced son. But look what happened. They elected Walid. I was astonished. Had they decided to give him a trial period, after losing hope in the elders and notables who had filled the post before him? Who can tell? But who and what am I to measure my own judgment, a father's judgment, against the wisdom and judgment of the entire village? They elected Walid. They must have known what they were doing. Is it my fault they elected him?"

A sense of discomfort spread among the notables. They shifted on their seats and cleared their throats. No, no, God forbid. They had no intention of blaming old Abu-Hana or suggesting that he hadn't brought up his son properly. No thought was further from their minds. Allah forbid. On the contrary, he had sons to be proud of. The pride of the village. Walid, too, would turn out all right. Abu-Hana had spoken the truth — the villagers had elected him. Everyone was certain that in time Walid would bring him much joy. It was only a matter of age. Youthful mischievousness. When he grows up and marries, he'll leave all this nonsense behind. But in the meantime, he is running wild. He needs a touch of the rein.

No, they would say no more. A hint to the wise. They could trust Salah Abu-Hana to know what to do. Who were they — dust at his feet in both wisdom and virtue. Who were they to teach him how to tame his son?

Salah Abu-Hana refilled their small cups, passed the tray of cigarettes and the bowl of sweetmeats, in no hurry to speak. One of the visitors — whose title of Hadj attested not only to his having made the pilgrimage to Mecca but also to his great age, for since the establishment of the state, Israeli Arabs had not been able to go to Mecca — spoke for everyone. Ah, ah, now that the matter was in good hands, a stone had been lifted from their hearts. From tomorrow on, it would be clear to one and all that what was permissible to notables was not permissible to all and sundry.

Everyone nodded.

Salah Abu-Hana did not nod.

The visitors exchanged anxious glances.

Abu-Hana spread out his arms, as if to say "There's nothing I can do."

They looked at him, surprised.

It was impossible, unimaginable, that he would publicly admit that his son would not obey him. He had to be joking.

One of the *sheikhs*, whose paunch rested in front of him, wrapped in a wide silk sash down to his knees, felt compelled to speak frankly. "Surely you know, *ya* Abu-Hana, how much we respect you. We are all convinced that you will be able to rein your son. We have come to place our anxieties in your hands."

Abu-Hana again spread out his arms. "You are my guests; my house is your house and all that is in it is yours. But what you ask me for I have not the power to give. No one knows better than I that my son is yet a colt. If one wants a straight furrow, one doesn't harness a colt to the plow. But I am not the one who elected him. You elected him. What he does in the council is by the power of the electors."

They could contain their displeasure no more. And what about our customs, our traditions? And the commandment of the Prophet, which makes fathers responsible for the upbringing of their sons? Is Abu-Hana exempting himself from all this?

Salah Abu-Hana hastened to retract. "God forbid," he said. "You mustn't misunderstand me. If I've failed, I beg your forgiveness. It was only my lack of wisdom that obstructed me. Now I understand that it's not my son who has failed in the council, but I who have failed in bringing him up. The fault is mine. I am grateful to you for having spoken so delicately, so circuitously, for not saying to me to my face, 'Salah Abu-Hana, how have you brought up this son of yours!' Now I understand everything. One thing I beg of you now — don't spare me anything else. Tell me clearly and explicitly: Has Walid violated the rules, or has someone else in my family — my wife, perhaps, or one of my daughters, or my daughters-in-law? Have you discovered, Allah forbid, that Walid has been severe with others and lenient with himself and his relatives?

"Have you discovered that in the Abu-Hana clan faucets have been turned on during hours not allotted, or that its members have deferred paying their taxes, or have received permits in preference to any other?

"If such is the case, please do not spare me, my guests — my brothers, friends, and mentors. On my head may it be. I solemnly assure you that if it is only out of respect that you refrain from telling me of my son's shame to my face, and therefore make hints only so as not to grieve me — if that is so, I renounce my honor. Please, tell me. And if this is what you are concealing from me, I can assure you my son will feel the weight of my arm. No longer will he be called my son, nor will he call me father, until he mends his ways."

They were furious, but they could say nothing. He had sealed their mouths, even though he had urged them to tell him what they felt. They glanced at each other, stammered, tried to conduct an ordinary conversation, but failed. Flushed and choking with rage, they started preparing to leave. Salah Abu-Hana urged them to have more coffee, tried to fill their cups, passed around the copper tray of cigarettes of all kinds — American, Israeli, Jordanian — but the guests were suddenly in a hurry to leave. They gulped down their coffee and hastily bade their farewells. Salah Abu-Hana looked at them all with a warm smile. They glanced back at him, trying to determine if he was mocking them. He seemed genuinely sorry they were leaving so hastily.

*　　*　　*

Walid continued to carry out his reforms, not sensing or not caring that he was making enemies both inside and outside the village.

One day, just as he was leaving the office of the minister for the interior in Jerusalem, he bumped into the prime minister's adviser for Arab affairs.

"Ho, ho, *ya ibni* [my son], what a pleasant surprise. What brings you here?" asked the adviser patronizingly, and clapped him affectionately on the shoulder.

"Money," replied Walid, smiling. "I've come to ask for money from the development budget."

"So why didn't you come to me? I told you, I'm always ready to help."

"He manages quite well by himself," a bemused voice said. They turned to greet the minister, who continued: "Believe me, another ten Walids, and you'll have to look for another job. They won't need your advising."

They all laughed; then the adviser hurried on his way, frowning, no doubt thinking that the minister was right. This kid's running too fast. He has to be bridled.

7

WALID'S SUCCESS embarrassed many who had so far made easy quarry of the Arab sector. The experts on Arab affairs were unwilling to admit that his election attested to significant developments beneath the surface. They hoped that by training or taming Walid, they would be able to preserve the status quo. But Walid refused to be taken in tow.

As soon as it became apparent that the young chairman knew a thing or two other than how to kick a soccer ball, and that he was even likely to succeed in his job, it was decided in the inner chambers of the ruling party that Walid Abu-Hana merited closer scrutiny. "This guy is worth some trouble. He has mass appeal; he has a nose for politics. The media favor him. Let's snap him up before somebody else does."

Thus began a short-lived honeymoon between the Labor Party and the young mayor.

The affair was doomed before it started. The party bosses took it for granted that Walid would change his tune as soon as some vague promises were whispered in his ear about the possibility of his being put on the party ticket for the general elections in the future.

They were not entirely wrong. Walid undeniably nursed a dream of becoming a member of the Knesset. However, he was not willing to trade his integrity for the Knesset seat.

The experts were quick to wash their hands of him and to devise their strategy. While party celebrities continued to praise the young mayor and assert their personal friendship with him, a vigorous campaign was begun behind the scenes to dismiss him from office.

There were eleven councilmen in the village, nine of whom had voted Walid into office. If four of these proved amenable to persuasion, that would be enough to unseat him.

* * *

Walid was hesitant when he telephoned Maya. He dawdled before coming to the point, expressing gratitude to her for the large feature article that had turned him, overnight, into a public figure throughout the State of Israel, then, in the next breath, apologizing to her for wasting her time. Finally, he came to the point: his situation had deteriorated sharply and it looked very much as though his political opponents would soon succeed in getting him out of office.

It was no news to Maya that Walid had plenty of political opponents, but she was taken by surprise to hear his dire assessment.

"I've been invited by Yitzhak Levi, the director of the Arab Affairs Department of the Histadrut, to come for a chat," said Walid. "As you know, he wields great power over Arab affairs and he's Labor's man all the way. I don't like the looks of it."

Maya smelled a rat, too. The progress that Walid had made in his short term as mayor threatened to upset the cozy arrangement by which the Labor Party was assured of malleable Arab leadership. Realizing that despite his sharp wit and political instincts, Walid was still something of a political innocent and no match for Levi, Maya decided to help him if she could.

"Would you like me to come with you?" she ventured. "Levi is bursting to give me a lecture on the error of my ways after what I wrote about you. He'll jump at the chance to have two fish to fry."

"Why, that would be marvelous. I certainly would feel better about it," exclaimed Walid, in candid relief.

Maya made a mental note that ordinarily her suggestion would have been unpardonable — a woman offering assistance to a man of some importance! Yes, Walid was different.

Levi sounded delighted when she reached him on the phone. "I'm very glad you called, Maya. I have quite a number of things to say to you concerning what you wrote about Kafr-Hama, but I keep in mind that you're young. You wrote a lot of nonsense, but we won't make an issue of it. The important thing is to find time for a serious conversation, and then you'll understand what we're doing here. It's not as simple as journalists think."

Maya said that she would be pleased to learn more about the subject and especially wanted to know if there was any truth in the rumor that the establishment was joining forces with the Arab communists in order to depose the young mayor of Kafr-Hama.

"I'm glad you asked me that," said Levi. "But that's not something we can talk about on the phone, you understand."

"I really thought that you'd try to help Walid Abu-Hana," said Maya.

"Of course we're helping. In fact, I'll be meeting him tomorrow at nine. You can come, too, to see how much work we're putting into this young fellow."

The next day, in Levi's room, she watched Yitzhak Levi exercise his expertise on Walid.

First of all, Levi explained to Walid that he had got himself into a fix from which only the affection and compassion of Big Brother, the Department for Arab Affairs of the Histadrut, could extract him. Then he systematically proceeded to quash all Walid's hopes for a political future. Every now and then, he would retreat slightly, adding a touch of encouragement. "Don't take it to heart, Walid. Politics isn't something you learn in a day or two. We were all young once, and we thought the world could be divided into black and white. But life teaches us to compromise. We know your intentions are good. We all admire your work. But really, be serious, how long do you think that we can give you credit simply because we like you? Public life is responsibility, and you've destroyed a wealth of good will that took us years to establish. It doesn't matter that your intentions were good . . ."

After about an hour of grilling, Walid was willing to admit that he himself was indeed responsible for his precarious position. At this point of absolute despair, Levi threw him the life line. "Look, I'll tell you straight, both common sense and public responsibility force us to dump you. You made this mess; now you'll have to clean it up. But I have to admit that I've got a soft spot in my heart for you; I've seen you growing up here, right before my eyes. So you've made some mistakes. But I believe that you're still capable of winning back your place. I'm willing to take a risk. And I won't conceal from you that the odds are clearly against us. Still, I want to give you a chance. A man has to take some risks in his life. The fact is, I'm sorry for you. There's only one way of sparing your father and your brothers the shame of your being turned out of office. Sign this letter of resignation. I'm willing to do this for you. You don't have to thank me. I believe that you'll appreciate it. So that's it. Let this be a lesson to you."

Fascinated, Maya followed the conversation and watched how Levi casually passed the letter of resignation to Walid, who pulled out a pen and hesitantly raised it over the space left for his signature.

She felt like an observer watching a man about to be eaten by a shark. At the very last moment, just as Walid's pen touched the paper, she cleared her throat. "Just a minute, just a minute, tell me, Mr. Levi . . ." Walid's hand rose from the paper, and Levi looked at Maya with murder in his eyes.

Maya swallowed a laugh and continued, her face all innocence and bewilderment. "I don't understand something. If Walid signs, he loses his position and it'll look as if he admits failure, right? So why is that better than being deposed? It's as if he were signing his own dismissal."

Levi explained — in a torrent of words. But all three of them recognized that the decisive moment had passed. Walid had recovered. "I really appreciate what you're trying to do for me, Yitzhak, but I want to think it over," he said calmly.

In the corridor he sent her a grateful look, wiped his forehead, and said incredulously, "It almost worked. I nearly signed."

After this experience, Walid began to trust Maya as a political ally, taking her into his full confidence.

To mark this turning point in their friendship and celebrate the young mayor's reprieve, they retired to a café not far from the Histadrut headquarters. This café was a meeting place for soccer players, though in the morning hours well-to-do housewives liked to sit there and gossip while the Yemeni cleaning women scrubbed their floors.

As they sipped thick, syrupy-sweet Arabic coffee, Walid elaborated on the efforts to unseat him. Maya knew that he served as chairman of the town council only at the discretion of the other councilors, and that a vote of no confidence could turn him out of the chairmanship any time a majority could be mustered. If that happened, he would still be a councilor, but he would lose the power and prestige of being chief executive of the town administration. Still, she was concerned when he reported that such a motion of no confidence was soon to be put to the town council, and she was shocked to hear Walid say that the votes of four councilmen had been bought for five thousand pounds apiece. She could not avoid noticing that for an Arab politician to report to a Jewish journalist a case of graft among Arabs was also extraordinary. Now she had no doubt at all that he trusted her.

"It's a scandal," said Maya. "You have to make it public."

"Make it public?" Walid repeated. He sounded bemused. "It's taken for granted that bribery figures in such important matters. You can't expose what everyone knows, including my self-appointed mentor, Mr. Levi."

"The Supreme Court. We have to take it to the Supreme Court." Maya was fuming.

Walid pondered this new suggestion. There were so many unknowns and obstacles. The Supreme Court costs money, and this money would have to come from Walid's pocket, or, more precisely, from the family's pocket, from his father and brothers. The decision itself was also difficult — publicly to accuse respected Arab figures of giving and accepting bribes. To hang dirty laundry in public simply was not done.

The Abu-Hana family bravely arrived at their decision. Rasem, Walid's older brother who was studying economics at the Hebrew University, suggested that they approach Advocate Greenbaum, who had once been state attorney. He believed that the public reputation of such a figure would make a lot of difference.

From the moment the rumor spread that the young chairman was soliciting people's signatures on sworn declarations about their knowledge of the bribes, the village was in a furor. This young brat, they rumbled, who wasn't even married and still played soccer, who belonged to a family that did not even carry the weight of a full-sized clan; this fellow had not only dared to get himself elected chairman of the council, but was now challenging respected and respectable agreements among the elders of the village and was threatening to drag them by their ears through an Israeli court.

Elders and notables stormed through the streets of the village with angry expressions on their faces, calling on heaven and earth to testify that never had such a thing occurred before.

Everyone discussed the matter fervently and endlessly, as they waited with bated breath for the date of the council meeting that would depose Walid Abu-Hana.

It was not easy to obtain sworn declarations. It was one thing to pound the table in a coffee house in the middle of the village and declaim bitterly against the wretches who were willing to sell their souls for five thousand pounds; it was something else to sign a document to that effect in a notary's office. Finally the testimony was collected and the documents presented, and a date was set for the hearing in the Supreme Court, requesting the issuing of a show-cause order. The request was to be heard in Jerusalem on the morning of the day the council scheduled its afternoon meeting.

The race against time began. Even if the order was granted, there might not be time to bring the documents issued by the Supreme Court to Kafr-Hama and deliver them personally to all of the council members before the time appointed for the vote.

Maya worried about the timing as she hurried from the newspaper building in Tel Aviv to Kafr-Hama. She was excited, tense; she had almost passed the first houses in the village when it dawned on her that something strange was going on. The village seemed abandoned, empty. The cafés were shut down; the windows, doors, and shutters of most of the houses on the main street were closed, too. Kafr-Hama resembled a ghost town, devastated by epidemic or war.

Then she heard distant voices, like the sound of approaching thunder. Shouts. After the last turn in the street leading to the council building, she saw them. A sea of people. Young men, old men, adolescents, and even women. A solid human mass, marching and yelling. At first she could not make out the cry rising and falling rhythmically, excitedly, from hoarse throats. Then she heard the words: "With our blood and our souls we will redeem you, Walid. With our blood and our souls we will redeem you, Walid."

The multitude of people formed a tight ring around the council building. Maya saw Walid raised on the shoulders of the crowd like a human battering ram with which they intended to break down the walls of tradition and backwardness. She recognized Taufik, Walid's trusted lieutenant, standing head and shoulders above the crowd. His voice was leading the chorus while his eyes anxiously followed the aerial progress of his friend.

She met Walid's gaze. His excitement was obvious.

Taufik signaled to Maya to park the car and hurried toward her. They didn't speak. There was no need. All three of them would have liked to force the clock to move more slowly. Each passing second increased the tension. While the crowd outside swore its allegiance to the young council chairman, the members of the council who were already inside, waiting for the meeting to convene, tried to ignore the voices.

The hands of the clock approached four, the hour set for the meeting. The crowd continued its cries, increasing the tempo.

Walid's face was pale.

"Wait another five minutes," urged Taufik, pleadingly.

"I have to go in. The meeting has to start on time," said Walid.

Taufik looked angrily at the clock. "Even if the order doesn't get here on time, those old men won't sleep well," he said to Walid. "Even on their wives' bellies they'll hear the echoes of this demonstration. They'll be afraid of you."

Walking heavily, as if they had weights around their ankles, the three of them climbed the narrow stone steps into the council building. The crowd became silent.

They understand, thought Maya. No one has explained it to them, but they understand that the miracle hasn't happened. That the strong hand of the court has not reached their village on time.

Walid opened the gate leading to the council hall. The men inside looked at him with open mockery, triumphantly. Then the silence outside was clearly penetrated by the noise of a vehicle.

Everyone spoke and shouted at once. "Conduct the vote," shouted the prospective new chairman, flushed and choking. "Conduct the vote!"

"I would like to ask all the council members to sit down," said Walid, imbuing his voice with all the authority he could muster without revealing his excitement.

Outside, the crowd parted as if an order had been given, allowing the small car to park right beside the steps. To Maya, viewing the scene, this small, dusty green car could have been the modern incarnation of the Messiah's white donkey.

From the car emerged a man with a large paunch, panting, clutching a file of papers. His face was red and dripping with sweat. He was trailed by a strikingly handsome young man with a mop of black hair, full of the importance of the moment and of self-importance, while trying to appear as if these matters merely constituted a routine day's work for him.

This, then, must be Rasem, thought Maya, the Abu-Hana brother who studies economics.

The crowd breathed a collective sigh of relief.

"Supreme Court, Supreme Court, Supreme Court," the crowd chanted, tasting the sounds and rolling them around their tongues, savoring them as if they were precious and exotic. Not everyone knew what secret they contained, but it was obvious that it was a great magic charm.

"Supreme Court, Supreme Court, Supreme Court."

Maya didn't even feel at first that she was digging her fingernails into the palms of her hands. "Taufik, let them in, Taufik. Don't let anybody block their path."

"We're voting to depose the chairman," shouted the prospective new chairman.

Walid spoke. "I request the council members to be seated so that I may open the meeting."

From the street came roars of joy. Hasty steps, almost running, and then the two men were inside. Rasem and the paunchy lawyer, his tie flapping to the side. The council members were stumped, but reluctant to admit defeat. They started waving their arms about, shouting into each other's words. The prospective chairman placed himself in the path of the two men. "You can't come in here," he said. "Only council members..."

Walid spoke, quietly. "This is Advocate Greenbaum. My brother Rasem you all recognize. Advocate Greenbaum has brought the Supreme Court's decision. Rasem will translate. As chairman of the council, I have the honor to open this meeting."

"You *were* chairman," one of the members called out.

"I still am," said Walid.

"Quiet, please," said Rasem. "Advocate Greenbaum would like to say something to the members of the council."

"He has nothing to say to us," the members who intended to depose Walid shouted angrily. "We'll vote and that's it."

Advocate Greenbaum raised his hand.

"Honored gentlemen," he said, "I bring you an order from the Supreme Court. Each of you is personally ordered not to participate in a meeting designed to depose the chairman, and not to vote on such a matter."

"We don't need to take any account of that," several replied.

"Anyone who ignores an order of the Supreme Court is breaking the law. You are placing yourselves in contempt of court," Greenbaum explained, sweating and breathing heavily.

From his file he very carefully drew out documents covered with seals and markings, and laboriously read the name written on the top of each of them, with an inquiring glance at Rasem as he did so. Rasem then indicated which of the men sitting around the table was to receive the particular document. The first rejected the document with both hands, thrusting it away from him, refusing even to touch it. He started back as if defending himself from the evil eye, pushing his chair backward. And the others thrust their hands into the folds of their robes, as if afraid of burning them.

Fully aware of the electrified atmosphere in the hall, Greenbaum again explained that these orders represented a personal and explicit instruction of the supreme legal authority to each and every one of the members of this council, instructing him not to vote on the proposal to depose the chairman. He further explained that anyone receiving this order who did not act according to the instructions was committing an offense punishable by a fine and imprisonment. Similarly, anyone who refused to accept the order when it was handed to him was committing an equally grave offense. He explained what was meant by contempt of court and urged those present not to make matters worse for themselves by refusing to accept the orders after their significance had been made clear.

Rasem made a supreme effort to translate the lawyer's speech into Arabic. The prospective chairman and his supporters waved their fists in the air, shouting curses and insults at the young man of Kafr-Hama but not daring to offend the Jewish lawyer. Rasem tried to remain cool, to ignore their insults.

Those loyal to Walid reached out eagerly to receive the court documents. Among the others, some accepted the papers unwillingly or continued to reject them.

Everyone tried to silence everyone else. They jumped from their chairs and thrust their hands under each other's noses. Walid's voice broke through the din. He announced that since the only point on the agenda was the proposal to depose the chairman, and since the Supreme Court order prevented him from bringing the proposal to a vote, he was closing the meeting.

They went outside — he and his supporters, together with the guests — to the crowd still waiting. Again Walid was raised on the crowd's shoulders and the demonstrators cheered his triumph until they grew tired and dispersed to their homes.

Inside the hall remained those who had plotted to depose Walid. They decided to outsmart the Supreme Court. They held a meeting, voted to depose Walid, and elected a new chairman.

They realized, of course, that this gesture had no legal validity and that for it they might have to pay dearly, but they had to save face. Or perhaps they were wise to the rules of the game, and understood that no one would actually force them to pay the legal penalty for their blatant violation of the court order.

While the Abu-Hana family celebrated the victory of Israeli justice, a rumor spread through the village that a new chairman had been elected. Confused villagers consulted with each other, trying to discover if anyone could tell them which chairman's authority was the more valid.

Two weeks later the temporary court order was annulled, and after another two weeks a meeting to depose Walid was conducted without interruption.

The Abu-Hana family bore the costs of the legal exercise.

It was only much later that Maya understood the processes that had weighted the scales of justice against the valiant young mayor.

The defendants acquired the services of a Jewish lawyer from a Muslim country, who addressed the Supreme Court judges on "the Muslim mentality." He claimed that it was wrong for the Israeli regime to trample roughshod over the culture and tradition of a minority by arbitrarily imposing upon them the principles of Western law. And to top this, he pulled an argument out of his sleeve that confused Walid's lawyer, a native of Western Europe, and caught him unprepared. The lawyer for the deposing coalition claimed that one should not consider the sums of money that had changed hands as bribery, aimed, God forbid, at subverting the due processes of government. Such a view was an optical illusion, deriving from a European outlook. What was involved here was an ancient Muslim custom, carried out in good faith and worthy of respect. Its purpose was the depositing of monies in the hands of dignitaries so that they could later distribute it to charities. The case was not one of bribery, but of an ancient tradition of paying honor to elders, who were entrusted with the carrying out of the religious commandments, and whose task it was to distribute this money wisely and well.

The lawyer admitted that there was a casual connection between these sums of money and the decision to depose Walid, but the money was never intended for the private gain of any one of the public figures involved. And if it was true that the court's duty was to inform the elders of the proper processes of local government, it was not right to disgrace the village dignitaries as if they were receivers of bribes and to deem them unfit to carry out public functions. At least not in this case, the first of its kind, and one that would create a precedent. The best thing to do, claimed the lawyer piously, would be to allow the entire Arab public to learn lessons from this case, for future application.

"Tradition" is a magic word in the Israeli lexicon. Its place is secure in the pantheon of sacred cows. Even the Supreme

Court would not hasten to injure Arab sacred tradition.

At the same time, the judges recalled Walid's frank and convincing testimony; they were loath to disregard it.

How does one ensure progress without trampling on tradition?

It was then that the establishment flashed its trump card.

Unnamed agents of the Security Services requested permission to show the judges certain classified and very confidential documents, according to a procedure that allows for testimony pertaining to state security to be given *in camera* and without revealing the identity of the witnesses. Their version was that if the court decided against the dignitaries, Walid's life would be endangered.

Witnesses whose names were not revealed opened some files. The judges studied the documents. The files were closed. The witnesses left. The judges decided that the show-cause order should not be made absolute.

One of the Supreme Court judges, a well-known champion of liberal causes, spoke to the plaintiff apologetically. "You're a young man and you have a very active public life before you. Always remember that when we made this decision we were concerned for your welfare."

The case did not destroy Walid's charisma. Young men rallied to him, and his name became even more familiar. In the Arab sector, everyone understood what had really happened. The Arab public did not consider the affair of bribery in a more favorable light after the court decision. On the contrary. Many were disgusted with those involved in the matter, but everyone was delighted by the complex exercise involving the lawyer, the dignitaries, and the establishment. The villains had outwitted the judges; for that, at least, they deserved credit.

Walid's first term in office had two other legal repercussions. The elders, swelling with their first success, yet frightened by the powerful public support displayed for Walid, determined that he had to be squashed while he was still small. This was an intelligent decision.

They filed two legal complaints.

The first was against Rasem Abu-Hana. The complaint was that he had used vile language at the time he had brought the court's order to the council, thus injuring the honor of the elders and of the Prophet Mohammed. When Walid told her the news, Maya exclaimed, "But he did not!" Walid patiently explained that facts were immaterial. "The purpose is harassment of the Abu-Hanas; maybe they hope to goad Rasem into exploding in court. Rasem has a very volatile temper."

Rasem's defense offered twenty-six sworn statements, all testifying to Rasem's reputation, and several testimonials to the fact that he had not uttered one objectionable word at the meeting referred to, despite provocation. The complaint was dismissed, and the plaintiffs were ordered to pay a nominal compensation and costs. However, Rasem never forgave his accusers, and he held a grudge against the villagers from that time on.

The complaint against Walid was highly instructive.

The attorney, Hassan Antar, head of the most important feudal family in the village, son of the late Arab Knesset member, charged Walid with wrongfully exploiting his authority while chairman of the council, in that he had given instructions to have the flow of water to the plaintiff's house and fields closed. The plaintiff demanded a return of damages and compensation for the injury to his honor, for the insult, the inconvenience, the pain, and so on. It was disgusting, the complaint read, that an unknown rascal, from a family of no repute, had the impudence to raise his hand against the head of the most respected family in the village.

The debate was amusing, or perhaps sad. The esteemed lawyer, who argued his own case, admitted that he actually did owe many thousands of pounds to the council for water, and admitted, furthermore, that he had received numerous warnings before the water had been cut off at the chairman's instructions. But he insisted that "in our society it is inconceivable, Your Honor, that such a nobody will have the impudence to act against the Antar family."

The judge was astonished. "This man acted by the authority vested in him as chairman of the council."

"Your Honor is well aware that we quickly got that nonsense out of his head," said the plaintiff. "Who is he? He doesn't even have a family to speak of. Though his father's a respectable man, the family doesn't even merit consideration as a real clan in our village. They must be taught proper manners, Your Honor. How can a young brat who kicks a soccer ball around dare to cut off the water of the Antar family? Your Honor may ask anywhere in this country — everyone knows who Hassan Antar is. But no one knows this young upstart's family. It will be the end of the world if he is not taught his place."

The judge said quietly, "Do you know what the name of my family is, Mr. Antar?"

"Yes, Your Honor. You are Judge Shapira. Among us the name Shapira is well known; it's a very respected name."

The judge smiled. "But you know, Mr. Antar, perhaps that isn't my name at all. My parents perished in Poland during the war. I was brought here as a nameless orphan, with the Youth Aliyah. At the displaced persons camp in Germany, I met a woman who claimed that I was the son of Shapira, her neighbor in Lodz. I thought she might be right, and since then my name has been Shapira. But then again, Mr. Antar, I could be wrong. Maybe I am not Shapira by right, and perhaps I bear this name falsely. What then, Mr. Antar? Should the court adopt your criteria, I would have to face the loss of my good name and learn new manners. Well, you see, my esteemed colleague, that I have no choice but to reject your line of reasoning." His voice became clear and distinct: "The court rules that the prestige or eminence of ancestry will be no guide in the administration of justice."

8

WALID ONCE CONFESSED to Maya that whenever he or one of his brothers had to memorize something, his sister Leila would always learn it before they did by listening to them repeating the lesson while she washed clothes, cooked, or scrubbed the floors.

"Had she been given the opportunity to study, she would have put us all to shame," he said.

Maya agreed with him. "If only she could read and write, she'd be able to do that."

"Leila," Maya said one day, "let's make a deal. I'll teach you to read and write, and you'll teach me to speak Arabic." Leila's eyes glowed. "*T'fadal*," she said. "Today?"

They decided that during each of Maya's visits they would set aside some time for study, but somehow nothing came of it. Leila didn't want to press Maya, and Maya, though her offer was sincere and she had meant well, would always arrive pressed for time, and would leave with a solemn promise that on her next visit they would begin.

"What will you teach her?" asked Walid. "The Hebrew alphabet or the Arabic?"

"Best to do both," said Maya. "That way we'll learn together. She'll improve her Hebrew and I'll improve my Arabic."

It was a somewhat unusual situation, because Maya had studied Arabic at high school, and had been able to read a newspaper without difficulty. She did even better with children's books, which included the dots that stood for vowels. But over the years she forgot it all from lack of use and neglect. Every Israeli Arab child, however, was taught to read, write, and speak Hebrew. They even learned by rote

Bialik's poem "To the Bird" at elementary school in every Arab village. Maya didn't know whether to laugh or cry when she heard the poem, in which the Russian-born national poet of Israel had expressed his yearnings for Zion, pronounced in the guttural accents of the children in Kafr-Hama. She thought it incongruous that they were expected to memorize this poem while remaining ignorant of contemporary Arabic literature.

At any rate, Maya always delighted in the pleasure and surprise of young Arabs whenever she demonstrated her ability to write her name, and theirs, in the curling Arab script. Since meeting Walid she had regretted losing her facility with Arabic — especially because she could not hold proper conversations with Walid's father or with Leila.

Nevertheless, the two women became close friends. Leila received Maya joyfully with a hearty embrace and a kiss on both cheeks. They held long conversations with the aid of five words in Hebrew, three in Arabic, and a lot of good will. They would look into each other's eyes, and respond to the expression on the other's face.

"How are you?"

"In sh'allah."

"Kif halek?"

"Al-hamdu lillah."

After this, each would speak for a long time while the other nodded happily or made noises of grief, as the circumstances called for. When one or the other felt clearly that what was being discussed was not just an exchange of moods, but something specific and important, she would ask Walid or one of Leila's younger sisters, then studying at high school.

Walid's young sisters, who were still living in their father's home, were planning to become teachers, and dressed in Western style, or, rather, in its local version. For beneath their dresses they wore the standard narrow trousers of the village. But when they wore slacks and shirt, they looked no different from Jewish girls of their own age, except that they were much more restrained about baring their skin, always careful that their sleeves came right down to the wrist and that the top button at the neck was closed.

Leila dressed like the daughters of the previous generation, in village style; like her mother and her older sisters, who no longer lived at home. The traditional costume suited her to perfection, and Maya wondered if she realized that her beauty would have been dimmed by Western fashions.

Leila was the most beautiful of Salah Abu-Hana's daughters. Although the Abu-Hana family was renowned for its looks, Maya felt that the sons of the family were better-looking than the daughters. When Maya met Walid, his two oldest sisters had already been married for many years and had children of their own; the two young ones were still at high school. Leila was the middle sister. Maya always marveled at her radiant smile and graceful figure, and could not understand why she had not married, knowing that in this society for a woman to remain single was considered a disaster. Initially, Maya was convinced that Leila's single status concealed a love affair that was really a stirring drama. Later, when she became closer to the Abu-Hana family, she realized how wrong her conclusions had been.

When they first met, Leila was almost thirty. By the standards of the village, she was considered an old maid. The fellaheen were marrying the girls at eighteen. This was considered the most respectable time to be married, after the necessary delay for the sake of a high school education. If girls were not married by the age of eighteen, it was considered proof that she was not attractive enough to make anybody choose her for a wife. According to these same standards, she was supposed soon to be withered, wrinkled, and repressed from hard work in the fields and home, and no fun. A blot on the family reputation, which everyone tried to hide. Yet Leila Abu-Hana was the apple of her family's eye. Her younger sisters and her sisters-in-law showered her with affection.

Maya often teased Walid about his not teaching Leila to read and write. Yet despite the friendship and candor between them, Maya refrained a long time from asking why she hadn't been given in marriage.

Had Maya and Leila shared a common language, had she felt sure that she would be able to choose the right words, words that wouldn't injure, she should have talked about it with Leila herself. But in the absence of such a language, the riddle remained unsolved. For someone of Maya's inquisitive nature, it was an upsetting situation. One might have expected Leila to be somewhat bitter, sullen, withdrawn, aware that life had passed her by, and resigned to what this implied. But Leila was glowing. There was not a trace of bitterness in her.

Maya began to suspect that Walid was simply exploiting his sister's goodness and love. Without Leila, Walid undoubtedly would not have been able to remain a bachelor so long. The beloved and unwed sister filled the role of housekeeper for the young council chairman who was so highly favored by Jewish VIPs. Walid's house and guest room were always sparkling clean. Fresh flowers were always in the vases. As soon as visitors appeared in the doorway, there was someone to warm the pita, to prepare refreshments, to fill deep bowls with cubes of watermelon and slices of honeydew. Walid's shirts were always ironed and starched, and he was never short of clean socks. No faithful wife would have so pampered Walid and taken care of his guests' every need as Leila did. Always with a smile, always without noise or fuss, as if everything got done by itself. She never grumbled about the fact that Walid's guest room resembled the cafeteria of a busy railway station, open twenty-four hours a day.

Walid was very proud of his sister and never kept her hidden. On the contrary, he strongly encouraged her friendship with Maya.

Maya learned that the distinctive trait of the Abu-Hana family was its gift of absorbing innovations gradually and by choice, without rejecting old ways while doing so. Abu-Hana's daughters never entered the guest room and never sat with the men unless they were specifically invited to do so. For if among the guests there were local people of various ages, you could never be sure if one of them would not be offended by the presence of a woman, and consider this a rejection of traditional values. But when Walid invited his sisters, they always behaved with self-confidence.

Walid was not the only one who relied on Leila. In fact, she held the strings of the entire household. Actually, she shared this task with Tamira, the wife of her brother Hassan, the crafty and enterprising treasurer of the clan. Tamira, tall and full, had borne many children. She was a vivacious woman, hearty and affable. In the women's quarters, she filled the role her husband filled in the men's world. Tamira and Leila divided the housework between them, with never a tiff. Both of them took special care not to show disrespect to Basma Abu-Hana, Leila's mother, and consulted with her on every decision, major or minor. "Should we make the goat cheese today?" "Should we go to Tulkarm to buy the white gossamer muslin for the granddaughters' dresses?" "When shall we start spinning the wool?" "Should we distill the oil today?"

Walid's mother reigned in the large court, and under her watchful but kind supervision the chores were accomplished smoothly. The sound of women quarreling — brides with mothers-in-law, daughters with sisters-in-law — was never heard in the Abu-Hana household.

It was not for nothing that when a young man of the village had the good fortune to find a gracious bride, the villagers would say to him, "The star of Salah Abu-Hana has shone upon you!" And when it happened that a son disgraced the family, his father would sigh dejectedly and say, "Well, I'm not Salah Abu-Hana, am I?"

Maya longed for a dress like Leila's. A dress with a petticoat of the finest kaffiyeh cloth and over it a richly pleated skirt, with the waist tight over a blouse with puffed sleeves. Once when she expressed her admiration of a new dress Leila was wearing, and admitted that she envied her ability to sew her own clothes, Leila offered to make her a dress. Walid translated, to make sure they would agree on the color. Maya liked purple. After some time, Walid informed her that the dress was ready.

It was a terrible disappointment. Leila had fashioned a dress that was a miserable compromise with Western vogue. She had put a lot of work into it, embroidering the sleeves and the bodice with a dense cross-pattern. But the dress itself was without character or taste, and Maya wore it at home only in appreciation of the love and good will that had been invested in it. She confessed to Walid that she had dreamed of a real peasant's dress. "I thought that was what you meant," he said, "but Leila laughed at me and said that you're a journalist and surely wouldn't wear a thing like that."

Leila's spinsterhood often occupied Maya's thoughts. It's impossible, she thought, that no one has asked for her hand. Perhaps Leila had pined after some young man, and her father had not found his family worthy of her?

No, that's impossible, thought Maya, remembering Najami, the oldest daughter, who had been allowed her choice of husband. Maya had met her when she was already a worn-out woman whom life had not pampered. Her heavily scarred hands bore witness to years of hard work. But even then her blue eyes and her fair skin showed that in her day she must have been considered a beauty — all this in addition to the Abu-Hana smile, which from time to time banished the burden of age. Once, in an unguarded moment — and such moments were frequent with Maya — she asked why Najami had been given to a landless hired hand.

"Because she wanted him," Walid replied. "Father knew that he was the one she wanted. She would blush scarlet when he passed our yard, slowing his walk as much as he dared. Father did not find it in his heart to betroth her to someone else."

Maya somehow was not surprised that in Salah Abu-Hana's home the daughters, too, were treated as individuals, long before such a trend had become popular.

Abu-Hana was also one of the first to send his daughters to school when the Compulsory Education Act was passed, thus paving the way for others to follow. They must have figured that if Abu-Hana sent his daughters to school, it meant that no harm would befall them, and their chastity would remain intact.

But Leila had missed out. When the act was passed, she was already over the compulsory-education age. Walid often told Maya how their father had taken Leila with him wherever he went, proud of her beauty and her intelligence, "just as if she were a boy."

Whenever they talked of Leila, they left certain things unsaid. Maya was concerned about Leila's future, but she was afraid of intruding in an area that was not her affair.

One day Walid arrived at Maya's home in Tel Aviv, and from the expression on his face, she knew something was up. They talked a little about the day's news, and then Walid said, as if in passing, that he didn't know how he would manage without Leila to care for him.

Maya was alarmed. "What's happened to Leila?"

"We've decided to marry her," Walid explained.

The man Leila's father and brothers had chosen to be her husband was a widower of about fifty. His children from his previous marriage were married and out of the house. He wasn't particularly wealthy, but he wasn't poor, either. An educated man, still in his prime. Old Abu-Hana would reinforce the material base of his prospective son-in-law to make sure that Leila would not suffer for lack of anything. Walid added, "She deserves a better husband, of course, but in her situation . . ."

"Have you asked her?" Maya asked anxiously.

"She's quite pleased, in fact; definitely pleased," said Walid.

Now that the subject had been broached, they discussed it at length. "A woman of her age doesn't have many possibilities in our society," Walid said. "She might find a lecherous old man, a widower with lots of children on his hands, who needs a woman to raise them for him and to warm his bed at night, and she'd consider herself lucky at that. Actually, we're fortunate to find this match. He'll be a good husband to her. He is vigorous; he will cherish Leila."

"Why did you wait so long?" Maya asked. "Perhaps you'll tell me why she had to stay single at all?"

"It just happened that way," said Walid. "She felt good at home, so she didn't press us. And we . . . we were selfish. It was hard for us to think of doing without her. And so the years passed. Year after year. Father never did give the girls in marriage when they were very young, just after puberty. We loved Leila and kept her with us a bit longer. At first, when men came to negotiate for her hand, not one of them was good enough for her, in my father's view. Still, if the truth be told, I think that Father knew and she knew that during the military rule we had to keep her at home. All the men were away at jobs. Our situation then was strained. Leila was the only one whom Father could trust with the chores to be done in the village, exactly like a man. Later, as she got older, she became choosy. She wanted an educated man, someone who would be considerate. But our educated men weren't keen on taking a wife who couldn't read or write. And one day we realized she'd missed the boat. She was too old for those whose turn had come to marry, and older men had already set up homes. We didn't notice, because we really preferred her at home."

"What's past is past," said Maya. "But what's happening now? This marriage you're planning for her; is it for her good, or is it just to salve your conscience?"

Walid was offended. "You know how we love her. It's only for her good."

"But did you ask her? Are you sure this is what she wants?" Maya insisted.

"It's all right, Maya," said Walid. "Believe me, it's all right. When we found the man, we saw right away how happy she was. She'll have a home of her own and a man of her own. She'll be second to no woman, she won't feel unneeded."

The wedding was not a big affair, because the bride was no young girl but a woman past her youth who was entering the home of a widower and a father. Yet few brides were as radiant as Leila as she sat on her wedding throne, and Maya wondered whether she had ever seen a bridegroom so proud of his bride as was Leila's husband when he led her home.

Several months after the wedding Walid suggested to Maya that she come with him to visit the newly married couple.

Leila and her husband were delighted to see them. Maya, who had not formed a definite impression before, was pleasantly surprised to find the husband a solid, energetic man. He clearly appeared to appreciate the treasure he had obtained. He spoke Hebrew fluently, and made a great effort to impress the Jewish newspaperwoman, Walid's friend, by his knowledge of current events.

Leila looked happy. One could see a new pride in her, a sense of her own value.

On the way back, Walid asked Maya, "Do you know a good obstetrician?" And he added quickly, "For Leila."

Maya almost caused an accident as she jumped for joy while driving, and Walid had to grab hold of the wheel. "What's so exciting about becoming an aunt?" he joked, beaming.

The lady obstetrician assuaged their anxieties. "No cause to worry," she said. "As much as a doctor can predict anything, I foresee no complications."

The birth of Leila's son caused great jubilation in the Abu-Hana family. Leila's motherhood erased whatever guilt feelings there might have been and righted whatever had gone wrong.

Two years later, Leila's second son was born. The ties between her and her parents, brothers, and sisters-in-law remained strong and binding. Had it been up to them, they would have been even closer. It was Leila who took care to space her visits, to maintain a certain distance. Maya discovered that this was the pride of the poor. Leila didn't care to be showered with gifts. She didn't want her husband to be dutifully grateful. With her talents and energy, she soon raised his social and economic position. They turned his small plot of land into a flourishing greenhouse in which they grew choice cucumbers.

*   *   *

Once, some years later, Maya suggested that Walid take his wife, Nadia, and his sister Leila to Jerusalem to visit his brother Rasem and his sister-in-law. Nadia wore a long skirt and a fashionable blouse. An observer might have taken her for an orthodox Jewish woman, because of the long sleeves and the kerchief covering her hair. Leila, as usual, wore a festive peasant dress. When they reached Tel Aviv, they stopped for a short rest at Maya's. Walid suggested they do some shopping at the supermarket nearby. Maya, who stayed home, watched them from upstairs and was glad that Walid did not feel embarrassed by Leila's traditional dress.

Watching Walid proudly accompany his peasant sister into the modern supermarket, Maya grasped fully for the first time how valid was Walid's explanation, a short while after his own wedding, for marrying an unsophisticated girl from Kafr-Hama.

"I had many doubts about this matter. I knew what your reasoning would be: I should choose a girl with a career and your intelligence, somebody educated enough to challenge me to improve and progress constantly. I did not chicken out from a partnership with somebody who's my equal. I took a long time making up my mind. And I took a measured look at my priorities and decided that I would never marry a woman who might look condescendingly on my mother and my sisters."

When they returned from the market, Maya immediately noticed that Walid was upset. She was afraid someone might have passed a comment about the "Arab woman," or somehow insulted Leila. But it turned out that she was completely off the mark. When Leila and Nadia went to the kitchen to prepare refreshments, Walid got it off his chest.

"I can't bear to see how Nadia walks through the store like a lady, pointing at whatever appeals to her without thinking twice about the price, while Leila looks, ponders, and moves on. I pleaded with her to buy everything she needs, but her pride wouldn't let her."

However, Leila put no restraint on her own giving. Both she and her husband felt a double joy when they were able to share what they had with others. When Maya came to the village, they wouldn't let her leave without taking some of their freshly grown cucumbers. Maya tried to limit the gift, but when she reached Tel Aviv, she usually found two crates chock-full of fruit and cucumbers.

9

ONE SATURDAY in the spring of 1972, Maya dropped in, as she often did, to say hello to the Abu-Hana family. They were glad to see her, as usual, and they welcomed with real joy her twelve-year-old son, Nimrod, and watched, bemused, when he disappeared on the back of a donkey, together with the young Abu-Hanas. But Maya could sense that something was troubling them; that they were hiding something from her.

"What's going on?" she asked as she accompanied Walid to his apartment, while Leila hurried out to prepare a light meal.

"We're having problems with Mother. You know what Mother means to us. Mother is home. If Mother isn't all right, nothing's all right. She's got something into her head and we can't get it out. We're worried."

Maya didn't understand.

"It's all because of Omar, my oldest brother. You know, the one in Saudi Arabia. Since his visit here, Mother's got it into her head that if he doesn't come back, her life isn't worth living. She lies in bed and says that she won't get up until she sees Omar living at home. Father worries; he's going crazy, and we don't know what to do."

"Can I help in any way?"

"We've already asked for family reunification," Walid said. "Father got the forms and we filled them out and sent them to Jerusalem, to the Ministry of the Interior. Now we're waiting for a reply."

"Maybe I could put in a good word with somebody?"

Walid blushed. "I think it'll be all right," he said, mentioning the name of a cabinet minister's wife. She was active among Jews and Arabs, and a frequent visitor at the Abu-Hana home. "She was here last Saturday. Had lunch with us. Father asked her about it and she said it'd be all right."

Maya considered how hard it was for old Abu-Hana to ask a favor. She had never heard him request anything for himself or his family. She smiled to herself at the almost childlike faith of her hosts in the power of the minister's wife. But she didn't want to upset their confidence, for there was no reason to suspect that the request would not be granted, even without the intervention of the minister's wife.

Three months later, the matter was still pending. Then Walid unexpectedly visited Maya at her office. He was very upset.

Maya looked at him questioningly.

"They rejected the application," Walid said. "Yesterday we got the reply from Jerusalem. They gave no explanation."

"Don't look so crestfallen," said Maya. "That isn't the end of the line."

"Not the end? It's the end of the world. At home everyone's acting as if the first-born son is dead. No one looks anyone in the eyes. Mother cried all night, and Leila yelled at me, 'Where are all your friends now, where are they? All the important people who come to visit you! The visitors from abroad, from the Foreign Ministry, the people from the Histadrut, the Labor Party? Where are all those people I give food and drink to, the people you say are friends of yours? Maybe I don't understand, because I don't know how to read or write, but you, you went to the university, you're clever, so give me an answer so I can understand...'"

"She's right," said Maya. "You do have friends. Go to them; tell them you need help."

Walid looked at her with a trapped expression. "What should I say to them? Ask them to do me a favor, to pull strings for me? That way I'll be providing confirmation to all those who say that an Arab doesn't make friends with a Jew except to get something out of it. You always said I couldn't be bought. And now you're suggesting that I put myself up for public auction?"

"Easy now; I didn't say sell yourself. I said go to your friends. That isn't selling yourself, or putting yourself up for auction."

"Why can't I do it without friends? I'm a citizen; my father's a citizen; my brothers are citizens. Why can't I get what's mine by right, without friends? Why could the Jews bring their brothers over here from Morocco and Iraq? When the Russians refused to let Jews come here, you set the world on its head. But my brother has to remain outside; there's no place here for him."

"What rubbish. So you're a citizen, so what? I'm a citizen, too, but the police came and got me out of bed at three o'clock in the morning, banging on my door, because I'd forgotten to pay a parking fine. They came to arrest me. If they treated you that way, everyone'd be screaming that it was because you're an Arab or because someone wanted to settle a political score with you. The state works through officials, and officials are people, and people make mistakes. Maliciously or innocently. It doesn't matter. What matters is our capacity to right such wrongs."

Walid clutched his head with both hands. "I'm finished, Maya. I don't know what to do. I've had hints. From all kinds of places: come and see us; we'll fix something. You know, all those experts in Arab affairs. The counselor on Arab affairs in the prime minister's office and the counselor on Arab affairs in the party and the Department of Arab Affairs in the Histadrut. But I can't do it. If I play their game, I put an end to the hopes of all the people who trust me."

"Stop carrying on like a woman. I can't understand what's happened to you. Take hold of yourself."

"It's not me; it's Mother. I can't look her in the eye. None of us can. I feel as if the whole village is secretly laughing at us: 'You wanted to act straight with the Jews' state; you thought you had rights here. Well, now you're getting what you deserve.' In our village everyone knows everything; there are no secrets. Everyone knows that informers are able to reunify their families, as do all kinds of filthy characters who slander the state all the time and have connections with its enemies — because the state wants to buy their loyalty. But we're already in the bag, it seems; they don't need to buy us, so they don't give a damn about us."

"You're exaggerating. I can believe that sometimes they have to give some kind of *baksheesh* to informers, but I'm sure they haven't allowed dangerous people to be brought into the country . . ."

Walid interrupted. "I don't know if those they brought in are dangerous or not. I know that some families, who asked for and got family reunification, are not averse to sticking a knife in your back at any minute. I know that they're slandering the state all the time. I'm not telling you stories. I know what I'm talking about."

Maya reached a decision. "Listen, this isn't the Wild West. The mice may be having a banquet, but there's law and there's order. I promise you we'll get Omar back. Now sit down quietly and don't interfere. Let me try to engineer this affair to a happy conclusion."

"I will not compromise my principles," Walid repeated stubbornly.

"I thought you knew me better than that," Maya retorted. "Give me some credit. I wouldn't jeopardize your reputation. You may as well trust me — at least for your mother's sake."

Walid lowered his eyes, and Maya knew she had won the argument, for nothing was dearer to Walid's heart than his mother's happiness. Maya lingered fondly on the image of Walid's mother, who still moved nimbly on her sandaled feet and never sat idle. Walid was utterly devoted to her. He had once told Maya how for years he and his brother Rasem scrupulously did all their school homework, fearful of their mother's stern daily inspection. Once, when Walid was in a particular hurry to join his friend Taufik under the olive tree, he dared to cheat a tiny little bit. "Did you do *all* your exercises?" his mother asked, her stern look boring into his evasive eyes. "Yes," he said, "of course." She did not like the way he shifted his glance. "Give me your notebook," she said.

Because he was afraid of being found out, he watched her closely and discovered that his mother, inspecting his notebook, was holding it upside down.

He did not betray his knowledge of her secret to her, to his brothers, or to any living soul except Maya, many years later, and he continued to prepare his homework thoroughly until he left the Kafr-Hama school altogether.

Recalling the expression of tenderness when he had recounted this episode, Maya watched Walid's tense face and waited for him to make up his mind.

Walid capitulated. "OK, if you think it'll work."

Maya expressed an assurance she didn't entirely feel. "Of course it will work. Now go bury that mourner's face of yours somewhere and return to your village wearing a smile. If you smile, then your mother will believe it'll all work out, too."

The next day Maya set off for Jerusalem. She asked for an appointment with a woman who was a senior official in the Ministry of the Interior. The woman wasn't available, but she directed her to an official below her in rank, one who was directly in charge of such matters. This official, who Maya later discovered was of Iraqi origin, received her politely, but his manner bespoke suspicion and distrust.

"How may I assist you?"

"My name is Maya Gilead. I have a request. Perhaps you can explain to me the reasons for the rejection of the Abu-Hana family's application to allow their oldest son to return to their village . . ."

"Excuse me, Ms. Gilead. I see there's been a misunderstanding. Had I known this was why you were here, I would have directed you to the ministry spokesman. You know, I'm sure, that government employees are not allowed to give interviews."

"I haven't come here to interview you, Mr. Rajwan. I've come as a citizen, to receive an explanation."

"Excuse me, please, I don't understand what this affair has to do with you?"

"I'm a friend of the Abu-Hana family. I'd like to know the reasons for the rejection of the application."

"We don't generally explain the grounds for rejection. There's a public committee, and it deals with all applications. And if the decision is negative, there must have been good reasons."

"That's exactly it. It's those reasons I want to hear."

"We don't owe you any explanations," he objected testily.

"Really? And I think that you owe me — indeed, every citizen — answers and explanations to a lot of questions. According to what criteria does this committee reach its decisions? What requirements must an applicant fulfill to receive a positive reply? Who are the members of the committee?"

"We do not reveal the names of the committee's members. That would expose them to continual pestering, even to threats and real danger."

"You have a point there," Maya conceded. "But surely you can tell me what public bodies are represented in the committee."

"That won't change a thing. I can assure you that the request was discussed very thoroughly and received all the attention it deserved. If it was rejected, I repeat that there were good reasons for it."

Maya felt her blood boiling. She spoke quietly, too quietly. "I'm afraid I must differ. We're not talking about the mysteries of the holy Zohar. We're talking about a request made by a citizen to the authorities, and about a rejection of that request. The grounds for such a rejection should be available and convincing. That is a civil right."

The official behind the desk spoke drily. "We're not talking about rights. We're talking about a good-will gesture the state makes, beyond what the law calls for."

"There was an official announcement that family reunification would be permitted in every case that was found to be justified. What does 'justified' mean in this context?"

"In the case of the Abu-Hanas, it isn't a matter of family reunification. The person named in the application isn't a minor, or a woman whose husband is in Israel, or an old parent. This is a man in the prime of his life, a married man, a father of five children. Their purpose is not to bring a lost son back to the family's bosom. They want to bring an additional Arab family into the State of Israel."

"And what's so bad about that?"

The official removed his smile, like someone taking a coat off in a heated room. "Ms. Gilead. You have one perspective, and I have another perspective. I don't dismiss your views. But the government has a policy, and it acts according to this policy."

Maya tensed. "Mr. Rajwan, I ask you not to take what I say personally, because I really can't manage to dislike you. But you've been selling me lines for about half an hour now, and there's a limit to my patience. In my briefcase I have a list of fifty families whose applications the committee approved. In most of those cases you'll see it isn't a matter of a lost son or a wife living alone or an aged parent, but of entire families. Furthermore, one could place a very big public question mark beside the names of very many of those families whose requests were approved. I'm sure there were reasons, and I don't even want to know them, though I could guess. All I'm asking is that you tell me the reasons for the rejection of the Abu-Hana request. I don't think that's too much to ask."

"Ms. Gilead, I have great respect for the press, but I'm not prepared to be intimidated by it. Your remarks sound like a threat."

Maya took a deep breath and counted to three. "Mr. Rajwan, we can go on conducting a verbal duel and wasting both your time and mine. I have a suggestion. Forget for a moment that I'm a newspaperwoman. Assume that I haven't come here to get smart with you or to pump you for secrets 'off the record.' I believe that you do your work faithfully. I believe, without qualification, that the security of the State of Israel is important to you, and I should like you to assume for a moment that it's important to me, too. Are you willing to try to conduct our conversation on this basis, like two human beings with only good will between them?"

He scrutinized Maya anew, the pen in his hand knocking rhythmically on the desk. His eyes narrowed to smiling slits. "OK, Ms. Gilead . . ."

"Call me Maya."

"All right, Maya. I'm willing to take a chance. I know you from your writing. I'm a regular reader of yours. If you're conning me, you're a very sharp fox and you'd have tricked me anyway. I'm ready to play with the cards on the table, and I hope I won't regret it."

Maya beamed him the smile of a girl who had got lost in a railway station and then suddenly found her big brother. "Good. Let's start from the beginning. I'm a friend of Walid Abu-Hana. I know the whole family, and I believe that if their son isn't allowed to come back here, then someone among us, among the decision-makers, has taken leave of his senses. I really can't understand how it happened, and I'm sure that if you help me unravel the mystery, we'll discover that there's been a mistake."

"And what if we discover that there's been no mistake?"

"Then I'll ask you for guidance in doing what I must to change the decision. I'm willing to fight for this."

"Through the press?"

"I can't promise not to write about it. But I do promise you wholeheartedly that I haven't come here to gather material for an article, but simply to resolve this business."

"All right then, we'll begin at the beginning. Look in this file — it's the Abu-Hana application. Look. There are two documents: the application form and a letter from the wife of a cabinet minister, who says she knows them and recommends the approval of the request. I don't mind if you look at it; I'm sure it's not news to you. And now I'll show you a file with another request. Did you see where I took it from? From the top of the pile. They're all like that. You see — it's a whole book. A hundred, maybe two hundred documents."

Maya began to understand. "What's inside those files?"

"You can guess. Every deed, or every person, that can add a point in favor of the request."

"You mean the Abu-Hana application was too thin, not enough flesh?"

"Look, Maya, I've heard of Walid Abu-Hana, but I'm sure I don't know him as well as you do. Dozens of files go through my hands every day, and I can't always remember all the applicants. I imagine that the members of the committee are in the same boat. Let's say I'm the committee and you come to persuade me to approve the application. What will you say?"

"I'm starting to get the picture. Hold on a couple of minutes, and we'll do a dress rehearsal. I'll give you the reasons for approval one by one, and you'll tell me how to translate them into the language of application forms and committees. OK? All right then, we'll start with the story of Omar, the brother they want to bring home. He was twelve when the War of Independence broke out. At that time there was no high school in any of the Arab villages here. There was only Kadoorie — not the Jewish Kadoorie in Galilee, but the Kadoorie for the Arabs, in Tulkarm. He studied there as a boarder. When the fighting started, his father asked the Jewish commander of the area if he ought to bring his son home. The officer, a veteran member of a nearby kibbutz, knew Abu-Hana well. He advised him not to interrupt his son's studies. When the armistice lines were drawn, Tulkarm remained outside the State of Israel, in Jordanian territory. The military governor advised old Abu-Hana not to worry: 'Let him graduate. We'll not hold it against him; we'll let him come back.' Omar excelled in his studies. It was King Hussein, I believe, who awarded him a scholarship and sent him to the American University in Beirut. When he received his bachelor's degree, he returned to Jordan, married a lovely lady in Tulkarm, and went off to seek his fortune in Saudi Arabia."

"And he didn't do well?"

"He did fine! His family told me that Omar is the most senior Arab official in Aramco, the Arabian American Oil Company, in Saudi Arabia."

"And you mean to say he suddenly got homesick?"

"Not suddenly. All this time they've been in contact with him. For many years now it's been a very vague kind of contact. Once every two or three years they'd get a letter from him through some channel. They knew he didn't lack a thing, and from time to time they were notified of the birth of his children. I suppose they'd got resigned to the idea of never seeing him again. I don't have to tell you how it was up to the Six Day War. The borders between Israel and its neighbors were hermetically sealed. Even for Arabs who lived on different sides of the border, it was as if they were living on different planets."

"So what happened?"

"The map changed. We produced the miracle of the Six Day War. The barriers between Israeli Arabs and those living in the Gaza Strip and the West Bank collapsed, and they came face to face for the first time in twenty years. Then came the Open Bridges policy. You may remember that when Moshe Dayan made public the decision to allow Palestinians from all Arab countries to visit their families in the 'territories' and in Israel proper during summer months, he took us all by surprise. Among the tens of thousands of Palestinian Arabs who arrived to visit their relatives in Israel was Omar. That's when it happened. It was as if they hadn't been separated for twenty years. The next year he brought his children along. And suddenly he couldn't live without his parents, brothers, and sisters, and his parents couldn't endure another day without their grandchildren."

"If he has such a good life in Saudi Arabia, perhaps he'd be better off staying there. Life here isn't exactly like the Thousand and One Nights."

"That's their problem. Omar doesn't want to come here at our expense, and he isn't asking for a thing. He won't become a burden on the Jewish Agency or on the Ministry of Welfare. The Abu-Hana family doesn't need anybody's charity."

"That isn't enough. The members of the committee will want to know why they should change their decision. What can you say in the family's favor that would entitle them to special consideration?"

"All right, where do I start? Let's start with the father. Even before the establishment of the state, Salah Abu-Hana prevented riots against Jewish settlers. Today, all his sons work in cooperative projects with Jews. But the main thing in their favor is Walid: he's a one-man fraternity bureau. Everyone who's anyone in the Israeli establishment makes use of his honesty, his hospitality, his sympathies for the State of Israel and his commitment for Arab-Jewish co-existence. Every Saturday in their village is like a carnival of VIPs. Guests of the Foreign Ministry and of the Histadrut, guests of the party's political bureau and of other agencies. They bring their guests to Walid's, and they eat and drink and finish off their meal with a large dose of Arab Zionism. For all these purposes he's good, and we're proud of him. But when he asks us to let his brother come home, we ask, 'What on earth for?' Well, what does this make us look like?"

Rajwan tapped a brown finger on the slender file bearing the name ABU-HANA. "So why isn't all that in here?"

Maya looked at him questioningly. "You mean a letter from the Foreign Ministry and a letter from the political bureau and so on and so on?"

"Precisely. And the whole story you've just told. The more the better. Every bit of testimony that will help convince the committee not only that approval of the request is in the state's best interests, but that a rejection can do us harm."

"What's the procedure?"

"An appeal. You appeal the decision and you prepare the material to support the appeal. Without stinting on quantity."

Maya rose and shook Rajwan's hand. "Thank you. May I give you a call if I need some advice or guidance?"

"I'll be glad to help. Believe me, I'll be glad if this works out well."

*　*　*

Maya thought a great deal about how to obtain the letters of recommendation without turning Walid into a debtor. First of all, she compiled a list of public personalities and officials who made regular use of the Abu-Hana family's hospitality. The list resembled a *Who's Who* in Israel's political establishment. Then she began a series of telephone calls. Most of the people on the list knew Maya, at least by name. She took care to point out that she was calling on her own initiative. Some offered to write a letter of recommendation if Walid asked for one personally. In such cases, Maya's affable tone turned into one of professional dryness: "Walid doesn't want to ask anyone. I'm the one who's asking, because I'm ashamed that his request was refused. I thought that you would feel the same way. If I was mistaken . . ." At this point the person Maya called volunteered a letter.

Her talk with the secretary general of the Histadrut was truly gratifying. "I'm glad you called me," he said. "I didn't know there was a problem of this kind, and I really think we should all thank you for your initiative. I'll send you my letter today."

Soon Maya had accumulated a thick file of letters. When she met with Rajwan, who had become an ally, they agreed that the appeal now rested on an absolutely sound base.

Maya paid a visit to Kafr-Hama. From her elated mood, everyone understood that the matter was going to work out.

Several days later the phone rang. Rajwan. "Maya, when do you think you'll be coming up here?"

"You bastard, stop stringing me out. Have they approved it?"

Rajwan spoke haltingly. "The committee hasn't met yet. But I think we should have a talk."

"I'm coming right away."

Rajwan was distressed, and admitted it. "I don't know

what to do. You managed to convince me that it's right to let this fellow come back. And if I had any doubts that you might be prejudiced, these letters here prove that you weren't exaggerating. And that's what's so strange, because I think someone's putting a monkey wrench in the works. The committee hasn't met yet, but someone's interfering. I don't know who. I don't know if it's the counselor for Arab affairs or the special branch of the police, or the services. You'd better do something before the meeting. If the request's rejected again, that's the end of it."

Maya's face fell. "Thanks. Thanks for telling me."

So that was it. Somebody saw a chance to extract something from Walid.

All the way from Jerusalem to Tel Aviv, Maya feverishly mulled over in her mind all possible lines of action, and rejected them one by one. The services? What services? Military Intelligence, the Security Services, the Mossad, maybe. Go chase the wind. And what could she say to them? 'I heard that you're opposing . . .' 'Where? Who told you?' And suddenly she began to have doubts. She tried to ignore them, but there was no evading them. After all, she didn't know Walid's brother. Maybe Omar found his vocation with the PLO? Perhaps Omar Abu-Hana is the brain behind some of the activities of George Habash or Hawatma, the extremist Palestinian terrorist leaders. She couldn't be sure that the intelligence services didn't have restricted information about him.

And then the solution occurred to her.

She came home, sat down at her typewriter, and wrote a candid letter to a chief of one of the intelligence branches. She didn't know him personally, but in his few public appearances this high-ranking army officer had made a strong impression as trustworthy, honest, and brilliant. Maya listed everything she considered relevant to the Abu-Hana request. She explained her own involvement in the matter, recounting the steps she had taken so far, and finally explained the reasons for this letter.

I believe [she wrote], that the good of the state requires that this request be granted. I also think this is the state's duty. I believe that petty officials must not be allowed to interfere in this process. On the other hand, I have no idea whatsoever whether one or another of the intelligence agencies has information that may disqualify Omar Abu-Hana from returning to his family. Therefore, I'm appealing to you. I'm asking you to look into the matter, for I am not equipped to do that. If you discover that there are no grounds for your interference, and that whoever is working against the approval of the application is justified in his actions, I promise that I will wash my hands of the matter and will not ask for any clarifications, either privately, as a citizen, or publicly, as a newspaper-woman. But if there is no information disqualifying this man, and if you agree with me that the request should be approved, please act accordingly.

No answer, not even an acknowledgment of her letter. Then Rajwan called excitedly. "Maya, I don't know what you did, but it worked."

The day Maya brought the news to Kafr-Hama that the committee had approved the request for Omar's return was one of the happiest days of her life.

10

THE DAY SET for Omar Abu-Hana's return was very hot; there was a *khamsin*. Early in the morning, a convoy of cars left Kafr-Hama, heading for the Allenby Bridge across the Jordan River. Maya set out from Tel Aviv with a photographer from the newspaper. They drove in the photographer's car, of German make and air-conditioned. Maya, who scrupulously avoided buying any product manufactured in Germany, scoffed at herself, but she would enjoy the air-conditioning in this Audi. As the sedan threaded its way through the arid hills west of Jerusalem, Maya became momentarily lost in the rushing sound of the air-conditioner.

The landscape became a coffee-colored blur, and she recalled a conversation with a minor German diplomat whose pomposity had increased the contempt she instinctively felt for German officials. She had called him for his comment on a news item. The attaché had asked to meet her and at the start of that meeting had remarked, "I can't understand why we haven't met before at one of our diplomatic parties." Maya had responded drily, "There's nothing surprising about that, because I've never been to a party held at the German Embassy or under its auspices." The smile had vanished from the attaché's face as he said, "I wonder if there is a reason for that." Maya hadn't played at diplomacy. "Six million reasons at least," she had retorted.

The attaché was determined to prove that he didn't have any of the complexes of the Holocaust generation. Pointing to the telephone on his desk, he asked, "Do you boycott the telephone company because part of the equipment is of German make?" Maya regarded him without anger, as if he were a relic from the Stone Age. "I'm willing to speak to you at any time about my attitude to Germany, if and when we set a time for that. At this stage let me just point out that the equipment you mentioned is, as far as I know, part of the reparations agreement. I didn't object to that agreement. I believe that a very partial restitution of Jewish properties is in no way reparation or compensation for a single drop of blood. A criminal who returns part of the loot is not entitled to expect warmth or friendship in return, even though for some reason this fact is not clear to the government and leaders of Israel."

Her pensive mood was broken by the sight of an Arab herdsman driving his flock of sheep across the highway ahead. She happily immersed herself again in the excited anticipation of the reunion on the Allenby Bridge.

The trip from Tel Aviv to Jerusalem passed quickly and pleasantly, for Maya had insisted on setting out very early to avoid heavy traffic. As they drove toward Jericho, the heat outside was blazing, but with the windows closed and the air-conditioning running full blast, they moved like a bubble of cool air on a blazing strip of lava. The photographer asked for details of the work awaiting him. Maya's replies were fragmented and, unusual for her, agitated. Approaching the Jordan River, Maya suddenly realized that she wasn't making haste as a journalist, on a journalist's mission, but as a member of a family awaiting the return of a lost brother. It was relatively quiet on the bridge. The crossing from Jordan to Israel had become a routine matter. Still, the presence of the military governor and his deputy suggested that the event was unusual. Maya knew that the governor, Yonah, from Kibbutz Rishonim, had also come as a friend and not in his official capacity. He wanted to ensure that nothing would mar the family reunion, and perhaps also to share its happiness, as an observer.

A long line of cars, trucks, pickups, and vans attested to a full turnout by the Abu-Hana family. Near the bridge, in a small booth designed for people waiting for arrivals from the other side, sat Salah Abu-Hana and his portly uncle Hadj Jusef Abu-Hana, whose silver beard rested comfortably on his impressive paunch. Walid and three of his brothers also sat in the booth; the two youngest had remained at home to help the women prepare the banquet.

Maya smiled at Walid, who was as excited as a youngster on the eve of his high school prom, and also at Rasem. Rasem was the only one of the Abu-Hana family with whom Maya occasionally felt ill at ease; there was a vague and unsettling factor in her relations with him. A mutual caution existed between them, a kind of reserve. Maya had not even been certain that she would find him among the reception group. But this morning she met a different Rasem. He too was excited and happy; he too got up from time to time to bring a bottle of cold soda from the adjacent booth to his father and his uncle.

Rasem had tried to cool his family's enthusiasm about his brother's return. Not that he was not concerned for Omar's welfare. On the contrary. He believed that it wasn't fair to influence the older brother, the first-born son, to leave his Saudi luxury and his American limousine for the sake of the right to live with his own family. Rasem was the only one of the entire family who doubted whether life in Kafr-Hama was preferable to the treasures of the petrodollar. He had insisted on his own right to give Omar, during his visit in Kafr-Hama last summer, a not very glowing description of life in Israel, and had stressed the very real danger of a drop in his standard of living.

A touch of disquietude had been apparent in Rasem, as if he was no longer convinced that to be a member of the Abu-Hana family from Kafr-Hama was the best thing that could happen to a person. In a subtle way, he maintained a measure of distance from his fellow villagers, and Maya suspected that were it not for his devotion to his family, the handsome economist would not miss Kafr-Hama. Rasem was also the only member of the family who had not become dejected when the application for family reunification was turned down. But when he saw his mother consumed with grief, his father stooped with despair, and his brothers all pining for Omar's return, he stopped raising doubts. He even tried to influence Walid to bend a fraction, saying angrily, "If you want him back all that much, then don't be afraid of dirtying your hands a little. You're like a virgin who's eager to get married, but doesn't understand what the man is looking for between her legs."

Hassan, the financial wizard, could not contain himself. He was darting from one group to another, exasperating Noori, the younger brother. Noori was in charge of the farming, and his earthiness and tranquillity reminded Maya of his father.

The waiting was prolonged, and they all tried to help each other cover up their excitement and impatience by calmly discussing matters requiring a settled mind, like the herds of livestock and the tobacco crop and trading cars for later models. The governor, Yonah, ran toward them, forgetting the dignity of his status, to inform them that Omar had arrived at the bridge. They reacted as if a bolt of electricity had struck them. They walked in a strange manner, intentionally slow, in order to get as close as possible to the point of entry without appearing to hurry, without injuring their composure by overenthusiasm. The procedures on the bridge took a long time. The large moving van was loaded with all the material benefits that East and West had produced under the aegis of the petrodollar. Rolled-up Persian carpets; huge copper trays, engraved and embossed; furniture inlaid with mother-of-pearl; coffee services made by master craftsmen. And beside them television sets, a washing machine, a huge refrigerator, a dryer, a humidifier, a stereo set, and many other Western marvels. One of the customs men observed, "It's like Ali Baba after a robbery in New York." The customs inspection advanced rapidly and without difficulty under Yonah's surveillance. The problems began when a dozen heavy crates, of uniform size, were unloaded from the truck.

"What's this?" asked the customs man.

"Books," answered Omar.

"So many books?"

"What I had."

The crates were opened. The inspector thrust his arm into each one, pulling out a volume in English or Arabic, and peering at it from every angle. The inspector's gaze darted from the books to the "new immigrant" and back; the man was trying to make up his mind if the connection between them was reasonable.

"Are all these books yours?" he asked Omar, this time in English.

"Yes, and my children's. The big ones go to high school."

"All right then," said the inspector, still staring in wonder at the intellectual cargo that had arrived from the direction of Amman. When all the documents were signed, and only then, Omar's wife and children emerged from the luxurious car that all this time had been parked on the Jordanian side.

They hurried through the checkpoint, the mother holding the youngest daughter in her arms, and approached the Israeli side.

Maya was unable to restrain her tears. Old Abu-Hana stood waiting; the uncle and the sons were some distance away, behind him. The group coming from the bridge moved forward as if in slow motion. Omar bent down over his father's hand and kissed it with reverence. The father raised his arms to embrace his son, and then they stayed locked in embrace for a long moment without separating, biting their lips so as not to cry like women. Then Abu-Hana greeted his grandchildren and his daughter-in-law. Only when Salah Abu-Hana raised Omar's youngest daughter in his arms did the tears flow without inhibition. He lavished kisses on the little girl and didn't stop embracing her for a long while. Her father stood to the side and cried too, not even bothering to hide his tears.

After that there was much hugging and clapping on the back and kissing. Omar's sons and daughters tried to mask their anxieties and their fears of tomorrow. His oldest son, a smartly dressed and handsome teen-ager, looked coldly and suspiciously at Maya and announced that he considered himself a Palestinian. There was a lot of confusion in his eyes.

Maya stayed at the fringe, her eyes moist, after having instructed the photographer to be as invisible as possible. Suddenly, she saw Walid approaching her. He led her to his father. Old Abu-Hana took her hand and introduced her to Omar. "She is your sister," he said. "A new daughter in the Abu-Hana family. She arranged for your return and now she is one of us."

Then the arrivals were introduced to Yonah, and the young ones among them stared in disbelief when Walid and Yonah exchanged playful shoves with their elbows and made jokes at each other's expense. Yonah promised to visit them on his next leave to celebrate Omar's return.

Maya reminded herself that the real difficulties would begin only now. She wondered how Mona, Omar's wife, would get along with the Abu-Hanas and adjust to village life, and how the older children would adapt to their new circumstances.

When the belongings were loaded onto the trucks and the pickups, everyone got into the different cars and the convoy set out for Kafr-Hama.

On the way they stopped at a roadside inn close to a cool spring bursting from a rock face and down a steep slope and gathering in a shallow pool paved entirely with water-melons, which the proprietor placed there in order to serve them cold and refreshing to his clients. The little children splashed cold water on each other, and sunbeams reflected in every drop. The adults delighted in their joy and sprinkled their own hot faces with the cold spring water.

Just outside Kafr-Hama the convoy slowed, organized itself, closing distances between the vehicles so that they would enter the village ceremoniously. There were staccato bursts from the car horns and much excited hand-waving. Children and adults ran toward them and around them, waving their arms and yelling loudly, "The son of Abu-Hana, the son of Abu-Hana!" When they neared the parents' house, the convoy stopped in the large space outside the iron gate between Abu-Hana's house and Walid's.

The gate was opened wide and in the entrance stood

Omar's mother in a white kaffiyeh and a white dress. Surrounding her were her daughters and daughters-in-law, all in ceremonial dress and flashing a radiant welcome with the white teeth of the Abu-Hanas, which were like a family trademark. Again, everyone was restrained until Omar approached gravely, kissed his mother's hand, and she raised her arms to him. They embraced for a long while. After that everyone embraced everyone else, caressing each other, laughing, crying, and talking all at once. The neighbors and the aunts gathered around, wiping tears from their eyes, rhythmically tapping their lips as they emitted the traditional ululations.

Afterward, Maya did not remember the order of events. Had the convoy first brought them to the new house that had been completed hastily for Omar's return, or had they first sat down to the family dinner? And when had the reception taken place for the local dignitaries and elders who began streaming into the house, according to their importance and relation to the Abu-Hana family? The entire day had been charged with excitement, blurred by high tension; and only the smiles, the gleaming eyes, the laughter, and the tears remained engraved in her memory.

11

THE PERIOD immediately after Omar's return from Saudi Arabia was a long carnival of visits, ceremonial dinners, and trips to the country. In all the excitement, no one gave a thought to what Omar would do for a living, or to other elementary problems of his readjustment. From morning to evening it was one continuous rush to welcome guests, to embrace, to kiss, to respond to questions, or, alternatively, to don festive clothes, cram into a car or two, and visit Tel Aviv, Jerusalem, or Hadera.

True, the question of a livelihood was not so pressing. The Abu-Hana family was not needy, and they adhered to the kibbutz rule of "from each according to his capacity, to each according to his needs." Since old Abu-Hana had never been a Marxist and was no blind believer in any absolutist theory, he applied this rule with a good deal of flexibility. If one of his sons, in order to prove his independence, opened his own bank account or managed his own affairs, no one made an issue of that. But when the very same son decided to make a large purchase that his private bank account could not carry, like buying a car, for example, he would turn to his father. The old man would then finance the purchase after consulting with the other sons, to stress the fact that what was involved constituted a family matter, not just a financial transaction. No one would mention that just a short while ago this very member of the family preferred to go it alone. The lesson was usually well absorbed without its being discussed.

This being so, it was clear that the family larder would take care of regular supplies in Omar's household, and that his wife would never lack whatever she needed to feed her family and her guests. But Omar's self-respect required that he find an occupation appropriate to his status, his education, and his executive experience.

During the first months after his return Omar continued to talk enthusiastically about the freedom and equality enjoyed by Arab citizens in Israel. Maya interviewed him about the life of Palestinians in Arab countries. The interview appeared anonymously, because Omar was still waiting to receive a sizable sum from Aramco and did not intend to jeopardize his chance of receiving the money due him. He described with much pain the existence of Palestinians among the "sister countries." During that interview he said, in reply to a question, "The only place where a Palestinian Arab can say he feels at home is in the State of Israel, and nowhere else."

For a long time Maya would swell with pride and optimism on remembering this sentence, which had been spoken in good faith and not for the sake of flattery. Whenever she fell into a black mood, she recalled that conversation, like someone reaching for a bottle of energy pills. Later it became sadly apparent to her that if Omar were to be asked the question again, he would give a different answer.

Maya and Omar had lengthy conversations about his life in Saudi Arabia. His was a style of life typical of a Palestinian who had established himself economically but lacked acutely a sense of home and belonging. Initially, Omar stressed the bitter aspects of the lives of Palestinians in Arab countries in contrast to their sense of belonging in the State of Israel. He didn't try to distort the picture in order to please Maya. This was a natural distortion of the prism through which he contemplated his recent Saudi Arabian past and his Israeli present. The material prosperity he had enjoyed in Saudi Arabia seemed natural to him, but secondary when evaluated against the insults he had suffered and the bitterness that had accumulated in him. Somehow he found it easier to speak about his Saudi Arabian period to Maya than to his brothers and his father, who felt so much pain at the very mention of his long isolation among strangers that he wanted to spare them as much as possible.

Life in Israel seemed to him at first to be beautiful. So beautiful as to be dazzling, because it was so different from what he had expected, after listening to reports in Arab countries. In addition, the warmth of his reunion with his parents and brothers somehow protected him from the disappointments that still awaited him in his old-new homeland.

In Saudi Arabia, he had taken for granted the American standard of living, which he felt befitted his rank in the company, where he had demonstrated an uncanny talent for diplomacy while acting as liaison between the Americans and the Saudis. He lived, as did his American colleagues, the fairy-tale existence of Aramco senior employees; they were housed in an exclusive, hermetically sealed supermodern city within the medieval Saudi desert kingdom. Which explained why, contrary to expectations, Mona was not bewitched by the day-to-day life of an Arab village wife and mother. Everybody expected her to feel like a liberated lark, coming from the strict Muslim state where no woman is allowed to uncover her face or her ankle, and where even a royal princess was stoned for cohabitation. But Mona had lived an altogether different kind of life there. Behind the walls of the Aramco private city she had enjoyed the privileges of affluent American suburbia. To her, life in Kafr-Hama represented a definite step backward.

Maya knew that the awakening would soon begin. It was necessary to act quickly. The first alarming signs came from the children. The school year had begun. The older children came back from the school at Kafr-Hama completely astounded. They couldn't believe that a high school English teacher could be such a complete boor. They didn't know whether to feel embarrassed for him or to be angry, and they were very confused. They didn't know whether and how to complain to their father, because they had learned that respect for teachers and elders was a commandment of the first magnitude and felt that to expose the teacher's ignorance was a serious violation of it. But Omar, who had been trained as an English teacher, very soon found out for himself. And not only with regard to English. The situation with Arabic wasn't much better, and in other subjects it was catastrophic. He brought his discoveries to Walid.

Walid shrugged his shoulders and sighed. "That's how it is. The standard of teaching is low, teaching methods are outdated, and, worst of all, the teachers obtain their posts through personal connections and not as a result of their education or suitability for the job."

"And you are content to put up with that?" Omar fumed.

"I'm fighting, but it isn't as simple as it seems," Walid admitted. "You'll find out for yourself. When the children get a bit older, we'll take them out of the local school at the first opportunity and send them to Jewish schools in Hadera or Pardes Hanna, and after a while they'll catch up with what they've missed."

"I do not intend to accept that," Omar responded. "I'm not prepared to let my children stay even one more day in that retarded institution. They'll lose all respect for teachers; all the values that they've acquired over the years will be destroyed."

That Saturday the family called a war council, to which Maya was invited. This was the first serious crisis since Omar's return, and it had to be resolved quickly and efficiently.

Maya was prepared. She had been mulling over this problem ever since she encountered Omar's family at the Allenby Bridge, had heard the fluent and impeccable English of Omar's children, and admired their good manners and their evident intelligence. Maya suggested that the two older sons should be sent to the high school in Pardes Hanna, where Walid and his brothers had studied. Omar's sons didn't understand Hebrew, but neither did the new Jewish immigrants. Their knowledge of English and their achievements in science would compensate for their handicaps in Hebrew and related subjects and would assure their successful integration in class. The girls presented the more serious problem. By the popular standards in Arab society they were almost mature. Their pronounced beauty posed an added responsibility. Would the family agree to send them to a co-ed Jewish high school?

The solution of Pardes Hanna for the boys was quickly accepted, since this formula had been tested in the family several times before.

Rasem — who had come from Jerusalem to attend the meeting — surprised everyone with his suggested solution for the girls: a convent school in East Jerusalem. "They'll learn manners there and turn into real ladies," he argued. Old Abu-Hana appeared to be staggered by this solution and made no remark. The others also remained silent and undecided.

Before she had time to consider her response, Maya broke the silence. Afterward, she wondered if she would have behaved in the same impulsive manner if the suggestion had been made by Walid or his father.

"Have you gone crazy? Isn't it enough that they have to adapt to the transition from Saudi Arabia to Israel, from life in the modern sanctuary of Aramco to the life of fellaheen in Kafr-Hama? Now you want these two young girls to be thrust into the additional conflict of Muslims being educated by Catholic nuns?"

Rasem flushed with anger, and Maya suspected that were it not for his father, he would have advised her to mind her own business. But old Abu-Hana sent her a relieved look, so it seemed that her words had fallen on attentive ears.

"Well, Maya, what do you suggest?" asked Rasem when he was able to control his anger.

"I suggest you check out if Kibbutz Ein Ganim is willing to admit them into its school," said Maya.

They all exchanged glances, trying to guess each other's response. Walid was the first to speak. "That isn't a bad idea. The standard of studies is high; the company is good; and the intimate setup will allow them to be introduced to Israeli life from its most friendly side. Because they're two, it won't be so difficult for them. And, most important, they'll be close to home."

"They don't have to sleep at the kibbutz." Hassan was

musing aloud. "We can take them there every morning on our way to pasture and bring them back in the afternoon."

Rasem didn't protest, because he realized that the issue was closed. His brothers were pleased with Maya's idea. He knew that Omar's daughters felt like complete strangers in Kafr-Hama and that if they went to school in Jerusalem they would never strike roots in the village society. Paradoxically, attending school in the kibbutz would make it easier for them to adapt to their father's birthplace and to the family's life style. He kept silent, but his expression indicated that he did not think that much good would come of his nieces' learning to like village life.

Walid summarized the discussion: "I think we should check it out. Hassan and I will go over to the kibbutz tomorrow and have a word with Dan, the schoolmaster. We have to see first of all if they have any vacancies," he added, as if trying to appease Rasem.

The two girls who were the object of the whole discussion awaited with curiosity and anxiety the meeting with their Jewish peers in the kibbutz. Even Omar's wife did not object. It seemed that the issue was settled.

Surprisingly, the kibbutz leaders recoiled from this attempt at co-existence.

Maya was indignant at the kibbutz's refusal to accept the two Arab girls. "They preach the brotherhood of man, equality, unity of workers. They should not be allowed to get away with this. Listen, Walid, I'm sure we can do something. I shall demand some explanations. If this is their attitude, let the public read about it and judge how they practice what they preach."

Walid hedged and stammered and did not look Maya in the eye. "Do me a favor and drop it. Let's not make an issue of it."

"You're willing to let this pass?"

Walid looked at her. There was a mixture of affection and pity in his gaze. "Sometimes I can't make up my mind if you're stupid or naïve. Life isn't elementary mathematics.

It isn't two plus two. People are just people. We have to compromise."

Maya continued to insist, refusing to admit she'd made a mistake, hurt that her interference had brought disappointment and distress to her friends.

Walid spoke frankly. "Maya, do us a favor and leave this matter alone. We work with Ein Ganim; we do a lot of business with them. The family isn't interested in starting a feud with them."

"I'm an idiot," Maya confessed. "Dumb. How did I forget the story of the kibbutz girl who married a young Arab who had done training at Ein Ganim? I didn't question their explanations, that the kibbutz had rejected the couple's candidacy for membership because of 'social inadaptability.' Probably they threw them out because underneath their socialist soul their Jewish separatism awoke. This way they were spared the confrontation with the offspring of such a marriage. I'll bet they were afraid that the kibbutz children would call them 'dirty Arabs.' "

Walid spoke. "Don't scoff. It isn't simple. Dan said that if the girls were younger, there'd be no problem. But they're at the age when the kids start pairing off at school. The whole situation could become embarrassing not only to them, but also to us. Perhaps it really isn't a good idea to conduct social experiments with the lives of these two girls."

But Maya wasn't consoled. She continued lashing out, as if trying to atone for the insult to the Abu-Hana family. "Those hypocrites," she said. "They're worse than the religious fanatics. Beautiful souls."

The Abu-Hana family didn't hold this failure against Maya. It was decided that the girls would be sent to the high school at Pardes Hanna, where the boys were going.

When the time came to discuss the future of Omar himself, they again admitted Maya into their councils, and again accepted a solution that had been suggested jointly by Walid and Maya. Omar was an experienced executive, but Israeli Arabs were not eligible for many executive jobs. The large companies had no use for the services of senior Arab managers. Some of the biggest corporations supplied services or products to the defense forces and did not employ Arabs. Since almost any activity in Israel — economic or otherwise — had some bearing on security, this became a standard pretext for barring Arabs from positions of responsibility. White-collar Arabs competed for teaching jobs in primary and secondary schools in the Arab sector and for the few jobs the government offered them from time to time in reward for services. There were several lawyers who opened offices of their own to serve the Arab populace; there were several doctors — most of whom had studied abroad — and an insignificant number of minor functionaries in the local branches of government departments.

The rest were either independent farmers or small manufacturers, and the vast majority were a cheap labor force for agriculture, building, and industry in the Jewish economy. Omar was not fit for any of the very few "prestigious" positions because of his lack of knowledge of Israeli conditions and because he could not speak Hebrew. Some occupation had to be found that would offer him an agreeable challenge while he learned the language and became integrated into the society.

"The university," Maya suggested. "That's it, the university," Walid seconded with alacrity.

Omar registered as a student of English literature at Tel Aviv University. He enjoyed instant popularity. He was the most handsome man in the department. Tall, dark, with a brilliant white smile. A Hollywood star incarnate. The Oriental Prince Charming in the dreams of Western girls. But the real sensation occurred during the first Hebrew lesson for new immigrants in the department. Everyone was asked where he was from, and when Omar answered "Saudi Arabia," there was a general commotion. A life-sized Palestinian in an Israeli institution of learning.

He was pleased with the university. He enjoyed studying, and if he had been given the opportunity to study all his life, he would have been very happy. The curious, longing, and encouraging looks of the women students flattered him, and all in all it appeared that being a carefree student several hours of the day and a paterfamilias at night suited him wonderfully.

After the first round of examinations, his self-confidence increased greatly. He achieved high grades and became one of the central figures in the department. His company was sought not only because he was striking and mysterious, but also because he was an excellent student and generous in extending help.

Often Walid would drop by to pick up Maya, and they would meet Omar for snacks or lunch on the campus. One day Omar looked depressed and withdrawn, which was unusual for him. "What's the matter?" asked Maya. Walid answered quickly for his brother. "It's nothing; it doesn't matter. He's had a brush with some stupid woman."

Maya didn't leave it at that. After being pressed, Omar showed her the pages of his last paper, on English medieval poetry. Written in the margin was the grade, 75, and a written comment: "This is fine work and deserves an excellent grade, but I don't believe you wrote it yourself."

When Omar had got the paper back from the lecturer, he didn't understand her remark, so he had asked her for an explanation. The bitter-faced woman, with lips always compressed into a straight, tight line, barked at him angrily, "You're an Arab, right? I've never yet met an Arab student capable of producing work like this. I don't believe that you did it yourself, but I was willing not to make a case of it and to give you a grade that isn't bad at all."

Omar, who had worked for years as a teacher, had been so stunned that he was momentarily speechless.

Maya demanded that they mount the barricades at once. Demand a clarification, demand an apology, demand the teacher receive a letter of censure from the head of the department. But it seemed as if all Omar wanted was to bury himself and forget. Walid, too, preferred that the matter be forgotten as quickly as possible.

Omar completed his B.A. in English with distinction, but

Maya always felt that his honeymoon with Israel and the university had been irrevocably ruined by that unfortunate encounter with one wretched and narrow-minded woman.

The incident was not mentioned again in Omar's presence, but in conversations between Maya and Walid it came up more than once. Walid emphasized that it was no more than an insignificant episode and should not be blown out of proportion. He pointed out to her that most of the Arab students wouldn't have passed the entrance exams if they weren't Arabs. Arab students always claim that the examination doesn't reflect their knowledge because of their difficulties with Hebrew, and the universities are afraid of being accused of discrimination against Arabs, so they accept students who should not be accepted.

"That doesn't make it any better," Maya objected. "They shouldn't give in to such blackmail and they shouldn't close their doors to the capable. Let them treat Arabs the way they treat everybody."

Walid wasn't impressed by Maya's reasoning. "Who's everybody? There's no way they treat 'everybody.' They treat students from North African countries one way, discharged soldiers another way, new immigrants another way, and Arabs yet another way. A method of treating everybody equally seems beyond our grasp. It's all built on a system of different attitudes to different kinds of people. Arabs don't have any special privileges, so they try to squeeze the last drop out of the establishment's fear of being accused of discrimination. I'm against this attitude. Not because I have an anti-Arab complex, but because it causes us to think of ourselves as inferior instead of trying to do the best we can and competing on equal terms."

Maya refused to drop the matter of the lecturer. "Leave the philosophy. I'm talking about one specific lecturer. Can you justify that stupid cow?"

Walid flashed her a pacifying smile. "A stupid question. She's just a dumb, miserable woman. She has a small brain and a small heart, if she has one at all. I think you ought to learn not to use up your ammunition against such nobodies, because you'll find they're everywhere. You have to learn to ignore them. It's just a pity that it happened to Omar. He was hurt."

Omar found it difficult to return to the village every day, an hour's drive in the small Renault the family had bought him, and then to get back every morning for his studies. The suggestion was raised that he live in Tel Aviv or rent a place where he could sleep over two or three times a week. But there was no chance of obtaining a place in the student dormitories. The quota allocated to Arab students was full, and there was a long waiting list. Walid was afraid of exposing Omar to landladies who might say to him, "You're an Arab? I'm sorry we don't have a room to let." Maya suggested that Omar stay at her place when he felt like it. He lived there for about three months, and Maya had never had a house guest who was less trouble.

*   *   *

Omar's estrangement from Kafr-Hama was slow but certain. When Walid and Maya tried to discover where they had gone wrong, the whole process began to seem inevitable. Whichever side they examined it from, they always reached a dead end.

For example, Omar's work. At the conclusion of his studies in the university he was offered a scholarship for his master's degree at an American university, but the money was insufficient to maintain his large family, which had been increased by another son. To travel to America alone did not even occur to him; he could not leave his wife alone for years, and of course neither could he leave his sons and daughters. Not that this made it easy to give up the scholarship. Omar seemed to feel that he was sealing a permanent divorce from all his dreams of scholarly, academic life, which he wanted more than anything in the world. Had he found an interesting and challenging position, he might have been consoled. But there was no such work for him.

He obtained two teaching posts, one full time, one part time. One was in the high school at Kafr-Hama and the other at the college for Arab teachers near Netanya. The work depressed him. At first he tried not to feel contempt for the ignorance of the teaching staff, the low educational standards of the pupils, their lack of manners and ambition. He tried to arouse them to intellectual activity, but very soon gave up. The teachers shunned him because his presence exposed their boorishness; the pupils rebelled against his heavy demands; and their parents began speaking against him in the village, arguing that he wanted the impossible from their children and thus was intentionally placing stumbling blocks in their path.

His hope that new teachers, of the younger generation, would change the situation was quickly dissipated when he became acquainted with the new teachers at the college where he taught. First, he was shocked; finally he was in despair. The fact that one of his sisters studied in his classes did not help him, even within his own family. She protested that she had always earned A's in English from all the other teachers, and here was Omar, telling her she didn't know anything.

On the strength of his qualifications, he should have been made director of the high school. But it quickly turned out that he could have the post only if he accepted it as a favor to his family from someone in the Ministry of Education. If he insisted on competing for the post, without making any gestures of flattery or giving dinners to which the person in question would be invited, it was no dice. He tried nevertheless to obtain the job on his own merits, and immediately someone started a rumor in the village that the Abu-Hana family was exploiting its privileged status with the establishment in order to push their son into a cushy job, shoving aside the poor fellow who had given his best years to provide the children of the village with a good education.

Omar did not take this easily. He applied for a post as headmaster of a college in East Jerusalem, where the standard was far higher than that of the village high school, and was warmly received.

When Omar, with the help of his brothers, started packing his books for the move to Jerusalem, their father appeared in the yard and summoned his sons to him. "What's this?" he said. "What are you doing?" His face was pale.

"Packing my books, Abuya," Omar answered.

"Are you going somewhere?" asked the father.

Omar lowered his head.

"He'll need the books for his work," said Walid.

"If he needs books in Jerusalem, let him buy them there," said Salah Abu-Hana. "If he needs money, it will be found. But this is his home," he added, looking his son directly in the eye. "We dreamed so long of having you and your children in this house, next to the houses of your brothers. This house will remain your home, even while you're working in Jerusalem. You are not taking anything from here. You finished all your packing when you returned home."

The house remained intact. Every day one of his sisters-in-law cleaned the floors and the carpets. Whenever Omar arrived with his wife and children, or when sometimes the children traveled alone to spend the day at Kafr-Hama, the house was waiting for them.

Omar's oldest son, Fawzi, surprised everyone. A tall lad, well built, good at many sports that boys his age at Kafr-Hama had only heard about, such as tennis and fencing, a brilliant pupil — he was highly aware of all the political complications of the Palestinian problem. It was clear that Fawzi would be a hard nut to crack. He was, of course, careful not to offend his grandfather and other members of his family, but he did not conceal his views about the Israeli "conquerors," about the dispossession of Palestinians from their homeland, and all related issues.

But it was Fawzi who was accepted most quickly in the Israeli high school in Pardes Hanna.

Fawzi's extreme pro-Palestinian views quickly led to a confrontation in class. A classmate had said, "You don't like it? So get out of here! We did not ask you to come here, anyway." And Fawzi retorted, "This is my country. What are *you* doing here?" "Dirty Palestinian," the Jewish boys shouted at him, and blows followed. There was a fight; Fawzi won and was sure that the others would snitch on him and he would be expelled from the school. But his classmates decided that he was OK, had balls, and had the right to think whatever he wanted to. At the elections for the class committee four months later, he was elected by a decisive majority as chairman.

Later, when Omar's daughters were enrolled in the same school, the earlier fears were allayed. The girls did very well in their studies, were liked by all, and were soon being invited to the homes of their new Jewish friends.

When Omar obtained the post in Jerusalem, he transferred all his children to a school in East Jerusalem. Everybody tried to act as if it was nothing more than a simple move, necessitated by his new office. Actually, all were aware that it was an important change. Since the formal act of annexation by the Knesset, the Israelis considered East Jerusalem an integral part of their state and capital city. But its inhabitants continued to regard themselves as Palestinians, living under occupation.

Now Fawzi found himself on the other side of the fence, occasionally using arguments aimed at chilling the Palestinian zeal of his new classmates. On one of the first days at the new school, he came home injured. He had got into a fight with a toughy, who had called him a "pimp for Jews." On his visits to Kafr-Hama he popped over to Hadera and Pardes Hanna to visit with his Jewish pals. But the ties between them gradually slackened. The Jewish boys were occupied with their impending military service, discussing what units they hoped to go to and with whom. Fawzi had nothing to do with all this, and the others felt constrained by his presence when they were discussing these matters, so central to their lives.

Because of the move to East Jerusalem, the girls finally ended up at a convent school, just as Rasem had suggested earlier. It was considered best for young ladies. Politics did not occupy them very much. At this age they were more concerned with fashion, grooming, and matters of the heart.

Also, they preferred to live in urban society, among the daughters of wealthier Arab families, who shared their views and had broader horizons than those of the girls their age at Kafr-Hama.

Happiest of all was Omar's wife. Mona, a beautiful woman, looked more like her daughters' older sister than their mother. She was not highly educated and at first blush seemed a quiet, retiring person. She came from a family of humble means in Jenin. Thanks to her marriage, Mona had escaped the hard and ungrateful life of the girls of her town. In Saudi Arabia, she had reveled in the luxuries accessible to her through her husband's position.

The large house they had occupied in the American reservation of Aramco was equipped with the best of advanced appliances. Like the American women, she wore fashionable Western clothes; she bought her provisions in the huge supermarket, which lacked nothing; and her children attended the Aramco school, where they studied in classes of five or ten, for which the company supplied the best teachers and the most sophisticated teaching aides, to compensate its workers for their enforced isolation.

Mona had been terrified by the thought of living in Kafr-Hama. She feared the authority of her mother-in-law and sisters-in-law. She was afraid that they would criticize her Western ways and her daughters' upbringing, but it did not occur to her to object to Omar's decisions. She wanted to please her husband's family, which was superior to her own in status, prestige, and wealth. She was used to cooking in small quantities, only for her husband and her children, with modern kitchen aids, and found it difficult to adapt to the cooperative cooking for the entire family in her mother-in-law's yard, with each wife taking home what she needed. In East Jerusalem, she could be again queen of her own kitchen. She regained her serenity and her self-confidence.

Perhaps it is a case of all's well that ends well, thought Maya. Perhaps she was wrong to hope for a different solution.

But living in East Jerusalem means living behind the

invisible mental curtain that separates this part of the "unified" Eternal City from Israel. The meetings between Omar and Maya became more infrequent.

Several weeks after Sadat's visit to Jerusalem, Walid suggested to Maya that they visit Omar; he probably hoped that this new political bridge would reintroduce a sense of intimacy on the personal level. Walid's wife, Nadia, joined them too, and so did Leila, who donned for the occasion a festive peasant dress. As they drove through East Jerusalem, a shower of stones suddenly hit Maya's car, which bore Israeli license plates. Maya screeched to a halt. She was about to jump out to chase the hooligans, when she suddenly realized that by doing this she would be offending Walid's masculine pride in front of his wife and sister.

"Be tough with them," she said to him.

"Let it be," said Walid. "No point making a fuss."

Maya turned pale. "I'm not willing to put up with violence, not even the violence of Arab hooligans."

"What do you think you'll achieve? They'll throw stones at you from behind the wall and you won't even know who did it."

Maya shot her friend a disappointed look. Without another word she got out of the car and walked resolutely toward the yard from which the stones had been hurled.

Walid bit his lip, got out of the car, and scolded the boys in Arabic.

They drove on in silence.

The meeting with Omar depressed them even more.

Why? Maya asked herself. Omar and his family had been glad to see them, the dinner had been rich and tasty, the embraces on parting had been heartfelt and sincere. But on the way back they hardly spoke to each other. Nadia and Leila fell asleep on the back seat.

"He doesn't look happy," said Maya.

"I wasn't able to cheer him up," said Walid.

"How have the youngsters got acclimatized?" Maya asked.

"I don't know," said Walid. "I don't think they know themselves. It's all confused. At the start I knew what was hurting Omar and I thought I'd be able to help. Now I find it hard to understand him. Sometimes I think we don't have a common language. I don't know what's eating him."

They remained silent for some time.

"I think I know," said Maya. "But don't laugh at me. I try to think about him and about you and to put my finger on the source of the difference between you two. He's simply a refugee, not in the sense of a person who has no permanent house, but like a person estranged from his environment. He doesn't feel he really belongs."

Walid looked at her for a long while, then repeated to himself, "Estranged, that's it."

As they approached Kafr-Hama, Walid said quietly, "Do you think we did the right thing, bringing him back?"

Maya wasn't sure, but she wanted to console him. "At least his children will grow up under your father's eye, and surely it's worth the risk."

12

IT WAS RASEM'S TURN to settle down. Maya knew that his choice had already been made, and she was curious about the intended bride. Yet when the opportunity presented itself, she almost missed it.

On one visit, after drinking coffee with Salah Abu-Hana, she went into the yard to say hello to Walid's mother. She saw she had come at the right time, when the goat cheese was being made. A large, round tray, perforated at its base, stood on a low stool. On one side of it sat Rasmiya, one of Walid's sisters-in-law, and on the other side sat a pretty woman whom Maya didn't recognize. She was taking white cloths of coarse cotton from a pail beside her and placing them carefully side by side in the tray. Then Rasmiya poured approximately two glasses of sour goat's milk from the pitcher at her feet into each square of cloth formed in this way. When Rasmiya finished filling one level, the girl placed another layer of square cloths on top of the first. When three layers were full, the two started tying the ends of the cloths together with loose knots, while the surplus fluid drained through the cloth onto the tray and from there into the receptacle beneath. Then they transferred the full squares of cloth into another vessel and began the process over again.

Walid introduced Hannah to Maya.

Maya's curiosity was aroused at once. Hannah was obviously one of the household, for a casual guest would not have been employed in making cheese. Even though she was seated, one could see that she was tall and well proportioned. She had dark flowing hair, large soft almond-shaped eyes, and olive complexion free of makeup. She wore a long dark skirt, a long-sleeved blouse closed at the neck, and flat sandals. From her appearance, she could have been Jewish or a daughter of Kafr-Hama. But not exactly. There was something in her self-confidence, in her ease with a stranger, in the way she looked Maya straight in the eye, that was different from what one would expect of an Arab village girl, even in the Abu-Hana family.

"Pleased to meet you," said Hannah, and continued with her work.

Afterward, when Maya and Walid were by themselves, Maya asked him about her, and learned that Hannah was Rasem's girlfriend.

"Rasem's Jewish girlfriend" was the thought that flashed through Maya's mind, and she immediately regretted not having spoken with her longer.

For Maya knew a lot about Hannah. Walid had often mentioned her, though not by name, and there were many unsaid things that she had guessed for herself.

Rasem and Hannah had met in Jerusalem when Rasem was studying for his master's degree. She was a new immigrant from America, the daughter of parents who were strongly Zionist and traditional in their customs and who had been filled with apprehensions by the procession of Gentile boyfriends, fellow students, whom she used to bring home.

"Can't you find a nice Jewish boy?" her mother would ask — though later she stopped asking when the question sent her daughter into a rage.

"Can't you understand, they're my friends," Hannah would respond. "I'm not getting married to them. They don't ask me if I'm Jewish, and I don't ask them if they're non-Jewish. This isn't Russia; this is America. Here everyone's recognized as a person in his own right."

"I'm not saying they're not persons," the mother would reply in defense. "America's a wonderful country. And they're all very nice, your friends. But you'll break your father's heart if you bring him a grandchild by a non-Jewish father."

Hannah's father, on the other hand, would say, "Maidele, my treasure, you must forgive your mother. She doesn't understand. She doesn't know these are modern times. But you should understand her. Her heart will break if she can't lead her daughter to stand under a bridal canopy in a proper Jewish wedding."

Hannah had no intention of getting married yet. It had always been clear to her that she would marry a Jew, that her children would have a Jewish father. But her parents' pressure drove her crazy. So when her mother suggested she go to Israel to study for her master's, she jumped at the idea. At least there nobody would pester her. And her fellow students would be Jewish, so she could not go wrong.

That night her parents slept peacefully.

When Hannah arrived in Israel, she hoped she would find her place among young Israelis. She thought they surely would welcome a young Jewish girl like herself.

In fact, she was in for a shock. Later she realized that had she waited patiently, she would probably have found those warm Israelis she had sought. But the social climate at first was hostile.

She was advised that Israeli men were bashful and soft as butter inside despite their rough manners. But she found them crude, inconsiderate, and impolite. The Israelis of her own age shared a common past, a common language, and a world of concepts based on common experiences in which she had no part. She hadn't served in the army with them; she hadn't been in the youth movement; she hadn't gone to school with any of them, climbed to the top of Mount Hermon on a trek, or spent a bivouac in the Judean desert. She was a stranger and remained an outsider. At the university, in arguments that developed during lectures or in the cafeteria or the library, whenever she criticized any aspect of Israel, she would be angrily chastised. How could she allow herself to express an opinion when she was new here? She didn't understand anything yet. And anyway, American Jews donate a few dollars to the United Jewish Appeal and think they own the Israeli Jews. If, on the other hand, she kept quiet during a discussion because she didn't feel she knew enough to participate, they would claim it was her duty and her right as a Jew to speak her mind.

Her loneliness oppressed her. She had never felt so alienated, so much a stranger, even when she had been practically the only Jewish girl in her class at school. When she met Rasem, all her problems vanished. This young man, with the sleek dark hair, the brown skin, and the dazzling smile, filled her whole horizon. His looks were of the kind that in the Middle East would be taken for granted, though in Scandinavian countries they would cause a traffic jam. To Hannah he was much more than just an attractive man; he was considerate and sensitive and gentle, and he smiled at her when she was embarrassed and always greeted her politely. His courting wasn't of the crude Sabra kind, which always left her slighted, shamed, and hurt.

The Sabras considered tenderness, flirting, the display of good manners in general, and male-female etiquette in particular a confession of weakness, not worthy of their self-image as the strong and silent type. They attempted to get her to bed in the crudest manner, and when she rejected their advances they hastened to mask their own inadequacy with wounding remarks and to reassert their male supremacy.

When Rasem introduced himself to her in the library, she didn't inquire if he was a Jew or an Arab. Perhaps she figured his name was that of a Jew from one of the Arab countries. At any rate, when he invited her to visit his family at Kafr-Hama, it came as a complete surprise that he was an Arab. When she thought it over later, she realized that she must have known from the first that he was, but it had made no difference. And suddenly it was a reality — of costume, of customs, of smells: an Arab village.

It was strange. Much stranger than dining at the home of a Protestant or Catholic friend in her home town. There, they spoke the same language, wore the same clothes, discussed the same subjects as her own parents. Here, she discovered an entirely different world.

Nevertheless, she felt at ease. She was received with open

arms, no questions asked, with love. When Rasem mentioned that she was in the country alone, her parents in America, his mother's eyes filled with compassion and she pressed Hannah to her breast. "Poor child," she said, and scolded her son for not bringing Hannah home sooner.

After she had visited several times, Salah Abu-Hana told his son that he would be willing to help Hannah if she would allow him to. The suggestion reduced Hannah to tears.

Until she met Rasem, Hannah had been very shy and reserved with her fellow students. They, for their part, hardly noticed her. Yet when she started seeing Rasem, she became a center of attention. Because she found an Arab worthy of her, they couldn't forgive her.

Rasem didn't allow himself to analyze his feelings for Hannah, and took care to keep their relationship on a Platonic basis. He didn't want her to be hurt. Also, he wanted to see how she withstood the pressure of her environment. How she responded to the responses of others to their relationship. Only then was he willing to ask himself and Hannah about the future.

It seemed that the entire Abu-Hana clan, not only Rasem, gave Hannah a new sense of dignity, a new life. She amazed them with the ease with which she had learned both Hebrew and Arabic. She became friends with Rasem's sisters and mother, felt that she was one of the family, with no barriers. In the Abu-Hana household she was accepted as a daughter.

The Prophet does not forbid his believers to wed Jewish wives. In Kafr-Hama a mixed marriage was not an unheard-of thing. The few mixed couples all came from the lower rungs of the social ladder, Arab men who left the village and met Jewish girls. Arab women had no option; they stayed home. There were many romantic flings between well-educated Arab men and young, well-to-do Jewish women. But those affairs didn't last long. Marriage occurred mostly in the cases where a Jewish woman was so socially undesirable that any marriage, even with an Arab, meant an advancement for her — like a young girl abandoned and working as a prostitute, whom a young Arab decided to reform. Mixed marriages among the middle class hardly existed, with a few isolated exceptions that flowered in mutually ideological backgrounds, like the youth movement of the Communist Party. Of the few such marriages familiar to Maya, all but two ended in divorce, with bitterness and resentment on both sides. Therefore, the case of Hannah and Rasem was an exception and involved a conscious risk.

Walid told Maya that when Rasem and Hannah approached his parents about their decision to marry, his mother had embraced her, and his father had kissed her on the forehead and asked, "And what of your parents, my daughter?"

Hannah blushed, stammered, and lowered her eyes.

Salah Abu-Hana said, "Parents who have only one daughter, and a wonderful daughter like you, surely miss her very much. They surely want what is good for you. Go home, my daughter. Tell your mother and father about Rasem and about us. Tell them how much we love you. I believe they will give you their blessing."

Rasem interjected, "It's not so simple, Father. A trip like that costs about as much as a whole year of studies."

Abu-Hana looked at him in amazement. "You are our daughter," he said to Hannah. "Rasem will buy you a ticket and you'll fly home next week. Good news mustn't wait."

Hannah returned the same week she set out. She didn't speak to Maya about the meeting with her parents, but perhaps she discussed it with Rasem and his parents. She stopped writing home after that.

No date was set for the wedding. When anyone mentioned marriage, Abu-Hana would sigh. "It's hard for a girl to marry without her parents' consent. We'll wait a little; perhaps they'll relent."

Walid's mother would gaze at Hannah's slim figure and sigh.

She continued sighing into her pillow, in secret. She had seven sons, each one of them unique and special to her. Deep in her heart she loved Walid best. He was in no hurry to get married and always laughed off her transparent hints in this direction. Rasem, who was older than Walid — Rasem, the successful, the handsome, the talented, whose framed university diploma adorned the wall of his father's guest room — had found himself a woman but was unable to rejoice in her. So she would sigh, and sometimes the sighing turned into real sobbing. She didn't believe that waiting would change anything. She realized they wouldn't have an easy time of it, and doubted if even love would be enough to see them through.

Rasem's mother loved the Jewish girl her son had brought home. Hannah was very much like Leila, and the two became close, like sisters. But Leila had been born to the fate of an Arab girl. And Hannah? Her parents denied her. Her friends would certainly reject her. True, the Abu-Hana house was wide open to her. But would that be enough for Hannah? Basma tossed and tossed on her bed, and at times she and Salah Abu-Hana would discuss the predicament long into the night. They were very concerned about both Hannah and Rasem. For Rasem was not like their other sons. If he had the opportunity, perhaps he would sever his ties with the village. Were it not for his parents and brothers, he surely would find visiting the village quite pointless. Salah Abu-Hana had often wondered about this strange phenomenon. He himself was like a plant that had grown in this soil. Even when he strolled through the streets of Tel Aviv or Jerusalem, or sipped coffee at one of the kibbutzim or Jewish villages in the area, he always felt as if his very being was rooted in this soil. He could not understand that anyone would not prefer the village. How could one want to breathe other air? Surely it wasn't easy for Rasem not to love his village. Had he found the woman he loved here in Kafr-Hama, his tie to his home, to his roots, would be much stronger.

Salah too had no doubt that the future held many hard tests for these two young people. He pitied Hannah more than Rasem. His son was tough, not easily hurt. But Hannah — she would have to find shelter in Kafr-Hama, and Kafr-

Hama, for all its warmth, was not the most suitable place for a young American Jewish girl from a vastly different culture.

Maya wanted to make friends with Hannah, but she wanted to be sure she wasn't imposing herself on Hannah, who, for her part, was friendly and affable but kept her distance.

Maya was curious about the fact that when she visited, the Abu-Hanas all gathered to welcome her, but Hannah never appeared. After the exchange of greetings, news, stories, and ritual responses, and after several cups of coffee, Maya would go out to the inner courtyard to visit the women. In the small room with the low ceiling, where Walid's mother cooked the family meals in large saucepans, she often found Hannah, almost indistinguishable from all the other women. At first Maya felt that there was something distasteful about this. She considered it an inappropriate pretense — this young, well-educated woman, trying to assimilate herself into a society alien to her mentality and views.

Later she learned that she'd been mistaken. Hannah had never sacrificed her own personality, her independence, or her vision of the world. She genuinely enjoyed the company of the Abu-Hana women.

For four long years Hannah, Rasem, and the entire Abu-Hana family waited for some change of heart in Hannah's parents. To no avail.

*　　*　　*

One day Rasem arrived alone for the weekend. He went into his father's room, kissed his hand, and announced, "We don't intend to wait anymore. We're getting married."

That night all the brothers assembled to discuss arrangements — especially about the khadi who would register Hannah as a Muslim, because in Israel a Muslim is not allowed to marry a Jew in a civil wedding ceremony. There are no civil marriages, and two people of different religions can marry only if one of them converts to the faith of the other.

For some reason, without any explicit discussion, the wedding plans were very modest, like a celebration in a house of mourners. It was Walid who asked, "What's got into you? Whom are we hiding from? The Abu-Hana family is marrying the best of its sons. Rasem is bringing us a bride we all love and are proud of. Let's not make this a modest wedding. Let's have a celebration that everyone will talk about."

Everyone's spirits lifted.

The invitations sent out to hundreds of people all over the country were decorated with the fairy-tale drawing of a bridal carriage drawn by four galloping horses. All the rules of ceremony were observed. Hannah sat on her bridal throne for the customary twenty-four hours, surrounded by her new sisters-in-law and their friends, and only her firm resolution not to shame the family helped her to get through this ritual in the midst of clouds of perfume and incense.

Maya was delighted for her, but surmised that the couple's worst difficulties were still ahead of them. Walid was optimistic that everything would work out.

"And their children?" asked Maya.

"May they have many," said Walid. "Nothing can go wrong. With a father and mother like them, and with the grandparents they'll have."

"Wait, wait." Maya laughed. "We're not so sure of the contribution of the other two grandparents."

But Walid refused to subscribe to pessimism. He was certain that most of their ordeals were behind them. What did it matter that the children would be considered Jews according to the Jewish code and Muslims by the Islamic code? By the time they grew up, these distinctions would not be important. They'd be Israelis, and what mattered most was that their parents would love them.

Socially, Hannah and Rasem found their place among the educated residents in East Jerusalem, where they were joined later by Omar and Mona. In West Jerusalem they formed a circle of friends from Rasem's schooldays at Pardes Hanna and his student days at the Hebrew University, as well as of Hannah's American friends. These young Jews, who had relocated to Israel in pursuit of a more meaningful and value-oriented life, were bewildered by a reality that was so different from the dream which had inspired it. They included members of the professions, university lecturers, artists, and scientists, who were always in the forefront of the latest fight for social justice: for women's rights, for blacks' rights, against discrimination on the basis of religion, against the incursion of religion into civil matters, against anti-Semitism.

Here they felt a bit ridiculous. For the first time in their lives they were unable to call things by name. Their dream country had laid a trap for them. It demanded — and received — from them unconditional loyalty and love. It forbade them to criticize. Whenever they dared to comment on, or express reservations about, anything as it was, they were immediately marked with the stamp of traitor. They maintained their unrealistic vision of justice, in the narrow frame of their own homes and immediate environment. For them, Hannah's marriage to Rasem offered unquestionable proof that they had remained true to their ideals, to their vision of human equality.

But even so, in this safe world between the family in Kafr-Hama and the friends in Jerusalem, East and West, an alien and grating note would sometimes be heard.

The discordant notes became more frequent and noticeable after the Yom Kippur War, in 1973, which wrought a drastic turnabout in public opinion. Rasem's wedding took place a few months before this war, when Israelis were still glorying in the 1967 victory, secure in the belief of their absolute military superiority. Yom Kippur shattered their equanimity. Arabs were enemies. It was no longer fashionable to underestimate them, to brush them aside as a mere nuisance. They spelled danger.

Rasem felt the change acutely. The roadblocks, for instance. Rasem constantly praised his wife's driving, but whenever they traveled together, he drove. When, however, the radio and newspapers reported terrorist actions, or when they knew from experience that they would have to pass a roadblock where suspicious cars were thoroughly checked out by Israeli security men, he would sit in the passenger seat, leaving the wheel to his wife.

"But you have Israeli license plates," Maya remarked when Rasem mentioned the checking procedures at the roadblocks.

"But he has an Arab face, too," remarked Walid, matter-of-factly.

"Your face doesn't change when you sit in the passenger seat," Maya said, as if she didn't understand.

"Show me one Israeli security man who'll believe that an Arab's willing to sit beside his wife and let her drive," retorted Rasem. "If the woman's driving she must be a Jew. So her husband has to be a Jew, too."

"You're being facetious," said Maya, getting annoyed. "You yourself have brought me to the homes of your friends on the West Bank, where the girls drive and wear pants and behave just as I do."

"True — and again not true," said Rasem. "They belong to the aristocracy. In their city, everyone knows them. But, first of all, they drive cars with license plates of the occupied territories, and second, they'll never drive into Israel proper without a male escort, and when there's a man in the car, he drives."

Hannah added, "Rasem can't forget how they ruined a whole week's holiday for him at one of the roadblocks. We were traveling in two cars. With Jerry and Rivka. You know — he's a lecturer in psychology, and she teaches retarded children. We'd driven up to the Kinneret and had had a terrific week. On the way back, coming out of Wadi Ara, there was a roadblock. Rivka and I were in the first car, and we completely forgot that they might stop the second car, which Rasem was driving. It simply didn't occur to us. We got to a gas station and suddenly noticed that the other car wasn't behind us. Rivka figured they might have had a blowout, so we drove back to look for them. At the roadblock, we saw that our car had been detained. You couldn't talk to Rasem for a whole week afterward."

Maya said, "The easiest thing is to say it's awful, and to identify with his justified anger. But I can't do that. I have no solution to offer. I hate the roadblocks, and I also think they're not very efficient. But if they prevent the entrance of even one terrorist or one explosive charge, then they're worth a hundred or even a thousand inconveniences, including the justified resentment of people who have been pointlessly delayed by the roadside."

Rasem glanced up, started to say something, then changed his mind. But everyone looked at him, waiting for him to speak. "It's not the way you describe it. If you were pulled up sometimes, and I at other times, or if they searched you just once for every three times they search me, I'd shut up. I shut up now too. But inside I'm furious. I'm not furious because there are roadblocks. I don't want terrorists bringing in explosives either. But every time I reach a roadblock I'm reminded that I'm not an Israeli citizen but merely an Arab, and all the talk about equality won't change a thing. Both of us drive on the road, and both of us could be smuggling in terrorist equipment, but you pass uninterrupted because you're a Jew and I get stopped because I'm an Arab, and not because I'm a smuggler or a terrorist."

Maya responded, "But it's a fact that the terrorists are Arabs and the objects of their attacks are Jews. A roadblock isn't a radar station. There's no way of searching everyone or of knowing in advance which car is carrying terrorists. The most that can be done is to stop those drivers there's some reason to be suspicious about. There's no getting away from the fact that Arabs and Jews are at war."

"So where does that leave me?" asked Rasem. "This war against the Jews is being waged against me too, as long as I don't take my stand on the other side. The Arabs fighting on the other side regard me as a coward or a traitor. That's hard enough to bear without additional burdens. If I only felt I were getting encouragement from this side, that my state considered me a citizen in fact . . ."

"When peace comes . . ." Walid sang the words of the popular song, to cut off the conversation.

They had rehashed this subject many times, and they knew they'd discuss it again in the future. Maya suddenly laughed. "You can take pride in the fact that you've got a terribly suspicious face, Rasem," she said. "They don't stop ordinary Arabs at the roadblocks. If you don't believe me I'll prove it to you. You all remember Asher, don't you? My friend from Chile, who read poetry in many languages and decided to learn Arabic poetry. Asher's an officer in the Civil Defense, and his men are in charge of manning the roadblocks in certain areas. To be brief, they decided to check the alertness of the guards. Asher took another fellow with him — a North African Jew, with a swarthy complexion. They put West Bank license plates on an old jalopy — with different numbers on the licenses. They drove through a roadblock and no one even looked at them. Down the road a bit they turned around, drove through the same roadblock once again. No response. They turned around once more, stopped beside the roadblock, and questioned the guards. The poor clods didn't even try to justify themselves. They explained quite seriously to the investigating officers that there was no need to check; the Arabs from the West Bank stop of their own accord."

They all laughed until tears streamed from their eyes. Rasem said, "It's pure nonsense. If it's to save the life of one child, I'm willing to stop at roadblocks even an hour a day. But you know that isn't what's involved. I'm not getting upset about roadblocks on the roads. I'm indignant about the roadblocks in the hearts, the minds, the newspapers, the policies. There are roadblocks all along the line. The Arabs from the West Bank have it easier; at least they know who they are. They are Palestinians. They regard the Israelis as occupiers, and they expect to be treated as enemies. But I'm supposed to be an Israeli citizen. To be treated as an enemy by my own country is a different kind of experience."

Walid grinned wryly. "In Pardes Hanna the Jewish history teacher discussed at length the identity crisis that Jews suffered from. Now we're privileged to see the transfer of this affliction from the Jews to the Arabs. The question used to be 'What are we first — Jews or Israelis?' Now it's 'What are we first — Arabs or Israelis?' "

Maya said, "What's your answer? Israeli Jews would contend that their attitude toward you would be dictated by your answer."

Walid replied, "Our answer depends on your attitude."

They all looked at each other. For a while no one spoke.

Rasem broke the silence. "Don't look so glum, all of you." His smile was tinged with irony. "If you weren't such godless infidels, you'd find consolation in the fact that the prophecy of the Book has come true. The inhabitants of the land have become the hewers of wood and the drawers of water."

No one smiled back.

Rasem was determined to change their mood. "I have a great story for you. Have you heard the one about the divine summit in Jerusalem? No? Well, the gods decided to have a summit, in the Holy City, of course. Jehovah, being the current landlord, was the official host. Everybody showed up. The Jewish God bade a gracious welcome to Jesus, Buddha, and all the lesser deities, and then said, 'Seeing that we are all gathered here, we may as well begin...' 'But where's Allah?' Jesus queried. 'Oh, he's here,' the host reassured him, and, turning toward the servants' entry, called out, 'Allah, bring in the coffee.' "

*   *   *

About two years after the wedding Hannah made a hasty trip to the United States. Someone in the family had called her because her father was very ill. She was on the plane that very day. Rasem was to join her the next day. They didn't know how seriously ill her father was, and he didn't want her to have to face it alone. She arrived home in time for the funeral. When she returned to Israel she received a long letter her father had written on his deathbed.

I'm sorry [he had written]. I'm sorry for the years I have lived in bereavement. If I could only bring them back. Try to forgive me, and ask the parents who adopted you as a daughter to forgive me too. If God wills, perhaps I will live to meet them and the husband you've chosen. If I don't, I want you to know I loved you very much.

Some months after Hannah's return, Maya happened to meet her in Abu-Hana's yard, sitting beside the metal tray of goat's cheese. Maya sat down on a stool next to Hannah and watched the process with intense curiosity. "I really can't understand," she said, "how from these heaps of sour milk such perfect squares of cheese emerge, all as uniform as if machine-made."

Hannah smiled at her proudly. "That requires a special skill. It's my mother who does it."

*   *   *

Financially, Rasem was thriving. He had left his position at the Ministry of Commerce and Industry to become an independent investment counselor and had opened an office in East Jerusalem. Very quickly his office became a focal point of economic ties between Jewish and Arab business-men, and between Israel and the West Bank. To the West Bank residents, Rasem was "one of their own" — he spoke their language, was familiar with their customs, and was the son of a respected family. A man one could trust. Even his Jewish wife added a point in his favor, for what better proof could there be of his equal status among the Jews. To the Israelis, he was "one of ours." An Arab, but with a *kosher* stamp. He wasn't just an ordinary Israeli Arab, an academic; there were numerous Arab academics. What was special about him was that he had attended a Jewish high school, had friends from the youth movement days, had worked in a high government post of a kind not usually reserved for Arabs. In short, "one of ours" who just happened to be an Arab.

Hannah, too, found herself at a crossroads between two worlds. After receiving her master's degree in archaeology, she obtained a position at the Israel Museum. Later on, her work brought her into contact with intellectuals and scholars from East Jerusalem and the West Bank. Hannah didn't force her friendship on them, but their incipient hostility crumbled very quickly. Her behavior made it clear that she had no intention of asserting arbitrary authority, nor did she try to ingratiate herself. Soon she won their respect and even their affection.

When they started searching for excuses to justify their affection for her, they found apparently contradictory arguments. Those who had decided to ignore completely that she was Jewish — an American who decided to immigrate to Israel and become an Israeli — thought of her as an American. Others commented that she was one of them. She conversed in Arabic and married an Arab.

Hannah learned the different attitudes of Jews and Arabs to mixed marriages.

Jews felt that because she had married an Arab, she had debased herself. She had betrayed the Jews.

The Arabs felt that because Rasem had married a Jewess, they should adopt her.

The more time that passed, the greater Maya's amazement at the success of this marriage, about which even relatives and friends of the couple had had forebodings. A mixed marriage is a risky venture in the best of times. But the times were far from good. The discord between Arab and Jewish Israelis was growing fast into uncompromising antagonism. The daily confrontation between the Israeli authorities and the population of the occupied territories escalated from hostile resentment into rioting and continual violence. Rasem and Hannah lived at the very intersection of all these mounting tensions and eruptions. Maya marveled at Hannah's ability to keep her marriage intact under such circumstances.

One weekend, when she and Hannah chanced to meet at the Abu-Hana home in Kafr-Hama, Maya gained some insight into Hannah and Rasem's predicament. The radio announcer reported riots and arrests on the West Bank. Hannah said, "Rasem's gone to Nablus. I asked him not to go. I try not to worry, but I wish he were back already."

On television they watched an interview with a religious

settler at Kiryat Arba, the controversial Jewish appendage to the Arab city of Hebron on the West Bank.

Hannah said, "This week we were supposed to go to Hebron. I wanted to postpone the trip, but Rasem said that we can't all put ourselves under house arrest. We went. We came to a roadblock built by kids, high school students. We couldn't continue. Meanwhile, other cars arrived, and we couldn't turn back either. An army command car arrived, with four young fellows in it, all about nineteen, commanded by an officer no more than twenty. They ordered all the people in cars with West Bank license plates to get out of their cars and dismantle the roadblock. Some of them were shaking with rage. An Arab taxi driver told the soldiers that they had no right to do this. The commander, actually, was nice. He didn't shout at the taxi driver; he smiled and said, 'We can't dismantle the roadblock for you because we have to hold our weapons. Otherwise someone will knock off our heads or steal our weapons and then shoot us down with our own guns. And the road has to be opened. And the kids who constructed the roadblock can't be found to dismantle it. So somebody has to do it. This roadblock wasn't put up against you, but against us. Your sons built it. You didn't stop them. So, please — pull the stones away.'

"Perhaps he was right," Hannah went on. "But I was ashamed about us sitting in our car while the West Bank Arabs worked." She suggested to Rasem that he help, but he wasn't excited about the idea. "If you don't clear the roadblock along with those old people, then I'm getting out of the car, and I'll go and help them." He went. Afterward, when they were driving again, he said, "It isn't simple. If an Israeli Jew gets out of his car and helps clear the roadblock, everybody calls him a fine fellow. But if I do it, it isn't just a political act of identification with the West Bank Arabs; it's as if I'm expressing objections to Israeli policy on the West Bank."

Hannah replied, "Rasem, I didn't send you to help with the work in the role of an Arab or an Israeli or a Muslim. It just bothered me that old people had to dismantle a barrier because they live on one side of it, but young people didn't have to dismantle it because they live on the other side."

"Hannah, get used to it," Rasem said gently. "Here, where we live, we're not just people; we're people with tags: 'Palestinian,' 'Israeli Arab,' Israeli 'Jew.' Israelis don't exist yet."

Hannah finished the account and looked at Maya with a pained expression. "Maybe it shows cowardice on my part, but I prefer not to go to the West Bank these days. I don't want to find myself in a situation where I'll be compelled to choose, to decide."

Maya responded, "We haven't had many opportunities to talk. But from the few meetings we've had, and from what Walid tells me, you don't seem like a coward."

Hannah gave her a grateful look and then continued, almost as if to herself, "I try, but I don't always know the right thing to do. Sometimes I find it hard to decide and afterward I'm sorry I didn't act. You know, some time ago we were guests of a very important family in East Jerusalem, and to this day I can't forgive myself for not opening my mouth on that occasion. I was afraid of being impolite. There were several guests, some from abroad. The hostess spoke with profound shock of her harsh experiences during the Six Day War, when the Israeli forces took the Old City. She pointed to her well-cultivated garden surrounding the house, and her voice broke as she recounted how the Jewish soldiers trampled on her flower beds when they searched the house, how they had stomped around in their hobnailed boots without regard or respect. Everyone sympathized with her, and the guests from abroad were shocked at the terrors of the occupation. And I didn't say a word."

Hannah's cheeks flushed at the memory of that scene. "You know," she said to Maya, "below the vestibule of that stately villa extends a refugee camp. Do you remember in what state of abject poverty we found those refugee camps after the Six Day War? I was ignorant then of the complex refugee situation, but I was shocked to discover how these refugees had been living under the regime of their brothers.

During all those years of Jordanian rule the grand lady in East Jerusalem had been able to see her Palestinian brothers in the refugee camp under her very nose, and hadn't been shocked at all. Her peace of mind was not troubled in the least, but how furious she became when a Jewish soldier trampled over a flower in her garden ... Still, I didn't open my mouth. I haven't forgiven myself since. I don't hold back anymore."

13

THE GUESTS kept arriving in the village in an unending stream, from the morning on. None of them needed to ask the way. They merely followed the cars in front of them. To the villagers they all looked the same: Jews. As for the guests, as soon as they spilled out of their cars, they examined each other with some curiosity to count how many belonged to the government party, how many to the opposition, how many to the Histadrut, how many to the kibbutzim in the area.

A stranger happening on the scene would have thought he'd come across a mass rally or a political assembly, not a family celebration — or, to be precise, a wedding.

Not just any wedding. Walid's wedding. His parents and brothers had almost given up hope that there would ever be one. It was only because of his special status and the absolute loyalty of his friends that his protracted bachelorhood had not given rise to winking and gossiping among the men of his own age, all of whom had by now established families. The young girls who had pined for him had already focused their dreams on a passionate and enchanting future for their daughters. Even Walid's own family had resigned themselves to the possibility that Walid's children would not grow up here, among them, in the village. That they would perhaps come for weekend visits or on festival days, with the chasm between them growing wider all the time. His family would have been almost reconciled to the idea that he might marry a foreign woman, a citified Christian Arab from Nazareth or a Jewess from Tel Aviv; at least they would see some grandchildren from him. And now he was getting married. Marrying a village girl. From time to time they would steal glances at him to make sure he hadn't changed his mind.

A pointless fear. One could see that no thought was further from his mind. Strained and uncomfortable in the dark, heavy suit made especially for the wedding from English wool of the highest quality, with complete disregard for the weather, Walid sent slightly embarrassed glances and smiles in all directions, and kept wiping the sweat from his forehead and upper lip with a fine white handkerchief, occasionally plunging into the crowd to greet some particularly distinguished guest.

Many guests, for whom this was their first Arab wedding, went searching eagerly for the bride. A futile quest. The celebration was for the bridegroom, for his family, and their guests.

*   *   *

All this time the bride, in a long white dress like those of Jewish brides, sits on a high, decorated armchair in one of the rooms of her parents' house. This is her throne. Here she is queen, for a day. This being so, the day has to be exploited to the fullest. She will sit on this throne, pretty, bejeweled, scented — for twenty-four hours on end. Surrounded by a tight ring of females — her mother, her sisters, her new sisters-in-law, aunts, friends, relatives, neighbors, and women who never stay away from such an event. No male intruder is allowed. The room is stifling. The women frequently sprinkle the bride with scents and perfumes, perhaps to restore her spirits, or perhaps to suppress the smell of sweat. They praise her beauty, her grace, and her virtues, and bemoan the childhood and youth from which she is parting forever. They lament the fate of the mother who must be separated from her now, and speak words of encouragement to her in her grief.

The bride sits as if she's in a swoon, eyes glazed, erect in the elevated chair, in heavy, exaggerated makeup, which she would not ordinarily wear. Her meticulously arranged hair rises in tiers above her.

She is eighteen years old. Only yesterday she attended school, fretting over grades or a teacher's scolding.

Today she is a bride. Walid's wife.

The crowd of women parts occasionally to clear a path for some Jewish women, who, out of a sense of duty or plain curiosity, feel the need to escape the main celebration for a few minutes, to feast their eyes on the bride.

"How are you?"

"All right ... thank you ... I feel fine ... How are you?" the bride replies in a low, pleasant voice, somewhat in a monotone, the Hebrew words slow to her tongue.

"She's lovely, really lovely," the women state as soon as they leave. "At least she finished high school," they murmur patronizingly, and hurry back to the large open space in the center of the group of stone houses of the Abu-Hana clan, where a full-sized and festively lighted wooden stage has been erected and where the revels are proceeding in full force.

*　*　*

The organization was perfect. All the men in the family had been recruited to greet the guests and show them to their places. Jews are accustomed to serving a complete dinner at weddings. Even though many hundreds were coming to his wedding, Walid had decided to treat them all to a royal banquet. Because there was no single large hall, three big rooms were converted into dining rooms with buffets. Walid's nephews were busily setting tables for groups of guests who appeared in the entrance, while others cleared away the dishes from those tables where other guests had finished their dinner.

Forty head of sheep had been slaughtered, eighty turkeys, and eight cows. The Abu-Hana clan had resolved that no one would rise from the table with a light stomach.

Haled Ibn-Abdalla and his two younger brothers had taken responsibility for the catering. Walid had wanted to pay them, but they were so insulted by his offer that only with great difficulty could he appease them. "It's our honor," they told him. "This is our present for your wedding." Haled and his brothers provided the secret formula behind the success of several roadside inns and restaurants that had done dazzling business in Tel Aviv, and the Jewish restaurateurs tried to outsmart each other by tempting the brothers to work for them.

No alcohol was served, since Muslims are forbidden to drink it, but the soft drinks flowed like water. Crate after crate.

Maya gulped down the food with gusto. The food was tastier than the meals that usually appeared on the tables of the Abu-Hana family. A fellah's kitchen was not distinguished by variety or refinement.

Absent-mindedly, Maya cast a perfunctory glance over the milling groups, but her son was nowhere in sight. She did not worry about him; he was probably helping out, along with the boys of the family, enjoying the excitement and the merrymaking.

She knew that she too should be celebrating, but she was sad — sad and perplexed. We've lost him, she said to herself. We've lost him, and this meal I'm eating is that of a wake, after the funeral of the dream of Jewish-Arab co-existence in Israel. Walid has decided that he has nothing to seek among us. And the trouble is, he's right, damn it.

What will he do with her, with this pretty girl with veiled eyes? What will they talk about? Why did he do this? He'd held out for so many years, and suddenly he folds. Maya feared that his choice signified his disavowal of political activity. As if he were telling them all, "I've had it. I don't need a partner for public life; just a wife and homemaker."

She recalled all the talks she and Walid had had on this subject. They hardly ever spoke of the possibility of his marriage with a Jew. Of all the Arabs Maya knew more or less intimately, Walid had a good chance to make such a marriage work. But somehow it had always been clear that Walid would not marry a Jew. Especially because he was so involved with Jewish society and felt so much at home there. It was important to him to show that he wasn't forgetting his roots. That he was an Arab and proud of it.

A redheaded woman wearing a lot of makeup, who had coiled her way onto the seat beside her, subjected Maya to a scrutinizing stare before asking if she was from the Histadrut or from the party.

Maya threw her a murderous glance and answered drily, "I'm from the bride's side."

Maya decided to forgo the final course. She got up and resumed her rounds among the guests sitting opposite the stage, which was decorated with colored bulbs and festive flags. A Druse dance troupe was performing a *debka*, and the loudspeakers carried the orchestra's music to the perimeters of the village. Maya observed the various groups, noticing that the former secretary general of the Histadrut was sitting in the front row. There's a real man, she thought. That's why he's a has-been.

She decided to take a walk in the village and immediately regretted it. There was no escaping the fact that she no longer felt welcome here. Of late she had not visited so often, and when she had come, she did not roam around the village freely. But the hostility surprised her. It was not something violent, tangible, dangerous. Not a stone raised, not even a threat. But it was in the air. In the children's glances.

*   *   *

As things turned out, she was glad Larry had declined her invitation to join her. Larry was a star reporter of a major American television network, and they were good pals. When Maya invited him, he wanted to bring along a film crew.

"This is a wedding of a friend, not an anthropological project," she chided him. He lost interest in the wedding.

If a blood-stained sheet were to be produced after the nuptials, or if there was a ceremony in which camels and sheep were exchanged for the bride, he would be begging to be invited. She smiled inwardly.

Maya remembered how amazed she had been years ago, after reading letters sent by Arab girls to a women's weekly, asking if it was possible to mend the hymen so that their shame might not be discovered on their wedding day, and how even more amazed she had been to discover that such an operation had actually become a fat source of income for gynecologists who specialized in it. At some point she had asked Walid about it. The bloody sheet was no longer brought out for inspection, he said, except among the most backward. But the family always knew, and blood revenge was a serious matter. Serious enough to justify such operations.

Maya recalled the Yemeni from the Palmach who had occupied family quarters in his kibbutz with his girlfriend. When asked years later why they didn't marry, he'd answered, "You crazy? How can I marry her? She isn't a virgin!"

She wondered how Jew and Arab managed to maintain such a distance when they're really so similar.

She recalled discussing the topic once with Larry. It had been during Purim and he had just got back from doing a television spot for his American network on children's costumes in Tel Aviv. He was in high spirits and full of stories about the imaginative finery. She asked him how many children had dressed up as Arabs, and he couldn't remember any. Maya said, "You see? It isn't natural. When I was a child, lots of us dressed up as Arabs. But these days, if a child comes to a kindergarten Purim party dressed as an Arab, the teacher suspects the father's a communist."

"That's not so surprising," said Larry. "It's quite natural in a war situation."

"What war? Where's the war?" she retorted vehemently, oblivious of his utter surprise at the intensity of her reaction. "I'm not talking about dressing up as Yasir Arafat. I'm talking about Arabs, Israeli Arabs, citizens of Israel, who live here and eat here and raise vegetables here and pay income tax. Can't you see it isn't natural? Something unnatural has happened here. In nineteen forty-eight we fought against Arabs, and during the nineteen fifties we went on hikes wearing kaffiyehs. What's happened to the kaffiyeh? That's what I want to know!"

Tonight, for example, is proof that Arabs and Jews can

mingle together, thought Maya, smiling warmly at new arrivals who greeted her. If Al Fatah set off a bomb among the guests at this wedding, they would really have a celebration. But Maya knew that no one here feared terrorism. Such incidents didn't occur at Kafr-Hama. Maya noticed that Taufik was not among the men receiving guests or escorting them to tables. This meant he was in charge of security — and he was certainly a man one could rely on.

What a strange world, Maya reflected. It was Jews who had sealed the friendship between Taufik and Walid. Had it not been for Jews, their paths might have never crossed. The towering Taufik, who always spoke in a soft, low voice, as if afraid that if he raised it he would bring down the walls of Jericho, grew up in a very poor family, sharecroppers who owned not a scrap of land. The Jewish instructor from the nearby Hashomer Hatzair kibbutz brought them together. They and several other boys their age used to steal away on appointed evenings to meet under the large fig tree on the lone hill several hundred meters past the last of the village houses, to listen solemnly and excitedly to the curly-haired young man in short pants and sandals talking about the brotherhood of nations, about national awakening, about the expulsion of the imperialists and about equality.

Walid had envied Taufik because his parents were glad to let him go off for a year and a half of education in the kibbutz. One less mouth to feed. Since that time they had shared the same dreams; they believed that they could change their world, determine their own fate, and work for a better future, together with the young men in the blue shirts and the short pants in the neighboring kibbutz.

Maya had tried to explain all these things to Larry, but it was obvious that he did not care. The only Arabs who interested Larry were the Palestinians.

In September of 1970, King Hussein determined to put an end to the Fatah organization in Jordan, and sent the Arab Legion to slay them by the thousands. Larry set out with his crew to cover these events, later referred to as "Black September," while Maya remained in Israel. Larry supplied memorable coverage of these one-sided battles, in which some 18,000 Palestinians were killed.

Maya envied him. Not him, really, but his professional advantages. It fired her imagination to think that any story of Larry's was screened from coast to coast, was viewed by millions, and influenced millions. If she had half that chance, she would make a documentary about Walid. Her theme would be: He is our hope, our bridge to the Arab world. If we turn our backs on him, we're destroying our future.

She had tried to sell Larry on the idea, but he shrugged it off. "Who cares about those Arabs of yours? Americans are aware of Israelis and Palestinians. Who even knows that there are Israeli Arabs, and who do you think wants to know?" When he saw how hurt she was, he relented and tried to soften his response. "Don't look at me like that. I don't tell you what to write, so don't you tell me what to shoot. I'm not underestimating your professional judgment; I'm just telling you that this isn't a subject for camera. It's too complicated. Maybe it's something you can explain in a book."

14

TOWARD THE END of 1975, the universities hit the head-
lines. The Israeli student is generally very conservative. He
makes noises on regular occasions, just before the announcement of tuition fees for the following year. Political issues
don't interest him. He's older than the American college
student, because he enrolls in the university after three years
of compulsory military service, sometimes longer. In many
cases he has a wife and children to care for, and has to bal-
ance his studies with his livelihood and saving for a home.
He has no time for games.

"Politics" is a dirty word in Hebrew. "Politicians" reminds
one of old ghetto-type people who did not make the grade
as officers and military commanders, who didn't manage to
earn big money, and therefore have no choice but to dig in
on the party front.

In the early days it was different. Politics represented revolution and pioneering. The first guard of politicians had wild
mops of hair, wore embroidered shirts and sandals, drained
the swamps during the day, and spoke at workers' rallies in
the evening. To finish off the night, they would dance a
hora, and discuss the new world being born, until the early
hours of the morning.

They were beautiful, wise, prophetic. The younger generation worshiped them and left politics in their hands, without
a second thought. The purpose the second generation set for
itself was to do, not to think. The thoughts had already
been thought before them, guiding their way. The second
generation had to be strong, courageous, and silent. To work
hard during the day and to sleep a toiler's sleep at night.
Doubts and indecision belonged to the period of the Diaspora.

So, too, in the universities. The serious student, the one who cared, skirted politics, leaving campus slogans and skirmishes to those who were fired by such nonsense: the Arab students. The Arab student is at least three years younger, his economic situation is usually better than that of his Jewish counterpart. He is not involved in student social life and has nothing to fill his spare time with, apart from fanning the sense of frustration among his friends.

A major source of friction between Jewish and Arab students has always been the problem of accommodations in the student dormitories. The number of places in the dormitories is small and the demand is great, for apartments off campus are very expensive. Using ordinary criteria, most of the Arab students are not entitled to dormitory rooms because they come from wealthy or well-to-do families. But they advance a different claim. They contend that because the universities are located in Jewish cities, those who rent apartments or rooms are Jews and are not willing to let the places to Arab students. The few who are willing to do so charge, in most cases, exorbitant rents.

This claim is not unfounded. The universities are well aware of this state of affairs, and to prevent a flare-up, they allocate as many places as possible to Arab students. This enrages the Jewish students, so the discontent continues.

This rivalry over accommodations had long caused ferment on the campus — but the issue of guard duty really fanned the flames.

Guard duty was instituted at the universities as a result of the rising wave of terrorist actions. A bomb exploded in the compus cafeteria; another was discovered on a university bus. A young Arab gardener was killed while attempting to plant a time bomb in the library. Every student was obliged to stand guard on a roster system. When a decisive majority of Arab students announced their refusal to participate, the Jewish students responded angrily. They had to serve in the army for three years while the Arabs relaxed in the university cafeteria. They had to give up three months a year for reserve service while the Arabs continued their studies. Now they also must guard the Arabs to ensure that they don't get blown up on campus, leaving them more time to conduct a campaign of slander ag~inst the State of Israel. If they refused to guard, then the Jewish students resented the burden of providing for their security.

The spokesmen for the Arab students protested over guarding against Palestinians. They themselves were Palestinians. Obviously they couldn't guard against themselves.

To this they added, in more private conversations, that the Jewish students have served in the army and carry weapons when they are on guard duty. The Arabs, on the other hand, have had no training with weapons, because the Jews don't trust them. Arab students would have to guard against terrorists with bare hands. Or travel in pairs, with a Jewish student carrying a rifle while the Arab servant walked beside him, holding a flashlight.

In November 1974, an anonymous poster had appeared at Bar Ilan University, bearing only the signature RESIDENTS OF THE STUDENT DORMITORIES.

The poster objected on numerous grounds to the residence of Arab students in the dormitories. It read, in part, "We fear the creation of a cell of Arab political activity, and of political friction with them. We are aware of security problems, that military information may fall into undesirable hands. We are aware of the differences of life style (cultural and religious) between us and them. We want to avoid a violent confrontation. We are aware of the ferment among the girls living in dormitories, who object strongly to the participation of Arabs in the cultural activities held jointly by the residents of the male and female dormitories, since such participation may give rise to unpleasant situations." The statement ended on a note of self-righteousness: "We want to reiterate that our objection does not arise from the fact that they are not Jews."

Walid was studying at Bar Ilan at the time. He liked this university and had been treated well there. He was stunned.

He brought Maya a copy of the poster and asked her to accompany him and witness for herself the reaction on campus.

In the center of the lawn sat a group of Arab students, demonstrating for their right to live in the dormitories. Around them stood a larger circle of Jewish students. The Arabs could hardly be heard. Occasionally, a Jewish student tried to object to the attacks on the Arabs. Two or three angry voices would turn against him: "Are you willing to live with an Arab?"

"Aren't you willing to live with an Arab?" Maya asked one of the speakers.

"Nobody is willing to live with an Arab," he answered, and added, "You know anyone who is willing to live with an Arab?"

"Yes," said Maya. "I."

"So what are you doing here? Go and f—— live with them."

"That's exactly what I'm doing here," said Maya. "I came here to live with them. That's what Zionism was all about. It called for Jews to come to live with the Arabs in Palestine. Have you heard of the Weizmann-Feisal correspondence?"

"Who's this crazy woman?" a brawny man shouted. "She must be from Matzpen [the extreme leftist pro-Arab faction] or a communist."

Maya smiled.

"Who does she think she is?" inquired a number of voices. "Throw her out of here."

Maya had time to notice that Walid was scanning the crowd with an anxious expression, looking for someone who could help rescue her if it became necessary.

A student standing to the side, in army uniform with the markings of a combat unit, interrupted. "Say, aren't you Maya Gilead?" The students stopped shouting and looked at her with curiosity. The soldier continued, "Leave her alone; she's Maya Gilead, the journalist. She's OK. I met her on the front line during the Yom Kippur War, in action. She really is OK."

Later Walid said to her, "That was lucky. I had one uneasy moment up there; I was afraid it would end up badly."

"Yes," said Maya, "but it's sad that the only certificate of approval everyone accepts is from the army and the war. 'She was in the war, so she's OK.' Anyone who wasn't in the war had better shut up." There was a pause. "Perhaps you could organize a number of Arab students for a symposium about guard duty on the campuses?" Maya asked, trusting him to follow her seemingly disconnected train of thought.

"You want students who will say what they think? That'll be a bit hard," said Walid. "But they might come for you. You, they still trust."

* * *

About fifteen Arab students gathered in the small apartment in Ramat Aviv, the trendy Tel Aviv suburb near Tel Aviv University. The apartment had been rented to Walid and accommodated five other Arab students. When Maya made it clear that she wanted to include in the debate only those who were willing to have their names and photographs printed, the number decreased to six. Walid preferred to stay out of it. All six declared that they refused to serve guard duty on grounds of conscience. After they had been comfortably seated despite their self-consciousness, Maya opened the discussion by asking them to define the moral basis of their objection.

"It all rests," said Nehela, a twenty-three-year-old, slim, and deceptively shy-looking girl from Nazareth who was studying for a master's in philosophy at Haifa University, "on the national Palestinian problem — the restoration of their legal rights."

MAYA: What has to be restored?

NEHELA: All the territories to the Palestinians, and all the Palestinians to their territories. Everything or nothing.

MAYA: You mean back to the 'seventy-six borders?

NEHELA: No. Jaffa and Nazareth, too.

MAYA: Your "everything" spells "nothing" for us. Do you expect us to agree to that?

Zahi, aged twenty, also from Nazareth, a second-year law student at Tel Aviv, sporting a David Niven mustache, was more moderate. "Not all the Arabs in Israel think that way. The majority favor a solution based on the nineteen forty-seven partition lines. The Communist Party slate proposes two states. It's in favor of co-existence, but the government claims that the communists are extremists, that they want to destroy the state."

MAYA: Are you a Communist Party member?

ZAHI: I'm in Mapam. It's a Zionist Party, but it is left. In Mapam, they say that everyone is equal, and I like that. When I was a little boy, we had a Jewish-Arab summer camp. The camp leaders of the Jewish children served in the army and put up wonderful tents in a jiffy, with electric lights and everything. Our leaders made miserable tents out of torn blankets. Since then, I've known precisely what equality is worth.

MAYA: No. I will not turn this debate into Arab-Jewish group therapy. Every one of us can tell of some bitter experience. Two of you have spoken, but not to the point. I repeat, what is your moral basis for refusing a duty that is essential to protect you as well as others? Please remember that when a bomb explodes in the dormitories, it won't distinguish between Arab and Jewish students.

Ibrahim, from a village in the Galilee, aged twenty-four, in the fourth year of his law studies at Jerusalem, said he had received notice to vacate his place in the dormitories following his announcement that he refused to do guard duty. He gave a familiar answer: "I'm not in favor of terrorist acts. But I'm not going to guard against Palestinians. I identify with the Palestinian struggle."

MAYA: The guard duty is meant to prevent terrorist acts, not to attack Palestinians.

IBRAHIM: You have to ask who's responsible for the terrorist acts. In my view, it's not the Palestinians. The government of Israel bears this responsibility because it leaves the Palestinians no other alternative.

Safwan, a tall, handsome, and intelligent-looking man, smiled broadly. He also was from the Arab city of Nazareth, and, at twenty-one, already a third-year medical student at Tel Aviv. He said, "The fact is that they, the Jews here, don't force us to serve in the army. If they understand that we have reasons for not serving in the army, why don't they understand that we have conscientious objections to standing guard?"

MAYA: I find it difficult to appreciate your position. You demand that the Jewish student, who arrives at the university three years late because of his army service, also guard your lives while he studies. Moreover, you also demand the right to turn your back when his life is threatened, while you study to your heart's content?

IBRAHIM: No one's doing us any favors. I have a right to go to a university because this is my country.

MAYA: Of course, and that's why you're a citizen and, as such, you have to obey the laws of your country and guard it against its enemies.

IBRAHIM: First of all, the state must treat me as a citizen, and then I'll see how I'll behave toward it. In the meantime, this state is sitting on my land. All the time I am a second class citizen, but when they want me to stand guard, they suddenly remind me of my citizenship.

MAYA: Why don't you ever speak up against the "discrimination" in your favor? Yes, I mean the advantage of the three years that you're not required to give. Why don't you volunteer for some kind of service during a corresponding period to the one the Jews serve in the army? Do something for your own people; put in equal time in the struggle against ignorance and illiteracy or the advancement of Arab women's rights?

SAFWAN: I'd be willing to volunteer for humanitarian service, but on condition that this wouldn't be part of Israel's security effort.

MAYA: You're studying medicine. Any work you'd do in the medical service would be humanitarian. What prevents you from being a doctor in the Israeli army?

SAFWAN: I'm not prepared to treat Israeli soldiers.

Maya was incredulous. "You're not prepared to treat Israeli soldiers, yet you claim the right to study medicine in an Israeli university?"

SAFWAN: I'm not prepared to wear an Israeli army uniform and by my work release other men for combat units.

IBRAHIM: I owe nothing to my Israeli citizenship. My Israeli citizenship is a fact I have to put up with. It is not something I have chosen. My self-determination is in my being a Palestinian.

MAYA: You're entitled to that. On condition that you're prepared to draw the necessary conclusions.

IBRAHIM: Such as?

MAYA: Such as renouncing your citizenship or at least giving up your place in the student dormitories.

IBRAHIM: Why? I'm not against the state, I'm against the policy.

MAYA: If there were a different Israeli government with a different policy, would you object to the Palestinians' method of struggle?

IBRAHIM: No, even then I would identify with them.

MAYA: Don't you see the contradiction between your Israeli citizenship and your opinions, which defy the existence of the State of Israel? Your view is not an expression of solidarity with the right of the Palestinians to self-determination; you're demanding the right to enjoy the state benefits while denying its right to exist.

NEHELA: Even the United Nations has now decided that the Palestinian struggle is legitimate and that Zionism is a racist movement. The whole world believes that the Palestinians should return and receive their lands back.

MAYA: I won't comment on the United Nations, but tell me, where should the Palestinians return — to Acre? Jaffa? Haifa?

NEHELA: That is their right.

MAYA: And what about our rights?

NEHELA: We won't hurt the Jews. We won't kill them.

MAYA: We don't hurt you either, and we don't kill you. Nevertheless, you demand the liquidation of the State of Israel. All this in the name of putting yet another Arab state on the map, to the exclusion of the only one we have.

NEHELA: It doesn't matter how many Arab states there are. Even if there were seventy, the Palestinians still have a right to a state of their own. This is clear, and it's something we will not give up.

MAYA: If that's so clear, why isn't it clear to you that the Jews are certainly not willing to relinquish their right to a single sovereign state of their own?

NEHELA: But why at our expense?

The group dispersed in a depressed mood. Maya heard them complaining to Walid in the corridor.

"What did they want from you?" Maya asked after they had left.

"They said I cheated them. They came because they had thought you were for the Arabs, and they couldn't understand why you didn't agree with them."

They looked at each other in something akin to despair. There was nothing to say.

After the proceedings of the symposium appeared in print, the Communist Party newspaper claimed that the students participating in it had been led astray. They had believed that the interviewer was sympathetic to their cause, but she had tricked them by cunning questions. Maya's colleagues, who generally dubbed her an Arab-lover, a Jew-hater, and other such endearing epithets, now smiled at her as if greeting the return of a prodigal daughter.

Maya said to Walid, "It's sad that the people who give me the creeps embrace me, but those whose rights I'm trying to defend give me a cold shoulder."

Walid responded, "Don't be patronizing, Maya. You don't have to like them. Even those who give you the creeps are entitled to their opinions. Nobody must be likable in order to be entitled to exercise his right."

"During that symposium," Maya said, "I kept remembering certain incidents from my student days in Jerusalem. We'd gone on a trip in a truck, and there were five Arab students among us. It was in the spring, and a sudden flood caught us in one of the *wadis*. Our lives were at stake. The water was rushing at us. The truck was bogged down, and everyone jumped out and started to push. Except the five Arabs, who stayed in the truck."

Walid protested, "Why look at me? You want me to assure you that I'm not proud of them? We're not Spartan; we don't throw our children into boiling water so that only the heroes survive. Comradeship, mutual aid, openness, esprit de corps — these are not qualities one is born with. These are qualities that have to be nurtured. For years, any attempt of the Israeli Arabs to organize themselves politically and to create a leadership has been stifled. Things that grow in the dark don't always look nice in the light."

"Where does it leave us?" asked Maya.

Walid chuckled. "Exactly where we want to be. You, Maya, you have the better deal. You stand up for what you believe in, and you can feel good about it. Even magnanimous. For me, it's not so easy. My people, those outside Israel, consider me a traitor. To them, anybody not actively fighting against Israel is a traitor. Somebody like me, who insists on contributing to the welfare and prosperity of Israel, isn't fit to live. You remember after the Six Day War, during my election campaign? The Fatah radio broadcast that their military court judged me in absentia and had sentenced me to death. I applied to the police for a permit to carry a gun. You know what they said? The chief of the special branch offered me a cup of coffee, said he was glad to review my application. He remarked conspiratorially that granting such a permit to an Arab entails certain services. No sweat; just keep my eyes and ears open. I got up and left. And you know, the funny part of it, at the same time the Communist Party daily, the one in Arabic, blasted at me nonstop, branding me as 'Jasus,' a paid police informer."

Maya, who listened spellbound, interrupted him. "You

never told me about it. You never said a word. Not about the gun, not about the slander."

Walid gave her a brotherly hug. "I couldn't trust you to keep your mouth shut. You would have plastered all over your paper the news about the death verdict, and then Al Fatah would have had no choice but to kill me to prove their credibility."

"Why didn't you react to the Jasus libel?" asked Maya.

"What was the point?" he retorted. "Every Israeli Arab realized that the commies were afraid that my anti-clan 'young generation' movement would lure away some of their followers. But that wasn't the major thing; I don't bleed over the defamation. This isn't the worst part of my predicament.

"We started with the Palestinians, who regard me as a traitor. What about the Israelis? Yes, the Jews. To them I am acceptable as a house pet — 'Look at our cute little Arab; isn't it cute, the way he talks about the virtues of the Zionist movement?' But the moment I stand on my hind legs and campaign for my rights and for Palestinian rights, they wag a finger at me, telling me I'd better mind my manners, or else."

Maya could not help smiling at the apt description, but as Walid continued, a note of real pain crept into his voice. "You know what's worse, Maya? The fact that I myself am not sure anymore. The worst part of it is my own doubt. I wish I knew for sure whether my faith is leading me toward a possible dream or toward a delusion."

15

In AUGUST 1975, a high Israeli official submitted to the government what came to be called "The Koenig Report," in which he advocated seizure of Arab lands in the Galilee. When its contents leaked out, the report galvanized the Israeli Arabs from passive hostility into energetic, outspoken opposition.

In the beginning of 1976, Maya evaluated the accumulating signs of unrest during the past months and noted, in a terse commentary in her newspaper, that Arab protest had sharply increased. Still, she half-expected the protest to die down, as it usually did. Judging by the overwhelming majority of reports in the newspapers, on the radio and television, Arab protest was indeed fading.

Only through her talks with Walid did Maya realize that the situation merited full attention. At the time, he was totally immersed in his studies in order to complete them as soon as possible and finally be financially independent. In loyalty to his friends on the Young Men's List at Kafr-Hama, he continued to head the list and had also been elected again to membership on the local council. He hoped this duty, however, would not consume much time. But Walid, it seemed, had been born to be involved in public matters. Even when he was not in any major official position, people solicited his views and responses. He was regarded as the representative of the younger generation. Maya had learned from previous experience that he always knew what was going on and which way the wind was blowing in the Arab street.

When Walid started worrying, Maya perceived that the situation was grave.

At about that time, Walid informed Maya that he intended to reclaim his position as council chairman.

"Right now, just when you're cramming for your exams at the university?"

"I have no choice," said Walid. "We're moving rapidly toward disaster. The Arab Committee has called the Israeli Arab population to stage a strike against the appropriation of their lands. They've already set the date — the thirtieth of March."

"I know that," said Maya. "But why are you upset? Don't tell me you see no reason for protest."

Walid grinned at her. "You know me better than that. Unfortunately, it's like lighting a match in a cellar full of gas fumes. Given the mood of the Israeli Arabs, the situation could easily deteriorate into a civil war. If I want to have any chance to influence the direction of events, I must sit on the Mayors' Committee, and in order to do that, I must be re-elected mayor."

Maya checked the urge to suggest that he was exaggerating somewhat; she knew Walid did not dramatize circumstances and events. Nor did she argue with his decision. They were both only too aware that land appropriations represented the most significant single factor in the tension-ridden Jewish-Arab co-existence within the State of Israel.

The thunderous alert in the Arab sector reached even the ears of the foreign press. Larry asked Maya to summarize the land question for the benefit of a young colleague who was new to his post. The man failed to understand the role of the Mayors' Committee.

Maya told him that the full name of this body was "The Committee of Mayors and Chairmen of Arab Municipalities and Local Councils." She went on to point out why an assembly of all the Arab mayors is tantamount to a representative body of the Israeli Arabs. She explained that Arab citizens in Israel live separately from the Jews, not by any segregating laws, but as the result of a historical process. In America, Jews have moved out of Brooklyn, and successful blacks have left Harlem. In Israel, there is no such mobility from the Arab realm to the Jewish. Even the names of the Arab places are Arabic, and those of the Jewish places are Hebrew. The division isn't socioeconomic; it's national. And though it is not absolute, it is decisive.

An Arab can sleep in any hotel in Israel. He can rent temporary lodgings in the city, and perhaps he can buy a piece of property in one of the large cities and move there to live. Perhaps. But most of the construction in cities is public and subsidized. When young Arabs in Jaffa, for example, tried to register for the apartments being built for newly married couples, they were turned away. Similarly, the Jewish agricultural settlements are subsidized by international Jewish institutions, like the Jewish Agency, and no Arab is admitted.

The Jewish agricultural settlements in Israel are on what is referred to as "national land." The settlers don't buy the land; they lease it. To qualify, they must satisfy certain criteria, the foremost of which is being "kosher" Jewish. This land was "redeemed" for Jewish settlement. Arabs have nothing to look for there.

The Jewish immigrants to Palestine before the establishment of the state, and even before the British Mandate, found an Arab population here. The immigrants didn't look for individual accommodations within the existing towns and villages; they wanted to create new agricultural settlements. New also in terms of life style, social structure, and political purpose. Thus, the kibbutzim and moshavim were built.

Among the Zionist newcomers to Palestine, a certain percentage preferred to remain urban. Some settled in established cities — in Jerusalem, Haifa, and Jaffa. Others created brand-new cities. In the course of time, the urban map became clearly defined: there were new cities, entirely populated by Jews, like Tel Aviv and Afula; totally Arab cities, like Nazareth; and mixed cities, which aimed for an ethnic mixture and achieved it, but in separate neighborhoods, like Acre, Haifa, and Jerusalem.

Had history taken a different path, it would have been

natural for the binational cities to have become more integrated. But the War of Independence sealed the division. The upper stratum of the Arab population — upper in terms of both education and resources, the traditional leadership and the leadership of the future — lived in the cities and possessed a high mobility. The wealthier Arabs in Palestine also had bank accounts, properties, and estates in Jordan, Lebanon, Syria, and Egypt. When the 1948 war broke out, they simply moved to a calmer location to wait until the storm died down. Their departure converted the binational cities into uninational ones: Haifa was emptied of Arabs, even though Haganah jeeps drove through the city with loudspeakers, calling on the Arabs not to abandon their homes. And with the exodus of the Arab elite, the Arab rural population was without leadership. This also explains why so many years passed before the national consciousness of Israeli Arabs took the form of political activity.

Some of the wealthy Arabs were personally involved in political movements that opposed the establishment of a Jewish state; some perhaps even fought beside their brothers, who arrived with arms from across the border to prevent the state from coming into being. But most of them probably figured that their departure was purely tactical, a temporary measure until the Jews were thrown into the sea. Then they would return to their homes in the wake of the victorious Arab armies.

While the members of the upper stratum climbed into their cars and moved, say, to Beirut, thousands of Arab farm-hands and city workers jammed the roads on foot or straddling donkeys. Some because they wholeheartedly believed the Arab propaganda that within days the "Yahoud" would be wiped out and the Arabs would return as conquerors; some from a natural wish to get away from a battleground. And there were others — and their existence should not be forgotten — Arab peasants who fled from their lands through fear of the Israeli army, which had risen overnight from its underground origins; as well as those villagers who were "encouraged" by the army units, or by the kibbutzim in their areas, to leave until the fighting was over. Had they been able to return afterward, they would have found their villages razed to the ground.

When the War of Independence was over, the newborn state welcomed its Arabs by confiscating most of their land and all of the land of their relatives and friends who were not there to be counted when the fighting stopped.

The struggle over land is a fateful one. Every state must appropriate land from individuals if it is needed for the common good, but in Israel the circumstances were different. The appropriation of Arab land was intended for the extension of Jewish living space, thus limiting the living space of the Arabs.

When the first round of massive appropriations of land to "Judaize" the Galilee began at the end of the 1950s, a strong protest movement arose. The voices of protest included many Jews. But in the end it all died down, the lands were taken, and a new city, Carmiel, was established.

Those who justified these measures emphasized that the state was created in order to provide a homeland for all the Jews. The Law of Return stipulates the right of all Jews to settle in Israel. Given its limited territorial resources, the state had no choice but to take over as much land as possible. Others argued that such lofty aspirations, however just, cannot be achieved at the expense of the basic civil rights of the Israeli Arab population.

While the argument continued, so did the preparations on both sides of the line. The danger of confiscation was not limited to the north of the country, though it got most of the public attention. In the Negev, in the south, the process of confiscation of Bedouin lands continued relentlessly. The southern nomads, who had previously resigned themselves to compromise and were making do with inferior pasture-land, were pressured by new restrictive measures to acts of despair.

Some observers feared that continued neglect of the Bedouin distress might result in a disastrous eruption more violent than the one that was being predicted for the north of the country.

*   *   *

Near the end of March, Walid was re-elected chairman of the Kafr-Hama Council. From the council meeting he drove directly to Nazareth, to address the Arab Mayors' Committee.

They listened to him carefully. Perhaps he was the only person who could voice these admonitions and spell out the dangers, and still command their attention.

"We must not create a precedent in which we, the Arabs, are on one side of the barricade, and the Jewish state is on the other, with us striking against the state," Walid said. "I'm not saying we have to be silent about the appropriations. I'm against them, and I'll fight them anywhere and any time. But we're citizens of this state, and we have to protest and demonstrate against the decision as citizens opposing our government, not as outsiders against a foreign government. It makes no sense for us to close down the government services in our villages. Those are *our* services. We must not accept the position of subcitizens, or citizens-by-compulsion."

They listened, but they no longer had any options. The die had been cast.

There were interviews on television and radio and meetings with the newspapermen; there were public meetings and house gatherings — and at all these Walid appeared, as the representative of sanity. His was the one voice that prevented the protest day from turning into an unequivocal declaration of war.

The Jewish establishment on Arab affairs immediately tried to claim him again as their own. Walid tried to shake them off as firmly as possible, and publicly reminded them of the many obstacles they had put in his path.

The functionaries immediately began to spread rumors that Walid was in fact opposed to all this fuss about the appropriation of lands. Walid was quick to repeat his vigorous opposition to the expropriations, which he regarded as violations of the fundamental civil rights of the Israeli Arabs.

March 30, 1976, has been recorded in Israel's history as Land Day. On that day, for the first time since the establishment of the state, the entire Arab Israeli population stood up together to speak for itself.

On Land Day, Kafr-Hama was the only Arab village in all of Israel in which school was scheduled as usual. Workers went to their jobs in the Jewish cities as they did every day; the local council opened its offices; and the council chairman announced that a teacher absent from work would lose a day's pay.

Walid's opponents had already prepared a guillotine for him; they wanted to declare him a traitor, but Walid upset their scheme. He announced that he would head a protest demonstration to be held in the village in the afternoon.

On March 30, 1976, a curfew was declared on the Arab villages in the Galilee.

A curfew? Someone pulled this hateful term out of the lexicon of the Mandate period.

It turned out that army vehicles that had been driven through the village of Sakhnin that morning had been pelted with rocks. Officers of the security forces had decided that it was unthinkable that army vehicles could not drive securely on Israel's roads, and that the appropriate response to such behavior was the declaration of a curfew. However, it did not occur to anyone to declare a curfew in Shekhunat Hatikva, the problem-ridden neighborhood on the outskirts of Tel Aviv, after crowds in the neighborhood went on a rampage outside the offices of the Football Association, injured policemen, and pelted police vehicles with rocks, in response to what they claimed was unjust refereeing against the neighborhood team.

But in Sakhnin the curfew was declared.

There are various versions as to what happened in the Galilee villages and in Nazareth on that day. Maya wasn't there. When she read the papers the next morning, she sorrowfully noted the disparity between the photographs and the reports. For example, according to a report, the soldiers who broke up demonstrations took special care not to break into the houses, but a huge photograph on the front page showed an armed soldier chasing a schoolgirl into a house.

The dry summary: Six were killed. Cause of death — shot by soldiers. The soldiers had supposedly fired warning shots into the air. The six dead were civilians, Arabs with Israeli citizenship. Among them, a boy aged six, a woman shot in the back.

This incident marked the first time in the history of the State of Israel that civilians had been killed by soldiers during a civilian demonstration.

Maya believed that the whole country would protest this outrage. She thought such a great flame would arise among Israel's Arabs and Jews alike that it would be difficult to put it out. But the country — the Jewish country — remained indifferent, except for a smattering of "noble souls." They were considered professional Arab-lovers, so their version was automatically suspect.

*　　*　　*

Immediately after Land Day one man singlehandedly stopped the avalanche. Walid was everywhere at once. He made himself heard loud and clear. He did not encourage the emotions of rage, and he consciously ignored this opportunity to make political capital and to ride the wave of frustration into the Knesset. Instead, he called for the establishment of a public commission of inquiry and managed to channel the bitterness and bereavement toward this legitimate demand. The press and the administration competed with each other in apologizing. For several weeks, the government adopted delaying tactics, inviting Arab dignitaries to Jerusalem, promising courtesy visits to their villages. Old budgetary requests long forgotten were unearthed and granted. All was well, as long as it took the heat off the demand for justice. To appease the chairmen of the Arab councils, the prime minister invited them to a meeting that was, of course, shown on television. Many noble sentiments were expressed, but the host took care to avoid committing himself. No investigating committee was set up.

A journalist interviewing Walid asked, "Why are you so insistent about the setting up of an investigating committee? Do you cast doubt on the veracity of the Security Services' statement that the soldiers did not shoot anyone intentionally, and that the victims were killed by shots fired in the air?"

Walid answered, "Far be it from me to cast doubt on the veracity of that statement."

"So why then do you insist on an inquiry?"

"Because since that statement was made, I can't sleep at night."

"I don't understand."

"As a citizen, I always slept well at night because I knew the army was protecting me. Now I am very worried. If our soldiers hit a six-year-old boy when they shoot in the air, then whoever taught them to use weapons should be summoned before a military tribunal. You understand, I am afraid that if they are ordered to open fire at the enemy, the bullets will fly into the air."

The experts on Arab affairs either didn't read newspapers or had no sense of irony. They stubbornly maintained their belief that Walid was a naïve young fellow who had fallen for their tactics. They figured it would be a good idea to use his naïveté and his courteousness to save their own skins. When the minister for police affairs was asked by newsmen why no investigating commission had been set up, as demanded by Arab leaders, the minister declared, in front of a television camera, that "even the chairman of the Kafr-Hama Council agreed with me that there is no need for such a commission."

The minister was certain that Walid would not refute him.

Walid responded publicly that the minister was lying.

16

A STRANGE THING HAPPENED. When Walid had attempted to win the support of the establishment and the Labor Party during his first term in office, they branded him a menace. Now the establishment tried with all its might to point to him as "our man," while Walid demonstratively made it clear that he wanted nothing to do with them.

He had no political backing, at home or outside the village. He was simply his own man, but everyone tried to claim him for his own. His popularity among the Arab population soared to a new high.

During this period Walid was repeating his first year of law school. Originally, he had completed this first year at Bar Ilan University, where he took his first degree in political science. But law was something else. The law school at Bar Ilan placed special emphasis on Hebrew law, which demanded vast knowledge of the Talmud. Most of the students, *yeshiva* graduates, were well versed in this field. Walid completed his first year successfully, but when he learned that the second year was composed almost entirely of Torah and Talmudic studies, he admitted defeat and decided to continue at Tel Aviv University. Tel Aviv University agreed to accept him on condition that he repeat the first year. There was no overlap between the two courses of study. Just as the exams were about to begin, preparations for Land Day started. Walid did not manage to take all his exams on the dates set and was informed that he would have to repeat the academic year once more.

Walid absorbed this blow in silence. He had become a very busy man, dividing his time between the village council, the committee of chairmen of the Arab local councils, his family, and the university.

When Nadia gave birth to a daughter, Walid was wild with delight. But Maya knew that deep down he was a bit sorry that little Yasmin was not a boy. He was incredibly proud of all her tricks, but suddenly he'd forget his grammar and say, "What a bastard he is, that kid." His plans, too, for enjoyment of the child's company were all designed for a son. He and Taufik would get up every morning at five and drive to the sea, "with the kid, and we'll make him into a great swimmer." When Walid was caught out, he would blush and freely laugh at himself. But there was no doubt about his love for Yasmin. She was the most looked-after child in Kafr-Hama. A little princess. When she was only a few days old they pierced her ear lobes and inserted shiny gold earrings with blue stones. Yasmin had large black eyes, from which peered the mischievousness of the Abu-Hana family.

Maya recalled how Walid and his wife had consulted with their Jewish friends about whether Nadia should continue her studies. This was shortly after the wedding. Walid was wondering whether they ought to rent an apartment in Tel Aviv, where they could both study at the university, or whether it would be better for Nadia to continue at the teachers' seminary near Kafr-Hama. The discussion took place at the home of Jewish friends in the fashionable residential area of Herzliyah Pituah. The hostess, a noted sociologist, tried to encourage Nadia to discuss the fields that interested her. Maya hardly participated in the long conversation. When the young couple left, the hosts said, with some satisfaction, "You were wrong, Maya. It's true Walid has married a village girl, but she'll go on studying. They'll be active together yet on the political scene. We should start scouting around for an apartment for them; it's a pity to waste time."

But Maya was convinced it would all come to nothing. Nadia would get pregnant at once, and from the moment she conceived she'd stay at home, filling the traditional role.

If she bore a daughter, she'd get pregnant again quickly. Walid was just over thirty; men of his age in the village are already surrounded by grown children, and he was expected now to prove his male prowess.

Their home was equipped with all the current household appliances on the market. These were among the symbols of the young couple's status, and it was ridiculous to ask Walid why they needed a fancy food blender with an array of parts, or a huge tea service, when the preparations for their large receptions were always completed downstairs, in his mother's realm. The questions were irrelevant. A bridegroom who respected himself would bring his bride to a kitchen equipped with an obligatory list of the best available, and the more there was, the more praiseworthy he was.

It hardly needs mentioning that there was also an automatic washing machine. Yet Maya found Nadia kneeling on the floor of the shower early one morning, washing Yasmin's diapers in a large basin. She had got tired of waiting for the machine to do in an hour what she could do manually in fifteen minutes.

On the other hand, the beautiful Nadia lost the talent, possessed by her mother and mother-in-law, of carrying a load on her head. This practice had become a sign of the older generation. The younger girls were ashamed to train themselves to do it. A pity, thought Maya, recalling the erect gait of Leila.

Following the events of Land Day, Walid devoted most of his energies to village matters. During this period he attached minimal importance to his image among the Jewish public. "This village is my public base," he said to Maya. "This is the source of my strength. If I'm strong here, I'm strong everywhere." He knew the members of his village, their weaknesses, their way of thinking — and he acted accordingly. Among the practical goals he had set himself, the solution of the shortage of electricity and water had first priority. The village had increased several times over since it had been connected to the electricity network. In a house where several years before a single light bulb of fifty watts had burned, lighting up corners, there were now six or seven electrical appliances, and dozens of light bulbs shone in as many large lamps.

The supply couldn't bear the load. Many homes were not connected to the network. Getting connected cost money. The villagers do not easily part with cash. First they delay; then they wrangle, bargain, hope for a miracle: maybe they'll connect the house to the supply and forget to ask for payment. Walid decided to connect every house in the village to the network. To illuminate the streets. He drove to the electric company's offices in Hadera and revealed his plan.

Sure enough, it worked like a Swiss watch. In a matter of hours the rumor spread through the village that all those who had not yet deposited the full payment had lost their opportunity to get electricity and only Walid could save them. The villagers besieged their council chairman. With much ceremony he contacted the electric company, as if for the first time, and in firm tones expressed incredulity that the company refused to accept payment. Walid threatened an appeal to the courts and to the government if the company persisted in its refusal. The electric company remained adamant. The chairman pulled all his rabbits out of the hat, and finally a compromise was arrived at: the company would grant a ten-day extension during which payments could be made. Never in any settlement — Arab or Jewish — had payments been collected so swiftly.

And there was light.

The mayor of Kafr-Hama also worked wonders in getting the water pipeline changed, and kept another promise, as well. The village — originally built with only narrow alleys with enough room for pedestrians, two donkeys, and perhaps a camel to pass — had started bursting under the pressure of the trucks and private cars now passing through. During Walid's term in office a two-way road was built, complete with road signs and an adequate system of side roads.

Kafr-Hama became a model village, spoken highly of by anyone connected with the Arab sector. Walid, once the champion of the young generation and the protégé of the progressive Jews, had become an accepted leader among the Arab population.

The chairmen of the larger councils, and even the mayor of Nazareth, the biggest Arab city in Israel, saw fit to invite him to every local event and to shower honors upon him. He rekindled his ambitions to become a Knesset member. A new political party, which had come into being on the wave of general protest against the existing establishment, was courting him openly, hinting broadly that he would be offered a safe place on the party ticket. The ruling party also made it known that it was willing to bargain. Walid was in no great hurry to commit himself. He appeared wherever he was invited but always took care to stress independence while not offending his hosts.

It was very obvious that Walid found the authority resulting from his second term as mayor very gratifying. Maya was afraid he might get trapped in the work of local government.

Whenever Maya felt that Walid's power and popularity were going to his head, she would tease him: "Shh! The chief of Kafr-Hama is speaking!" and both of them would burst out laughing. This was a private joke between Walid and Maya, and it came about after a large public meeting in one of the villages of the triangle. When the number of interjections increased, making it difficult for people to pay attention, one of the local elders — formerly among Walid's main detractors — raised his hand, his eyebrows, and his voice, and roared very solemnly, "Shh! Hush! The chief of Kafr-Hama is speaking!" Since then, whenever little Yasmin cried at an inopportune moment, or whenever anyone expressed an opinion not to Walid's liking, friends would admonish, half-jokingly, half-seriously, "Shh! The chief of Kafr-Hama is speaking!"

Maya was not too pleased with Walid's public position during this period. The rift between the Jewish majority and the Arab minority was growing deeper, and expressions of hostility toward the Arab minority were becoming more frequent and more widely reported in all the media. Walid remained one of the few public figures whom the Jews regarded with respect and trust. Maya hoped he would mount a crusade to counteract the process of disintegration. He did not seem inclined to do so.

A year passed during which Arab leaders and several Jewish public figures continued demanding full investigation into the events of Land Day. The demands continued to be ignored.

However, when the first anniversary of Land Day drew closer, the media paid some attention. They remembered. The chief concern of the establishment was to prevent the "exploitation of Land Day by extreme elements for purposes of incitement." Maya discovered to her amazement that a mysterious hand had apparently produced a redefinition in journalistic jargon. Judging by the newspapers, it appeared that the communists had become a publicly responsible element that was averting the takeover of the Arab sector by undefined "extreme elements."

The information that was leaked by the security agencies indicated that the Land Day anniversary would be marked with quiet demonstrations and public rallies, "despite provocations by the extreme elements."

On the day itself, March 30, 1977, Maya stayed in Tel Aviv. Most of the foreign correspondents went to Nablus. There were rumors of demonstrations of solidarity in the occupied territories, and most TV crews had no doubt whatsoever that a demonstration in Nablus would be much more interesting than a protest meeting in Nazareth.

Walid was well aware that March 30 was a dangerous date for the Arab leadership. If they were ineffectual, they would be penalized by their Arab constituents. If they protested too effectively, the Jewish establishment would make them suffer for it. Walid made sure that Kafr-Hama was under control. He and Taufik did thorough work in the village for two whole days before the crucial date. Walid himself spoke to parents and teachers and made them personally responsible to him to keep the schools functioning. Then there were meetings with staff people from other institutions — banks, the local council, the local medical clinic — to ensure that they would operate without disturbances. Taufik organized all the young men in patrols and charged them with inspecting the village and reporting any suspicious activity to him. Everything was smoothly organized and under control. The chairman of the council was to make a speech at the protest rally scheduled in the village in the afternoon.

Walid had not neglected the smallest detail and should have felt reassured. But one thing gnawed at him: the war of nerves waged by the regional police. Several days before the anniversary he received a phone call from a senior police official who warned him "unofficially" that the police had reliable information that acts of sabotage would take place in Kafr-Hama on Land Day. Walid thanked him and expressed his confidence that if the police had valid information, it was surely possible to arrest those involved before the Land Day anniversary. The official advised Walid to request a special police unit to be stationed at the council building on that day to protect it. Walid politely rejected the suggestion, saying he felt quite secure without police protection.

The next day he got another call, this time from the regional police commander. Again a warning, again hints about classified information, and friendly advice to ask for police reinforcements. This time Walid was more unequivocal: "Last year I demanded that no police enter the village, and I promised that order would be maintained. And it was. If you don't send police, there'll be no problems. I want your promise that there will be no policemen in the area. If I don't get this promise, as I was assured I would, I will announce publicly today that I will not be responsible for whatever happens in Kafr-Hama."

The police official was taken aback.

Walid sensed that the police were trying to create an atmosphere of tension, to pressure him into asking for special police forces. He and Taufik increased their precautionary measures. Until late at night they patrolled the alleys, went into the coffee houses, paid heed to every rumor. All was quiet. They conducted an additional swift operation, getting rid of the discarded rubber tires from the vicinity of the main road. Old tires were very much in fashion in the more violent riots and demonstrations. They burned easily, made a lot of mess, and were visually very effective.

The next day Walid had an appointment at the Ministry of Education in Jerusalem. He and Taufik decided that there was no reason for him not to keep the appointment. The deputy chairman was informed that he would fill in for the mayor until his return. Taufik conducted a final morning patrol, and Walid set out. It was six o'clock in the morning.

A carpenter driving to Netanya at seven remembered, as he was driving, that he'd left some documents at home, and returned to the village. He stopped first at Taufik's to report that five kilometers from Kafr-Hama there were a lot of soldiers on the road, plus police and border patrol men. And the special antiriot units.

At that moment the telephone rang. Walid wanted to know if everything was under control. "Everything's quiet so far," said Taufik. "People have gone to work; all the kids are at school. But Hamid the carpenter's here, and he says there're lots of army men on the road. I don't know if it has anything to do with us."

Walid didn't hear the alarm bells either. It never occurred to him to connect the army with Kafr-Hama. He said he would get in touch again around noon and would get back to the village by four, in time for the rally.

A short while after this exchange the rioting started.

*　　*　　*

All day Maya listened carefully to the reports on the radio and television. The anniversary of Land Day had passed quietly except for some minor disturbances.

The next day the newspapers reported that the Arab population had demonstrated self-discipline, disappointing inciters, except for minor incidents in Kafr-Hama. Walid's number was constantly busy. Maya could not reach him.

Finally, she got hold of him. "They killed us," Walid

stated flatly. "Army, border patrol, police. They killed us. They came down on the school with a helicopter and dropped tear gas. They killed us."

Maya wanted to cry. Instead, she shouted at Walid, "Stop talking like a Fatah spokesman. Who killed whom? Who killed you? Speak to the point!"

Walid's voice was absolutely colorless, an old man's voice. "They beat children and chased them into their homes. They frightened women. It was a pogrom."

"I don't understand," said Maya, her heart beating wildly. "Don't settle scores with me. Simply tell me exactly what happened."

"You think I understand what happened? I wasn't there. To this moment I don't understand. Tomorrow I'm holding a press conference."

At the press conference Walid reconstructed for newsmen the Land Day anniversary at Kafr-Hama, based on the testimony of villagers.

At eight-thirty in the morning, some young people — not schoolchildren — lit two tires at the entrance to the village. At that very moment a police unit, reinforced by the border patrol, arrived. The tire-burners fled in all directions. Within less than half an hour, police and army forces poured into the village, fanning out through the streets and workshops, yards and houses. A helicopter landed in the schoolyard (the police claimed the fugitives had run in the direction of the school), and uniformed men rushed into all the classrooms, where studies were proceeding in an orderly manner. Panic erupted in the school building as pupils fled from their classrooms, screaming, and ran toward their homes. Their screams frightened the whole village. No one knew what was happening, to whom, or where, but every mother ran about like a madwoman until her child came home. Most of the men were at work, as usual, in the Jewish settlements and in the cities.

Walid produced a lot of testimony, including that of two teen-agers, brothers, suspected by the police of "participating in the riot." They were chased into their older brother's workshop and pulled out by their hair, beaten with clubs, tied to an army jeep, and dragged behind it as it drove through the village. Maya saw the head of one of the boys. It was covered with fresh stitches, like a patchwork blanket. Another boy, twelve, who had held on to the door of his house, was beaten on his hands with sticks. Three of his fingers had been broken. Altogether, more than thirty were wounded, their testimony verified by medical reports. All the wounded were schoolchildren in school that day, so it was impossible that they had been involved with the gang that had set fire to the tires. Walid took some of the wounded to a private doctor for written certification of their condition.

Maya deduced that this manifestation of violence had not been accidental. This had been a planned and sophisticated operation. The forces involved in the operation were not regularly stationed in the area. Their composition and number were ample proof that someone had been interested in provoking a riot in Kafr-Hama. Someone wanted to prove that there was no Arab village that was loyal to the state, and that the only language which could assure the loyalty of the Arab minority was the language of force.

Whoever hoped to achieve this goal had been successful. He proved to Walid that he had no one to talk with on the Jewish side. He proved to all those young Arabs who esteemed Walid as an example to follow that his way was not the right way. He proved to the Arabs that the Jews desired to communicate with the language of police clubs. But the most important and most dangerous lesson the Kafr-Hama affair taught the Arabs of Israel was simply that the Israeli Arab was not going to be treated like a citizen. He was guilty until proven innocent. To the State of Israel, the Israeli Arab was first of all an Arab, always suspect, always to be considered guilty, unless he could manage to prove his innocence.

Maya was stunned. Graver than the act itself, she felt, was the conspiracy of silence that followed it. Even those newspapers which reported Walid's press conference did so with great restraint and obvious reservations. All of them reiterated at great length the clarifications and explanations given by police and military spokesmen. They also published interviews with public figures who declared it unthinkable that Israeli citizens could be prevented from free movement on the country's roads. No one asked how it could happen that Israeli schoolboys could find themselves dragged behind a police jeep through the streets of their village. The minister for education did not demand an investigation to find out who had been responsible for the landing of the helicopter in the high school yard.

For Maya herself, the most painful result was her sense of estrangement from the Abu-Hana family. Walid tried to pretend that nothing had changed. But the affability, the warmth, the trust, had vanished. They spoke to each other like strangers. Politely. Maya tried to touch him and found an empty space. Walid talked with her — but his mind was elsewhere. For the first time she felt real despair. More than that. She was afraid.

She recalled horrors she had experienced during her first years in the country. At the beginning she had still heard the sound of hobnailed jackboots on the stairs at night. Until she had started believing that her new life was real. Then there had been other fears. She had started fearing a confrontation with an unknown person whom one couldn't speak to. He would appear in the form of a madman who didn't understand her. She would wake up with a sense of helpless dread. She had always believed that if it was possible to articulate one's thoughts, then two people could get through to each other. But if she couldn't talk with Walid, it meant there was no chance for communication.

The Israeli public was willing to pass over the affair. Even the foreign press evinced no particular interest in it. Maya called Larry, who answered with some impatience. He still wasn't interested in Maya's Arabs. "You have a Jewish complex about perfection. You think Israel should be a state of absolute justice. Absolute justice occurs only in a utopia. The State of Israel is overburdened with problems. You yourself have told me of the residents of poor Jewish neighborhoods, compared with whom the Arabs of Kafr-Hama are tycoons. The Indians of Wounded Knee would be delighted to trade places with your Walid."

"Walid's father didn't scalp his neighbors from Kibbutz Gan Shoshanim," said Maya. "Racists in Israel speak about Israeli Arabs as if they're the ones who conducted the riots in Hebron, as if they're the terrorists who organized the massacre at Lydda, or murdered the mothers and children at Kiryat Shmoneh, or hijacked the plane to Entebbe. And that's one of the things I'm afraid of. Collective classification, collective punishment, collective attitudes. These Arabs, who are Israeli citizens, are Israeli citizens because they didn't leave the country, didn't fight against us, and didn't enlist into Kaukji's gangs in the war of 'forty-eight to murder and to loot. They're here because from the outset they accepted the idea that it's possible, and acceptable, to live in a Jewish state, among Jews, as citizens with equal rights."

"Equal rights are not something you get on a silver platter," Larry said. "The Indians, the blacks, the women, are fighting for them in the land of unlimited opportunities. And here, every one of you wants everything to come ready-made in bolts of thunder and lightning, like the tablets at Mount Sinai. If your Arabs want equal rights, let them fight for them."

Maya said bitterly, "You don't even hear what you're saying. On the one hand you say they have nothing to complain about because they have equal rights, but when they treat this notion seriously you say they've got cheek to demand equal rights without fighting for them. And if they do go out and fight for them, even people like you, who consider themselves impartial, will say, 'Look at those bastards. How can you give them equal rights if they're fighting against the state, especially in its beleaguered security condition?' "

"I don't envy them," said Larry, "but this problem isn't my major concern."

Maya tried to arouse her colleagues at the newspaper.

"I'm beginning to understand how the Holocaust happened. We've prepared the time bomb that's going to blow up the entire Zionist project, and we did it with our own hands. It's already ticking under our pillow, and all we do is turn over on the other side."

Some of her colleagues, who generally adopted a mocking tone of superiority toward her whenever she spoke of Israeli Arabs, this time took an overtly hostile stance. "You're sick," they said to her. "You're simply sick. You don't know what you're talking about. The police have explicitly stated that there was no abuse. Some reasonable precautions were taken to maintain order. Some hysterical kid got hit on the head and you want to turn the country upside down. You're simply deranged. How can you speak in the same breath about the Holocaust and a few brats from Kafr-Hama? You've completely lost all sense of proportion."

Others responded self-righteously, "Really, Maya, we're surprised at you. How can you possibly make such a comparison?"

She despaired. They were comparing the results while she was trying to make them aware of the first symptoms of moral indifference.

Maya was not one who cried easily, but she swallowed tears. She almost — almost — said what she so much wanted to say. No. What she didn't even dare to think, yet thought all the same: that her own people had become receptive to Hitler's ideology. For when they said "How can you compare," it meant "We can't be compared with anyone else; we're different." It didn't matter that one had meant you're different and therefore subhuman, and that the Israelis or the Jews thought we're different and therefore superhuman ... But this she didn't say, for she knew that if she said it she'd lose every friend, and her only hope was to talk until someone would hear.

If it goes on — this silence, this apathy, this lack of response — there'll be a disaster, she thought.

She sat down at her typewriter.

Only one newspaper would publish this article, a dissident weekly, which had always supported co-existence and self-determination for the Palestinians. Her title was I AM ASHAMED, MY BROTHER WALID.

She wrote with her heart's blood. Not to the subscribers. She was writing to him. She was trying to suture a broken heart.

As soon as the weekly appeared on the stands, the phone started ringing. Calls from angry, upset, and furious people. They didn't share her hurt. They heaped insults on her, threatened her, yelled coarse streams of foul words. Some wanted to know what exactly she did with her Arabs, where and when. Some offered her their own services instead. There was a call from a policeman's wife who asked her if she knew under what difficult conditions and for what a meager salary her husband carried out his duties, and whether he deserved being mentioned in the same breath as Hitler's troops. She didn't wait for Maya's answer; she slammed down the receiver.

At the newspaper she was received with cold silence. In the cafeteria she was ignored.

Maya waited.

Walid arrived the next day. "You've brought the village back to life," he said. "At home we've started laughing again. You know how we all felt? Cheated. Fools. As if we'd lived for thirty years with a rag covering our eyes. For thirty years we've been building something, believing in something, and suddenly it turns out to be a fraud, nonexistent. They kick you in the ass and laugh when you fall. It isn't just the affair itself. Believe me, when I summed up what happened that day in the village I was shocked and furious, but I wasn't in despair. We sat together and planned how we'd stand this state on its head. How we'd bring the entire story to the Knesset, to the public. How the whole country would demand that justice be done and the responsible people brought to trial. And suddenly we realized there was no one to talk to. That this wasn't an accident, an isolated incident; it was policy. You know how I felt? I wanted to bury myself in the ground. I felt guilty of fraud, of having preached to hundreds of young people who believed me and bought my merchandise and suddenly discovered that I'd sold them an empty bag."

"You didn't even believe in me," said Maya. "You weren't willing to talk to me."

Walid tried to protest. "What do you mean, I didn't talk to you? I did talk to you."

"As if to a stranger," said Maya.

"True," Walid admitted. "I can't deny it. I'm sorry."

The next day the secretary of Gan Shoshanim called a meeting of the secretaries of the kibbutzim and moshavim in the area. There was a heated debate.

One speaker said, "For thirty years we've lived here in neighborliness. Not in a state of cold war. In true friendship. We helped each other. And suddenly they throw this incendiary bomb in our home. If we remain silent today, after the beating of children at Hama, what right will we have tomorrow to ask our neighbors' help to trap the terrorists who come to blow up the kindergarten at Gan Shoshanim?"

There were contradictory views, too. "What was done there was criminal," said another secretary, a young man. "I don't justify it. We all know that those who did it caused much harm to the state. But what will it look like if the kibbutzim and moshavim of the area condemn the activities of the police and the army? You know what delight the PLO propaganda office will take in that. Our enemies will be able to say jubilantly: 'Even the Zionists themselves object to the activities of the Zionist state; you can imagine what terrible things really go on there.' "

An older man supported him. "We shouldn't exaggerate. Israel has no policy of mistreating minorities. We're a law-abiding state, and this is a case of violation of the law. We shouldn't lose our sense of proportion. We mustn't forget that we're at war, surrounded by a sea of mortal enemies. That's no ornate phrase, comrades. We are defending ourselves against forces that outnumber us many times over, and whose sole goal is to destroy us, and we mustn't forget that. We're not the ones who initiated this war, and we're not the ones who wanted it. So we can't allow ourselves to weaken the position of our armed forces when we should be strengthening it. Who are our armed forces? Our sons, our children. Are we going to compare them to Nazis? To fascists?"

Then Eyal spoke. He had been born in Gan Shoshanim and had won renown as one of the bravest regimental commanders in the army. Since the Yom Kippur War his name had been frequently heard in the political arena. His was one of the strongest voices against war.

"I serve in the Israeli army, and I'm proud to serve in the Israeli army, and I will continue serving in the Israeli army whenever I'm called to do so. But I am not willing to have my service used in order to justify what was done in Kafr-Hama. I'm fighting a just war, and my war will not be a just one if in its name children's skulls are cracked and women are frightened and studies at school are violently interrupted and my neighbors — whom I also defend when I go to war — are treated as if they're my enemy, only because they belong to a different national group."

"And a different religion, too," someone shouted.

"A different religion?" Eyal asked in wonder. "Since when have I had a religion?"

"But you're Jewish," they shouted at him.

"Yes, I'm Jewish," he said. "And I think that at least here, where we're all members of secular kibbutzim and moshavim, I don't need to go into the old dispute about whether the Jews are a nation or a religion. I think we're all agreed that Zionism is a movement of national renaissance that we came here not in order to build a synagogue to pray in, but a homeland where we can live as a free people, following the humanist principles of the dignity of man, the equality of man, and the spirit of man."

"That sounds very beautiful," someone called out. "Try telling that to Yasir Arafat!"

"I'm trying to remind *you* of it," Eyal replied quietly. "The beatings we're discussing weren't landed on Yasir's head. If there's even a chance to catch him, I'll be there.

But now we're talking about the beating up of our neighbors' children. The children who brought us watermelons and cigarettes and lemonade when we visited their homes.

"I'm not asking you to debate the future of Zionism. The question before us is a very simple one: Will we be able to look our neighbors in the eyes tomorrow? And the day after tomorrow, will we have to go to sleep behind a mined and electrified fence, or will we be able to go on as we have until now, in mutual trust and cooperation?"

"What cooperation?" another secretary shouted at him. "Have you forgotten that three young fellows from Hama were found guilty of membership in Al Fatah and of placing an explosive charge at the central bus station in Tel Aviv?"

"I haven't forgotten, and I'm glad they're in prison. But I also haven't forgotten the blood donations given by young men of Hama to the Israeli army, during the Six Day War. I haven't forgotten that during the Yom Kippur War they came, on their own initiative, to operate all the branches of our kibbutz economy while our men were away fighting. And I'm not forgetting that I've lived here with them, beside them, every day, for thirty years now, and at nights I can drive home without fear. I'm not forgetting that if I go to war, I can fight the armed enemy at our borders without worrying what will happen to my wife and children at home. I know that the rear is safe."

Eyal paused for a moment, and a silence ensued. Then he raised his voice. "And this is the question you're being asked to answer today: If there's another war, will we be able to concentrate all our forces to fight the enemy outside, or will we have to divide them, so as to protect our rear from enemies within?" He lowered his voice and his eyes. "I can assure you all — if today I were one of the young men of Hama, and I saw you all deciding to forget, to pass over what has happened without an outcry, then the first time I got a rifle in my hands I'd aim it straight at you."

Someone yelled, "You're deluding yourselves if you think they love us, or that they ever loved us. It's time we stopped being so self-righteous. We should face facts: we're sitting here on their land, and no fine words can hide that or change that."

Then a woman rose to speak. She had given this land her husband and her two sons. She could not speak heresy. "I only want to say that I agree with everything Eyal has said. I'm not going to war anymore. When I was young, in nineteen forty-eight, women were allowed to fight too. A lot has changed since then — that too. Now we wait for our sons and our husbands to return. I wait for the sons of other mothers. I try very hard not to speak in the name of the fallen, but this time I have to. I know that if Erez and Gilead were with us here today, they'd have said exactly what Eyal said. They fell in a just war. We may not desecrate that war by using it as justification for despicable acts. We may not remain silent. If we remain silent, then all the justification for our struggle to survive here disappears. If we remain silent, what can we claim we fought for? For the right to do to the Arabs what the Gentiles did to the Jews?"

They listened to her in silence.

Actually, there were no differences of opinion among them. All of them were shocked by what had happened. All of them condemned it. All of them agreed that the use of armed forces on the Land Day anniversary at Kafr-Hama had destroyed relations that had taken thirty years to build. But some were afraid that a condemnation of the act would be exploited for harmful ends by hostile elements, and others felt that it was wrong to issue a condemnation before an investigation was concluded.

They formulated an agreement. They would demand vigorously that there be a public investigation into the events of that day and would emphasize the good relations existing in the area since the establishment of the state. They would also express a strong hope that those responsible for the violence be brought to trial and that relations might continue as before.

The communiqué issued by these kibbutzim and moshavim caused an uproar. Knesset members began to arrive, meeting villagers, talking with them, promising to support their demand for a public inquiry. An occasional sympathetic voice appeared in the press.

Maya's newspaper sent a senior writer to conduct a "balanced inquiry" in Kafr-Hama.

His story opened with the words "The inhabitants of Kafr-Hama are not Zionists."

No public commission of inquiry was instituted.

17

AFTER THE FIRST THREE turbulent but uninterrupted years of Walid's second term, Maya believed that this time all would end well. He would complete the full four years as mayor of Kafr-Hama and bring to fruition some of his cherished projects.

She was wrong.

Unexpectedly, he phoned her at six o'clock one morning. "Hello, Maya? Starting today, you can address me by my first name. No titles."

She sat bolt upright in bed. "What happened? Don't play practical jokes on me."

"Cross my heart," he said.

"How come?" She still could not believe it.

"Simple," said Walid, his voice showing more surprise than disappointment. "Nothing changed basically in local politics. One of my staunch supporters wanted his son appointed schoolmaster. The guy is OK but has no academic degree. The father, who sits in the council, schemed quickly and persuaded a majority to unseat me. It cost them fifty thousand pounds. This time I didn't wait to see the end of the movie — this time I resigned."

"Shit."

"I'll come to Tel Aviv to celebrate my discharge from slavery in the public service. We'll have a long talk; we haven't had one in a long time."

As they started talking, Walid remarked, "He's so lucky, that jackass who's taken my place. I pulled all the carts out of the mud, and now he's going to lead the procession through the gate. I'll bet you he'll say, 'Three years Walid was chairman and didn't get anything done. I come into office, and everything starts working like a charm.' "

"Good luck to him. You should learn from him. Next time, try to take over from someone who's already done all the spadework."

Walid laughed. "I'll be satisfied if they just don't leave me scorched earth. I can do without their spadework. But this time, even this imbecile won't be able to spoil anything. Everything's signed and settled."

On a visit to Hadera, Walid dropped in to say hello to several acquaintances at the electric company. They informed him that some of the villagers had come by asking if it was possible to cancel the contract and get their money back.

Walid returned to Hama and started listening to the young men's conversations in the café. They were surprised that he didn't know about the new chairman and his flunkies going from house to house, on a whispering campaign, advising everyone who paid for electricity to change his mind and salvage some of his money. Walid heard an account of such an argument from a friend.

"What's the good of that to me? I don't want the money; I want electricity."

"You donkey son-of-a-donkey, no wonder they conned you. You deserve to be conned. You want electricity? And what about honor — is that nothing? To have everyone know that you can be led by the nose? You say you weren't conned? Of course you were conned! Think for a moment; look at it logically. If you want to buy a truck, what do you do? You go to Jenin, to Hadera, to Tulkarm, to Nazareth — you check things out, compare prices. One says this; one says that. You sit down and bargain. You bring the price down a bit here, a bit there, until you're satisfied. Right? Right. And what did Walid do? He went to the electric company — they told him a price, and he didn't even argue. What they asked for, he signed. What does he care? Is it money out of his father's pocket? No, it's from my pocket and your pocket. What do you say? There's no other way?

One can't bargain with the electric company? That's exactly what I'm saying. It's a monopoly. They force you to get your electricity from them. So of course they hoist the prices. So what can we do? We can refuse to buy.

"They conned you. They made a deal with the electric company and split the four thousand pounds fifty-fifty. What? Is Walid a thief? Who said that? Did I say he's a thief? It's probably his assistant, his deputy, and the official at the electric company who did it. Now there's nothing to do. I understand you. People need electricity. But a man's honor shines in the dark much stronger than electricity does. Yesterday I heard people laughing at you. I said to them, 'What're you laughing at? What can a man do? He has to have electricity.' Of course you have honor. I told them right away that I'm sure you'd be willing to tear the contract up in their face and take your money back, even if you lose half of it. I told them you have honor."

The rumors spread through the village. When they reached the housewives' ears, the women descended on their men like bristling cats. "God forbid! Don't do it! We need the electricity! For years we've been ruining our eyes and our hands. You bought a washing machine, didn't you? The most modern on the market, eh? You told the whole village about it! And there it stands, laughing at me while I wear my hands out. It stands there doing nothing. It can't work without electricity. And I have to work, whether there's electricity or not. You don't care about me. Your honor? Doesn't my condition have anything to do with your honor?"

The water program was also attacked.

Under Walid's chairmanship, the council had signed agreements, committed itself to payments, and, by wrangling and persistence, had obtained special budgets from the Ministry of the Interior. They had also drawn up a very detailed implementation plan.

The Water Authority had approved the implementation dates. They had studied the map of the village and checked the area that had the severest water shortage. They had pinpointed the most problematic neighborhood, on a hill, built in recent years, with no local wells. The faucets were dry most hours of the day. The first large water tower would be built in the troubled neighborhood. The site for the tower had been located; work was about to begin.

As soon as the new chairman assumed office, his agents invaded the neighborhood, which had already celebrated the news of the water. Walid's administration was accused of defrauding young couples by building the water tower in their vicinity.

The varieties of persuasion were reported to Walid. "You say they didn't take anyone's land? You're naive. So naïve. No wonder they're doing it here. And what if there's a flood? They'll build a water tower and a wall will break and flood your house and drown your children, God forbid. Think about it — what do you need? You need water, right? How much water? A few drops. To drink, to cook, to wash before prayer, to do the laundry. My mother used to bring all the water from the well, on her head, and it was enough. So what do you need a water tower for? Because the Ministry of the Interior gave us a budget? Have you ever known the Jews to give something for nothing? They'll probably build their water tower here next to our houses and then pipe the water off to their kibbutzim. We know them. They're sly. If they're building us a water tower, they must have their own reasons."

Agitation soon spread through the neighborhood on the hill. The few who tried to calm it were defeated. Heads of families went to the council offices every day, demanding that the work on the water tower be stopped.

Walid lamented that hundreds of thousands of pounds had been invested in the project.

Walid's third project also fell through. He had done the impossible. When the method of land appropriation had become streamlined and accelerated, and almost all the Arab villages in Israel were feeling the pressure of lack of land, Walid had managed to get nineteen dunams of land in the village area from the Israel Lands Administration, to build a Sports and Culture Center — or, as he and his friends referred to it, "our country club." He envisaged a center, alive with sporting and social activity, that would become a force in the village's social development and an example for other Arab villages to follow. It was his pet project, and it broke his heart to leave it. The Hama Council decided to hand over the land reserved for the Sports and Culture Center to — the Histadrut.

When he first heard the news, he couldn't believe it, considered it a bad joke. But the new chairman's agents quickly consolidated their campaign. "Does it make sense, the government giving us land? Whom are they trying to deceive? If they give us land, there must be something behind it. Of course, they say they want to build a soccer field. Why should they say anything else? Everyone knows that the young men in the village are crazy about soccer. How did Walid get elected? They kicked him in, a goal, straight from the soccer field. But why a landscape gardener, if what they want is a soccer field? For soccer all you need is to level the ground and to put up a fence. But anyone with any sense in his head will realize what they're up to. If they're making lawns [the speaker lowers his voice] . . . it's for the girls. Yes — they want to throw away all decent inhibitions. They want the girls to become completely wanton. They can't pet and fondle them on the soccer field — they need a lawn for that. The Jews aren't fools. They have corrupted our youth. They're working to undermine our moral basis, and they want us to pay for this lawn out of our own pockets, Allah forbid.

"You ask why we shouldn't keep the land as council property? Who says we're giving it back to the Jews? I know that this land was ours before the Zionists took it. But we haven't given it back to the Zionists. We've given it to the Histadrut. You think the Histadrut is the Zionists too? That it's the government? No, my friend, there's an Arab Histadrut now." And the speaker triumphantly pulled out posters duplicated by the Department for Arab Affairs of the Histadrut, studded from top to bottom with quotations from the Koran.

Walid could not stand by as his pet project collapsed before his eyes. He fought the land transfer at the council
meeting, but to no avail.

*　*　*

Walid started suffering from headaches. Maya was worried.
Walid had always managed to see the amusing side of any
defeat or victory. His headaches were appropriate to the
small frustrations of people closed in cubelike offices in Tel
Aviv office buildings. Not to Walid of Kafr-Hama.

Maya suggested that he bring his wife and little daughter
to spend two or three days in Tel Aviv.

"She can't travel now," Walid explained. "She doesn't feel
good when she travels, because of the pregnancy."

Maybe this time it'll be a son, Maya thought to herself,
smiling. Aloud she said, *"Mabruk! Mazel Tov!"*

"What do you think? Should I run for election again?" he
asked suddenly.

Maya wasn't sure how to respond. The wonder boy of
politics in the Arab sector was nearing his mid-thirties, was
married, with one child and another on the way, and had
not yet completed his law degree. Although he was well
provided for, anything could happen, and Maya felt that it
would be advantageous for Walid to have a profession. Sort
of an insurance policy against the unexpected.

Maya perceived that if anything happened to Hassan, the
brother in charge of the family's financial affairs, Walid
would take his place. Walid knew it, too. The future held
many perturbing problems, such as the fate of the Abu-Hana
family after the father's death. The family might decide to
preserve the status quo or the brothers might choose to divide the wealth, and then they'd all be left to their own
devices.

"Should I run for election again?"

Maya had no answer, but she said, "What for? What the
devil has changed between the first time you were deposed
and this time? The only difference is the price. Then the
opposition paid out twenty thousand to buy councilors'

votes, and this time they shelled out fifty thousand. If you take the rate of inflation into account, all we can say is that your price has gone down."

"Either I don't have a sense of humor or that isn't funny," Walid replied, but with a wry smile.

"Actually, how did they divide up the fifty thousand? Who got what?" asked Maya.

"Two councilors received honors; they got titles in lieu of money. One got electricity and water for his son who's getting married, at council expense, and two others divided what was left."

"You're a source of livelihood." Maya laughed. "Every few years they depose Walid and fatten up their bank accounts."

"Console yourself with the knowledge that these are not bribes. Just money put aside for charitable purposes."

"And what about the father of the son who's getting electricity and water? How do they explain that one away?"

"Judge for yourself. To marry off a son — is it not a holy commandment? And does not one need water and electricity in the house? That's it. That's the way the world goes."

"I'm missing one. Six voted against you. Two got honors, two bribes — sorry, charity — one's marrying off his son. What about the sixth?"

"The sixth's the Old Man," said Walid. The "Old Man" was their name for the councilor who had served as Walid's deputy during his first term. He was a notable from one of the largest clans in the village and was always elected to the council, automatically.

"I thought he liked you," said Maya.

"That's true. He told himself that he likes me, but he thinks his preferences shouldn't interfere with his livelihood."

"That fat old pasha! That sly bastard! Is he in financial difficulties?"

"He lives off the national insurance old-age pension," said Walid.

"So why are you surprised at him," Maya flared up. "No one can live on that pension!"

Walid burst out laughing. "I didn't say he lived off *his* pension; I said he lived off the national insurance pension. The Old Man was already quite old during the period of the military administration. The military governor was a nice person. He advised the Old Man to take out national insurance. We villagers don't like to pay out money now for promises of what we'll get later. But the governor convinced him, explaining that if he joined the national insurance scheme, he'd soon start receiving a pension for the rest of his life. The Old Man drew up a list of old men in the village who were close to pension age and who didn't have particularly clever sons. He then made a payment on behalf of each of them out of his own pocket. When the time came for one of them to receive a pension, he'd call on that man and say, 'If you give me a down payment of a certain sum, I'll arrange a pension for you for the rest of your life, but you'll have to pay me a third every month.' The old people kissed his hands. Come to the village on the day the national insurance payments come through and you'll see the Old Man standing across the road from the post office early in the morning. As each pensioner leaves the post office, he pays over a third to the Old Man."

Maya jumped up from the sofa. "Aren't you ashamed of yourself? You know about this, and you do nothing to stop it?"

Walid laughed, enjoying the sight of her agitation. "What can I do? If I lodge a complaint against him, all the old men he fleeces will come and curse me and my family. They're sure he's the Prophet's messenger, at the very least. Who'll bear witness against him?"

*   *   *

Several weeks later Walid was in Tel Aviv and made a quick stop at Maya's with his youngest brother, Mustafa, and with the cousin of his erstwhile deputy in the council. Mustafa, like Walid, had attended a Jewish high school in order to have an equal chance of competing for a place in the university. But during registration, he found he had no chance of majoring in the fields he wanted, medicine, pharmacology, or dentistry, and there was no department of veterinary science.

The wealthier Arab families had begun acting to a certain degree like English gentry from a previous century, leaving the title and the estates to the oldest son, preparing one son for the clergy, one for banking or politics, and so on. Every self-respecting wealthy Arab family wanted one son to be a lawyer, a teacher, or a senior official, and at least one in a solid profession like medicine or engineering. The trouble with engineering was that all the major industrial plants in Israel were connected one way or another to work that was classified, so the chances of an Arab engineer getting a position he could advance in were limited. On the other hand, there was no lack of patients in the Arab sector, even for a mediocre doctor.

A young Arab who was not accepted at the university did not need to explain in his village why he had been rejected. The reason was obvious: he was an Arab. They knew that hundreds of Jewish students with good grades were not accepted into medical school or into the natural sciences. They read the newspaper reports about, or interviews with, young men released from the Israeli army, sometimes officers, sometimes disabled men, who spoke bitterly about the fact that the state, which had taken a leg or an arm from them, forced them to plead for admission into universities in Italy or Germany. Most of the Arab students also realized that the quality of their secondary school education was lower than that of their Jewish competitors. However, instead of attacking the low teaching standards in the Arab schools, and demanding reform, they preferred to take pride in the names of the two or three Arab students who had excelled in their studies at the universities to which they'd been accepted. In a sense, the problem of the Arab students was similar to that of Jews who had come to Israel from

Islamic countries, whose schools also lagged behind those in the large cities or in the privileged settlements, like the kibbutzim.

Mustafa had been sent to study in Rumania, as had the deputy's cousin. The Eastern European countries had opened their universities to Arab students from Israel. The prime mediator in this arrangement was Israel's Communist Party (Rakah). Rakah preached a strange brand of communism, for, though communism was antinationalistic, the Israeli Communist Party had fostered Arab nationalism and built itself upon it. From its inception, this party had started sending young Arabs to study in the Soviet Union, and afterward in Eastern European countries. This possibility of travel was a magnet to many young Arabs, who felt stifled in their villages and the confining social structure within the narrow and sealed borders of Israel. After relations between Israel and the U.S.S.R. were severed, the stream of students kept flowing, both through the Communist Party and private channels, to east-European countries defined as "moderate," especially Rumania, which continued to maintain diplomatic relations with Israel. In Kafr-Hama alone, there were several dozen young men who had studied in Rumania.

"When we want to say something at home that we don't want anyone to understand," Mustafa said, laughing, "we speak Rumanian."

Maya recalled that Lior Ronen, the talented assistant of her vet, had studied veterinary science in Rumania.

Lior was the son of a famous Israeli soldier who had met his death chasing terrorists. He was following tracks to an area of caves on Mount Hebron. One of the soldiers in the pursuit squad was about to throw a hand grenade into a cave, but just then Lior's father noticed a young Arab woman sitting in the opening of the cave, breast-feeding an infant. He grasped the soldier's raised hand, and at the very same moment was hit by a bullet fired from a rifle inside the cave aimed just over the young woman's shoulder. Lior was seven years old at the time. When it was his turn to enlist in the army, he chose not an officer's course but a course for combat medics. She mentioned Lior's name, asking Mustafa whether they had bumped into each other in Rumania.

Mustafa said there was no chance that he'd met Lior; the Jews studied only in Bucharest. When Maya asked him about the social life in Rumania, the two younger men exchanged amused glances. "What social life? There we only study, eat, and sleep. The social life is dead. There's not an active student life, like here. There it's like our village. Nothing. Dead."

"But what do you do after classes? Don't you meet? Don't you go out?"

"There's nothing. Movies, opera, theater. We sit, talk, and that's it."

"That's exactly what there is here — movies, theater, talks among friends. What else is there here?"

The two "Rumanians" exchanged surprised looks and sent a questioning glance to Walid. "Here there're things happening all the time — petitions, politics, demonstrations — somebody gets arrested and everyone goes out to protest. Fun and games all the time."

"Are most of the students from Israel communists?" Maya asked.

"Anyone who goes to one of those universities comes back a noncommunist."

They returned to the subject of the forthcoming elections to the local council. Walid reported in a bantering tone about his opening campaign speech, which had gone on too long. "Do you think I should run for election?" he asked again.

Maya said, "What are you asking me for? You've just told me that you've started running. Do you want to chicken out after the starting gun's gone off?"

"Today I got the results of one exam," said Walid. "Not dazzling. I can't handle both the council and the university. But I've put so much work into the village . . ."

"You have to decide what you want. This council — it's like the work of a housewife. As soon as you finish washing the dishes, the sink's full again. When you were elected for the first time, you fought for electricity and water. And what are you concerned with now? Electricity and water. That doesn't lead anywhere."

"You yourself said that I can allow myself to be independent and strong because I have Kafr-Hama as a base, as backing."

"It's a base if you use it for a leap forward. When I first met you, I was convinced that, within two terms, you'd be in the Knesset. But you're not progressing; you're going around in circles. You push the village forward one meter, and the village panics and goes back two."

"That's the speed of progress," Walid replied. "The village is no worse than any other society. That's how it was in the French Revolution. They raised the banner of Liberty, Equality, Fraternity, and then they drowned all three in a blood bath. The Mensheviks and the Bolsheviks did the same. It's the same everywhere.

"Zionism got corrupted too. From the battle for Hebrew labor to a battle to employ Arab child labor. Apparently, there's no other way. But the fact is, there's always progress. Whatever you say, our people are living better today than they did ten or twenty years ago."

Maya wasn't convinced.

18

WALID DID DECIDE to run for election again. He was furious that the projects in which he had invested years of work and dreams were being wrecked. And perhaps he wanted to test himself and the support he had.

Or perhaps he decided for other reasons. This time the choice was between running for election and not being involved in public affairs at all — for he had closed many doors to himself. He denounced the duplicity of the Labor Party. He had no intention of harnessing himself to the communist wagon, and he was very skeptical about the efficacy of an Arab in a marginal Jewish party, no matter how noble its platform. Walid wanted to accomplish things, not to fantasize about them.

Or perhaps the choice before him now was either to run for election or to get out altogether, to take time out, to study for a few years in another country, another place. Maya suspected that were it not for Nadia's second pregnancy, that was the choice he might have made.

Behind his campaign existed the very real pressures of his followers, his friends and supporters who had stood behind him for more than ten years, and who without him were like sheep without a shepherd.

They wanted him to run, and he wanted to run for them, because despite all the disappointments and his vows to stop, he was a natural leader. He was a leader with roots, and his roots were sunk deep in the soil of Kafr-Hama. He believed that he could go far, but with the stubbornness of a peasant he was convinced that he could not progress even an inch if he did not base himself on the support of his own village. They supplied his foundation.

This time, there was the additional incentive that if he was elected, he would be able to function for a full four years, without the threat of being unseated hanging over his head.

This was the first time a council chairman was to be individually elected on a separate ticket, apart from lists of prospective councilors. Walid published an address to the villagers, calling on them to give him the opportunity not only to promise but also to implement.

Once again Walid plunged into the race with everything he had, convinced that common sense would win out. After all, he had fought for a better quality of life for his village, and he was sure that this fact would enable him to win.

In his enthusiasm, he disregarded a factor of no less importance — honor. When someone is elected chairman for a full term, that someone is awarded great personal honor. The large clans were convinced that this honor was their due, and they were not willing to relinquish it.

The election struggle in Kafr-Hama reached a pitch the village had not experienced for many years. The elders of the village unearthed an old institution that had disappeared from the spoken language, and breathed new life into it. When they realized that clan affinities would not guarantee victory to the large families, they suddenly remembered the h'ara, the neighborhood. This was a group of clans that, because they were related to each other, had chosen to live in close proximity. The institution of the h'ara had already lost all meaning long before the establishment of the state. Now, however, people suddenly started visiting their neighbors, announcing gravely, "We have to stick together, to support each other. After all, we belong to the same h'ara. And members of a h'ara are members of the same family. We are all brothers."

The elders waved this concept around like a magic charm. It turned out that eleven lists were running for the council, but the struggle for chairmanship was limited to three candidates — the representatives of the two largest clans in the village, and Walid Abu-Hana.

As election day approached, Walid's rivals threw caution and fairness to the wind. Their checkbooks appeared. On a conservative estimate, the two large clans spent about half a million pounds on "presents" and on buying votes outright. A record sum per voter, if one considers that there were three thousand voters in all, two thirds of whom were committed anyway, without being paid to vote for one list or the other.

Walid's followers almost declared rebellion against him the day before the elections because he turned away potential voters who wanted something in exchange for their vote.

"We don't buy votes," he declared repeatedly.

Even Taufik grew angry. "What's wrong with you? You want to be holier than the Pope? The big parties can do it, the establishment can do it, and you can't? And apart from that, lower your voice, don't offend some good people. This man isn't selling his vote. If he wanted to sell it, he'd sell it to the others. The way he sees it, he's giving you his vote free, because he believes in you. So hasn't he got something coming to him? To make him feel good? To make him happy?"

Walid remained adamant. "Either we do it the proper way, or I quit."

Hassan, the financial genius of the Abu-Hana family, allotted thirty thousand pounds on the eve of the election for expenses — drinks, gas to bring to the polls voters who had got stuck in the city. But when his followers pressed him to express his thanks in material form to several voters, Walid lost his temper. "Forget about money. From now on we aren't bringing any drinks, refreshments, sunflower seeds, chewing gum, or taxis. Anyone who wants to work for me for free can work. You don't want to work, go home."

"He's crazy," they said. "He's gone mad. He's been working too hard."

When Walid calmed down, he explained to them, "It's not the money; it's integrity that's at stake. I want the Arab voter to learn what his vote means. We have a tradition of selling votes. We also sell voices to extremist right-wing anti-Arab parties or to Jewish religious parties. And this has to stop. We have to prove ourselves worthy of democracy."

* * *

The candidate of the Mousmous clan had made a lot of money as a contractor of cement and other building materials. His people had made a list of all the young couples, and all the young men building houses in order to get married, and had presented them with bathtubs, toilet bowls, and bathroom sinks. Many of Walid's supporters had had to decide between their loyalty to him and a bathtub, and the choice had been a hard one. It is not a bribe, the candidate's messengers had explained; it's only a present, a token of our concern for the young couple.

In Taufik's coffee house, everyone was agitated because Walid's rivals tried to exploit a death to incite the villagers against him, the death of the youngest son of the Subhi family, a seventeen-year-old, gifted and brilliant, who had belonged to Walid's young guard. The mystery of the boy's death had not been solved, but among the young men in the village a version was circulating that many were willing to swear to. As the story went, it had happened on the day the boy's older brother married, and the boy had been sent on some errand. When Sid Mousmous sped down the busy street — for a rich man did not have to drive carefully — he ran over the boy. Sid Mousmous didn't have a driver's license. The injured boy was dragged into a nearby shed. Sid Mousmous had an emissary call the boy's father and brothers, and there was a lengthy bargaining session to determine how much money would buy the family's silence. All this time the boy was lying in the shed. The family didn't lodge a complaint, and the boy wasn't taken to the hospital. The exact price was never revealed, but the boy's father later added a new wing to his house.

No one knows if death came quickly, or if it took the boy many hours to die, or even if there had been a chance to save his life. Early the next morning, the father woke his wife and instructed her to bring food to the boy, who, he said, was tending the sheep. She searched until she found his body in the shed, under some sacks. The family then called the police. According to this version, the policeman who came also received something for his silence.

Walid and his friends were among the mourners at the boy's funeral. At the head of the procession walked the father, the brothers, and the contractor. Suddenly they noticed Walid. They pointed at him and whispered. The whisper ran through the procession: "That's the man responsible for the boy's death. He put new ideas in the boy's head, and that's why he's dead. Only because of Walid. Look at him, the way he walks in the funeral procession. As if his hands were clean. Anyone can see he isn't one of us; he's like an Englishman. Only the English killed Arabs and then walked in their funerals."

Before the body was lowered into the grave, there was an unexpected incident. A newcomer to the village, related by marriage to the boy, pulled aside the blanket covering the body. Addressing the police officer, he said, "I spit on your rank and on the badge on your cap. You have no shame. I'm a Bedouin. And I'm a tracker. But even a fool can see this wasn't a natural death, that the boy was run over." And he walked away rapidly. The father covered his son's body, the policeman remained silent, and the boy was buried.

Functionaries of the Labor Party also stirred the election pot by approaching the heads of two of the larger lists and advising them that it might be wise of them not to vote for Walid Abu-Hana.

When Walid learned about it, he reminded them that the Labor Party wasn't even in power then. But when voters got home they forgot Walid's remarks, remembering only that the government was opposed to Walid.

Walid could not get over this last episode. "I'm still a member of the Labor Party's central committee," he said to whoever would listen. "What are they doing this for? They're ranging all their artillery against me. Where's the logic in it?"

By election day, Walid, Taufik, and other activists of the

Young Men's List hadn't slept a wink for three days. Walid could hardly think straight. One of his most faithful supporters, who belonged to the ruling clan in the village, had been raided. His identity card, his wife's, and his parents' vanished. Without identity cards, they could not vote. He knew the names of the robbers and where the cards were being kept, but there was nothing he could do. "If you bring the police, there will be murder here," they had warned him. At another polling booth, one of the poorer villagers turned up; he had lived for years on the generous support of the Abu-Hana family. When he was sick he came to Walid. When someone bothered him, he came to Walid. At the polling booth he said, "I don't know how to put the slips in, and I don't want to make a mistake. I want to vote for Walid." They didn't give him the voting slips.

Many miracles occurred that day. People long dead cast their votes. Others, alive and breathing, managed to appear in two places at the same time, to be among the pilgrims to Mecca and to vote in the elections at Kafr-Hama.

The protests of the Young Men's representatives fell on deaf ears. They were outshouted by poll representatives of the big clans.

After the votes were counted, gloom settled on Kafr-Hama. Walid lost. He came in third. When the election fever passed, the villagers realized that, by not electing him, they had cheated themselves.

*   *   *

Maya was undecided whether to drive to Kafr-Hama or stay home. Finally, she decided to go. The village was deserted and empty. Then she spotted Taufik. He was walking along, staring at the ground. She called to him, but he didn't hear. She stopped the car, brakes squealing, right beside him. He raised his head apathetically. Several seconds elapsed before he recognized her. He got into the car.

"What's going on?" she asked.

"What do you expect?"

"Where's Walid?"

"Maybe at home, maybe in the office."

"How do you feel?"

"I think we made quite a good showing," he said, as if repeating aloud what he had reasoned innumerable times in his head. "Almost seven hundred votes, empty-handed, without money, without an organization, without a clan. Three hundred and fifty votes short of victory."

But his expression was sad.

Walid wasn't at home. Nadia said he was in the office. In Nadia's greeting to her, Maya heard real joy. Perhaps this was the first time that Nadia was really happy to see her. "I'll prepare something to eat for you and for Walid. He will be glad to know you are here. It will cheer him up."

Walid was sitting in his office in sandals, without socks. He looked as if he hadn't slept for many days. His supporters sat around, stooped, silent.

Walid hastened toward her. "What do you say?" he asked.

"I came to listen," she replied.

He continued as if the conversation had been interrupted. "I don't know, maybe I should have brought you here. During the last days I wondered whether I should ask you to come. We could have exchanged ideas and might have discovered a new angle for my campaign."

"It doesn't matter," she said. "It wouldn't have made any difference. Worse, they would have said you couldn't make it without outside assistance — and a woman's assistance, at that."

"Yes," he agreed, "they would have said, 'Look at him! He's brought in a woman to save him.' "

"And you wouldn't have listened to me anyway. What's your proverb? Listen to women, then do the opposite . . ."

"That's not my saying — it's the Prophet's."

They laughed and felt better.

In the office was a young man with a finely trimmed blond mustache. Had it not been for intensive work by Walid some time ago, he would have joined Al Fatah after being beaten by the police during a routine investigation. He had remained one of Walid's most loyal friends ever

since. Now he said to Maya, "It's a pity that you weren't
here yesterday. People sat here crying like little children.
Men, heads of families, crying shamelessly."

Eventually they were left alone — Walid, Taufik, and
Maya.

"If we don't consolidate our group, and don't draw up a
plan of action for our men, they will all get lost," Walid
observed.

Maya silently uttered a small prayer of thanksgiving.
Walid wasn't giving up. And she was almost certain that
after this defeat he would turn his back on politics for good.

"Maybe we should issue a declaration," said Walid, taking
out a writing pad.

> Friends [he wrote], have we been defeated, or have we won?
> That depends only on you. I want to thank you. The 674 votes
> given me are not just a number. They are 674 people who
> cannot be bought for money and cannot be broken by threats
> or by temptations. This is a great force, and I am proud and
> moved that such people have given me their vote.
>
> Such people can win any struggle, if they only persist in it.
> I, for my part, am willing to continue and to serve you.

Several days later, Walid's parents returned from the pilgrimage to Mecca, the first such pilgrimage since 1948 in
which the Riyadh authorities had allowed Israeli Arabs to
participate.

The Abu-Hana family welcomed their parents with a procession, a feast, and much joy. Walid was afraid that his
father would be very upset about his defeat.

Salah Abu-Hana listened and then asked, "So for four
years you won't be able to serve as council chairman?"

"Yes, Father, because the new rule states that the man
elected keeps the post for four years," said Walid, lowering
his eyes.

"*Allah Akhbar!*" The old man's eyes gleamed. "Four free
years to let you complete your studies properly and to take
joy in your wife and children."

Some time later Nadia gave birth — to a son.

Walid had often thought about a name for a son. "If it's a son, I'll call him Amir. That's a fine name, in both Hebrew and Arabic," he had once declared.

To Maya's surprise, she was informed that the son's name would be Muhammad.

"He was born with the name," Walid explained. "He was born circumcised. By tradition, a boy who is born circumcised contains the soul of a righteous man and should be called by an appropriate name, Abraham or Muhammad."

Walid chose Muhammad.

That there should be no doubt about who was who.

19

THE TEDIOUS DEBATE in the Knesset on the peace treaty with Egypt was an anticlimax to everyone. It seemed that since that miraculous hour when Sadat appeared in Jerusalem, since that Messianic, historic moment when national hatred was forgotten and hope for a peaceful future was rekindled, Israel's capacity to believe, to dream, had been exhausted. Now that the hour for signing the treaty had arrived, it was no longer fashionable to expect too much. Now was the hour for caution, skepticism, for prophecies of gloom.

At Maya's home several friends gathered to watch on television the ratification debate. Each Knesset member was allotted ten minutes, and it was reasonable to assume that no more than two or three good souls would give up their right to speak their minds to the nation and forsake the chance to be chronicled in the pages of history. Maya's friends sought refuge from boredom in each other's company during this long night of vigil. From time to time, when the Knesset Speaker announced the name of the next member to speak, they would turn the volume down and exchange impressions.

Arab Knesset members from the Communist Party made fiery speeches against Sadat's peace initiative. Maya couldn't restrain herself. "That makes my blood boil," she said. "How can they support that garbage?"

"They're not speaking for themselves; they're speaking for Moscow," Walid said, trying to calm her.

Maya would not be calmed. "What bothers them about our withdrawal from Sinai? A partial Jewish-Arab peace is better than a total Jewish-Arab war!"

"They're demanding that the Palestinians be kept in mind."

"Come off it," said Rafi, an Orientalist writing a doctoral thesis on the Palestinian refugees. "They know as well as I do, and perhaps even better, that in any war in the Middle East the Palestinians are the first victims. Today King Hussein is the darling of the Palestinians; yesterday he slaughtered them, during Black September. When a temporary respite came to the area, the Palestinians decided to let off fireworks in Lebanon, and started a great fire in which they themselves are now getting burned."

"So you sympathize with them," said Noa, another of Maya's friends, though an outspoken hawk. "The Palestinians behaved in Lebanon just like the scorpion who asked the frog to carry it across the river. The scorpion said, 'Be logical. If I sting you, we'll both drown.' The frog was convinced and let the scorpion climb onto his back. Midway across the river it felt the scorpion's sting. 'What have you done?' cried the frog. 'Now we'll both drown!' 'I couldn't help myself,' replied the passenger, sinking with the frog; 'a scorpion's a scorpion.' "

Boaz, Noa's boyfriend and her colleague in the documentary films division of Israeli television, said, "My parents are from Poland. And they're still amazed that only the Jews came to the aid of the Christians in Lebanon."

Miriam, an Arab student from Nazareth, who had hardly spoken all evening, said, blushing, "In Lebanon the war isn't between Muslims and Christians. That description isn't right at all. It's a war against the rich, for a more just distribution of property."

"That isn't precise either," said Rafi. "You're a Christian and you find it hard to reconcile your sympathy for the Palestinians with the fact that most of these Palestinians are Muslims and fought against the Christians."

Miriam with great feeling in her voice, interrupted him. "That isn't true. That's what the Zionist press writes."

Rafi smiled. "I agree with you that from reading newspapers it's very hard to understand what happened in Lebanon. But I don't think that the Zionist press, as you call it, has done that maliciously. I think that the newspapermen had difficulties in understanding, just as their readers did. Whoever says that in Lebanon Muslims are fighting against Christians is telling half the truth. And whoever says that it's the left fighting against the right is telling half the truth. And if anyone puts these two halves together, he still won't get the whole truth. It's much more complicated. But there can be no doubt that the Palestinians have played a central role in it all."

Noa said, "I'm sorry for what the Lebanese are going through, and I hope the world learns a lesson from it. Anyone who believed in any of Yasir Arafat's declarations can now see what they're worth. All that nonsense about a secular democratic Palestine, where people of all religions could live without discrimination. Lebanon was a democracy of that kind. Muslims, Christians, and even Jews lived there together. They opened their gates and homes to Arafat's people, and see how he's thanked them. If that's what they did in Lebanon, just imagine what they'll do to us if we give them the chance."

Walid added, "No one's suggesting inviting Arafat to Tel Aviv. But if the people living on the West Bank want him, that's their business."

Noa argued, "Today it'll be the West Bank, and tomorrow Haifa."

Rafi tried to direct the conversation into quieter channels. "Leave the West Bank for now. We'll have enough headaches over that when they start discussing the autonomy plan." Turning to Walid, he said, "I have the feeling that despite the declarations of the communist representatives, most of the Arabs in the country are happy with the peace initiative. I think that if this peace works out, Arab citizens of Israel will be able to breathe more freely too."

Walid agreed. "That's true. I also think that most of our people welcome this peace. But I'm not sure how it'll affect the Israeli Arabs' feelings as citizens."

"Tell me, Walid," asked Noa, "you're in favor of the establishment of a Palestinian state, aren't you?"

Walid smiled. "Of course I am."

"And if a Palestinian state is set up, then you'll leave Israel and become a citizen of that state?"

"No. I'll stay here."

"Then forgive me for saying this to you, but I think you're a hypocrite and a coward."

"I forgive you."

"You needn't take it personally. I'm just saying it's very easy to fight for a Palestinian state while enjoying all the advantages of Israel."

"Noa," said Rafi, "that isn't fair."

Walid stopped him. "I think it's very fair of her to say what she thinks. It's just a pity that she hasn't thought it all the way through."

"I think I have," said Noa, "but go ahead. Perhaps you can convince me that I'm wrong."

"Let's start from you denying me the right to support the idea of a Palestinian state," Walid began. "When you have to justify why I should suddenly be prohibited from doing so, you claim that an Arafatist state will try to destroy the state of Israel. But I didn't say that a Palestinian state has to be an Arafatist one. *You* said that, in order to reject, a priori, the idea of the establishment of a Palestinian state. I believe that the right of the Palestinians to a state of their own is no less valid than the right of the Jews to a state of their own. I don't understand how one can reject the rights of the Palestinians without destroying the moral basis of Israel's right to exist."

"That's cheap demagoguery," said Noa. "The Jewish people lost their independence two thousand years ago and fought for it for two thousand years, but the Palestinians are an accidental population; they began claiming they were a people or a nation only when the Jews managed to achieve their national independence."

Rafi tried to put an end to the argument by turning up the volume on the television set, but the others stopped him.

"Let it be as you say," said Walid. "Let's agree that the Palestinians aren't a two-thousand-year-old nation. I know several nations a lot younger. The Americans are only two hundred years old as a nation, and in achieving their national identity they also managed to oust another entity, yet no one disputes the Americans' right to a state of their own. Let's agree for the sake of argument that there was no Palestinian nation until the rise of Zionism, and that the Palestinian national movement — or the Palestinian national consciousness — crystallized as a by-product of political Zionism. So what? Does that mean it doesn't exist? Can you deny it for that reason? In nineteen forty-eight the representatives of the Jewish state-in-formation enthusiastically agreed to partition the territory of the British Mandate into a Jewish state and an Arab state. Why was that OK then, and so wrong now?"

Noa said, "You had a chance then and you didn't take it. So what do we owe you? You know very well that if the Arabs had won in 'forty-eight, there would have remained no trace of what you call the 'Palestinian national consciousness.' Our neighbors didn't invade the territory of the Mandate in 'forty-eight in order to set up a Palestinian state. Each Arab country came to grab as large a piece of the cake for itself as it could. The Egyptians came to grab the Negev, the Syrians hoped to annex the Galilee, and King Abdullah doubled the value of his kingdom and took over the West Bank as his own. What would you have done then? Would you have gone to the United Nations to demand the expulsion of the Arab conquerors, to give Palestine back to the Palestinians?"

"I don't know," said Walid. "On hypothetical questions your guess is as good as mine. Even if we accept your premise — if the entire area we call Palestine had been divided up among the Arab countries — the Palestinians would certainly have been faced with very difficult problems. But then the language of the regime would have been Arabic and the national religion would have been Islam, and the residents wouldn't have found their loyalty, their honesty, and their intelligence suspect just because they were Arabs."

"I'm glad you say that," said Noa. "You're confirming the

fact that there's no Palestinian nation, that there's only an Arab nation. You didn't contest my crucial point that there was no such animal as a Palestinian nation. It was created artificially to counteract the success of the Zionist movement, to stalemate the national revival of the Jews in their historic homeland."

There was a hint of bitterness in Walid's voice. "I didn't dispute the credentials of the Palestinian nation because it wasn't material. But assuming that anybody can pinpoint the birthdate of a nation, you should only be happy that the Palestinian nationhood did not take shape before the Zionists achieved independence for Israel. What would Theodor Herzl, the prophet of the political Zionist movement, have done with his vision if the ancient homeland of the Hebrews had already been claimed by a vigorous Palestinian national movement? He would have been left with no choice but his Uganda plan — a Jewish national colony in the African continent. Do you think that it would be easier for the Jews to deal with the problems of a Jewish Rhodesia than to come to terms with the Palestinians, their right for self-determination, and their desire for a state of their own?"

Noa said doggedly, "The Arabs have a state. Or, more exactly, they have several states."

Walid said, "Egypt is the Egyptians' state, Syria the Syrians', Yemen the Yemenis' — and in all these there is no solution for the Palestinians."

Maya, who had been listening attentively, sensed that Noa was receiving most of the sympathy. Noa sensed it, too. "Are you claiming," she continued, "that justice demands that to all the Arab states which exist one more state must be added, a Palestinian one? And what about justice for us? The Jews have no state, apart from Israel, of course. So must Israel apologize, 'Forgive me for being born, I'm sorry I gave you trouble,' and bow offstage?"

Walid was silent. "Go ahead, tell us," Noa urged him. "Tell us about your justice."

"It isn't my justice; it's just the claim you're putting in my mouth, without listening to what I have to say. I'm not denying Israel's right to exist. I've already said I believe in the right of national self-determination. If I'm a responsible citizen of a state, I obviously believe in my state's right to exist. But if the Palestinians have no state they see as their own, it makes no difference how many Arab states there are on the map."

"I think that we can deduce, from what you said earlier, that if the Egyptians were in control of Gaza, the Palestinians there would feel at home."

"Anyone living in his own home feels at home. But the refugee from Jaffa living in a camp in Gaza doesn't feel at home. And neither the Gaza dweller nor the refugee will feel good if he has to deal with a military administrator who speaks Hebrew."

"You speak Hebrew as well as I do, and you don't have to deal with a military administrator, but you're not happy."

"I'm not happy because you think that I should be grateful that I don't have to deal with a military administrator. I'm not happy because when I express a certain idea I'm thought a traitor, and you cast doubt on my right to Israeli citizenship, but if a Jew expresses the same idea, you don't voice any suspicion of his virtue as a citizen."

"That's not quite precise," said Noa. "I just demand that you be consistent. I demand intellectual integrity. If you define yourself as a Palestinian, that's your right. But then don't tell me that you're in favor of a Palestinian state, yet if such a state is set up you'll stay here."

"I'll stay here because I'm here not by anyone's grace. I didn't invade the place; I didn't receive anyone's hospitality. This is my home. I was born here, my parents were born here, my forefathers were born here. And, by the way, I didn't define myself as a Palestinian. Palestine isn't an Arab concept — nor a national or a cultural one. It doesn't appear in the Koran. It's a geographical concept, which names the population that lived in a specific area. That section of this population which was uprooted from the area, and has not found another place for itself and chooses to call itself Palestinian, continues to belong to this concept. I feel fully entitled to my Israeli citizenship, which means I've accepted Israel's right to sovereignty over the land I live in — so I can't call myself a Palestinian; I'm an Arab citizen of Israel. Being an Israeli citizen doesn't prevent me from demanding justice for the Palestinians. On the contrary, it's precisely because I'm living in my home, not uprooted from it, and because I'm a citizen of a democratic state where I'm allowed to express my opinion — it's precisely because of this that it's my duty to struggle for that justice."

"By placing explosive charges in the university cafeteria?" said Noa bitterly.

"Noa!" shouted Maya.

"I'm sorry," Noa said. "I didn't mean it personally."

Walid said, "It's all right. Sometimes it's important to forget about being polite, because you can be so polite that you don't say what you think, and you poison the atmosphere by what you don't say. No — not by explosive charges. I don't believe the end justifies the means. But I don't think that unjustifiable means disqualify a just end."

"You haven't answered my question. Why don't you go and be a Palestinian if you think their cause is so just?"

"I thought I had answered," said Walid. "I told you this is my home. I'm not a transient. I live here. If that's so hard for you to digest, let's take a different example. Why don't you object to American Jews calling themselves Zionists, and supporting the Zionist movement, even though they go on living in America?"

Miriam spoke. "I don't quite agree with Walid. I was born in Nazareth, but still I see myself as a Palestinian. I'm an Israeli citizen, but I didn't ask to be given that citizenship."

"You see," Noa charged triumphantly, "we can't have all these mental acrobatics. We keep coming back to the same point. Arabs against Jews. Whatever way it works out, they'll never be satisfied."

Dan, a very shy young composer who had kept silent so long that they forgot he was there, startled them with a blunt question. "What do you suggest? Should we throw them into the sea, or load them all into trucks?"

"Don't make me into a little Nazi," Noa snapped. "I'm no monster. I'm just a realist: I see what goes on and I don't want to delude myself. Don't get me wrong," she said, turning to Walid; "don't think I don't understand you. If I were in your place, I wouldn't speak so nicely, I wouldn't make such an effort to understand the justice of Zionism, of the Jews. I'd talk the way Miriam talks, and if I had the courage I wouldn't talk at all; I'd act, like Layla Khaled, the lady terrorist who hijacked a plane. That's the way it is. And we shouldn't deceive ourselves. Our rights are in conflict with your rights, and each side has to fight for its justice, to the end."

"Would that still be your view if you had any doubts about the outcome of such a war?" asked Walid.

"Listen," said Noa, "Maya told me that there are three kibbutzim settled partly on lands confiscated from your family. And she also told me proudly that your family's relations with those kibbutzim are good. Don't think that impresses me. I don't believe that your blood doesn't boil every time you see one of their tractors plowing that land. And if you have actually resigned yourself to that, then I'm afraid your son will one day demand the return of those lands. You say you're wholeheartedly a citizen, and I don't believe you." She paused for a moment and then added, "I'd like to believe you, but I can't."

Rafi said, "We're talking about Walid all the time, but the subject isn't Walid. We're talking about ourselves, about our own distress and discomfort with this situation. I'm sure that if a Palestinian state is established, everyone'll breathe easier. I just can't understand this fear of a state for the Palestinians. They'll be able to raise their heads a little higher. What's so frightening about that? Personally, I always feel better with someone who looks me in the eye."

"They won't be able to rest content with a state like the one you're talking about," said Noa. "They'll keep on eying us with envy. What future can there be for such a tiny, amputated state on the West Bank and in the Gaza Strip?"

"And what about Monaco and Luxembourg?" asked Walid.

"That isn't fair," said Dan. "You can't make that kind of comparison. First of all, those are states which live in peace with their neighbors."

"I thought we were talking about the possibility of a Palestinian state that would also live in peace with its neighbors," said Walid. "I'm sure it won't go to war with Syria or Egypt, and I find it hard to imagine it declaring war on Israel. If Israel wasn't afraid to stand up to all the Arab states put together, what's so frightening about a Palestinian state, which you yourselves admit will barely be able to stand on its own feet?"

"That's exactly it," said Noa. "It's because they won't be able to survive that they'll have to try to undermine us — out of resentment and envy."

"I really don't understand you," said Walid. "Do you think that when Israeli soldiers chase after high school students in Nablus there's less bitter resentment?"

By now they had completely forgotten the pantomime on the TV screen; they were all tensely attuned to each other.

Rafi said, "We keep going around in circles. You all know I disagree with Noa. But I also am not all that convinced that there's any viable solution of the Arab-Jewish conflict. Moreover, I'm not altogether certain that there's much hope for true harmony between Jews and Arabs within the State of Israel. I'm not too comfortable about this matter. Even if a Palestinian state is established, and even if you, Walid, don't find yourself in a conflict because of the struggle to establish such a state. I know you won't leave Israel — I agree with you that you don't have to leave, that it's your right to live here. But the question that really bothers me is this: Is there really a hope that you'll ever feel good about being a citizen of Israel? I haven't talked much about this with Maya. But I've read everything she's written about discrimination against Israeli Arabs. I agree that that's bad. But I don't know if there is a way to change the situation. I think that whatever happens, I'll always feel more at home here, in the Jewish state, than you do."

Dan said, "That's true. We have to admit that. I don't

mean to say that Arabs are second-class citizens, but of course they're not first-class citizens. Noa's right in that regard. If Walid wants justice for himself and his people, he should stand up against the State of Israel and its goals. Nothing will be able to make up for the fact that the kibbutzim are on his land. If every Arab in Israel decides to claim what is justly his, we'll all have to look for another place to live. And I don't think Maya is willing to go through that again — to be without a homeland, without a state. So with all due respect — and with all the sorrow it involves — we have to acknowledge that one nation's justice exists at the expense of another nation's justice. And we have to declare our priorities. As far as I'm concerned, my own welfare is more important than someone else's welfare. If I'm not willing to give up the existence of the Jewish state, I have to give up the luxury of being just to everyone else, and I have to accept the fact that Walid and Maya can be the best of friends on a personal level, but that on a national level they are in perpetual conflict. Do you agree with me?" he concluded, turning to Maya.

Maya noticed that Walid was tensely awaiting her reply, as if they had never discussed this matter together. "No, I don't agree. All this time, while you've been talking here, and they, in the Knesset, have been talking there, I've been asking myself on what grounds I don't agree with you. Because everything you've said is true. There's a conflict of interests and there's a national conflict and he's an Arab and I'm a Jew and I'm not willing to give up this state for him — not the state and not my right to live here. On the surface of it, we should be mortal enemies. But I've suddenly realized where the error lies. The flaw in thinking, in analysis. Both he and I begin from an acceptance of the existence of the State of Israel. And it's true that in this state, the way it is today, his citizenship is not equal in status to mine.

"But what you've omitted in this entire discussion is that all those reasons which affect his sense of equality are the very factors that distinguish between the state as it is and the state as I want it to be, the state as it was meant to be, the state envisioned by the Zionist movement, the state whose credo is reflected in the Declaration of Independence. When Noa doubts the possibility of Walid identifying himself with the State of Israel, it's not only because of her suspicions of Arabs, but because it really is difficult for Walid to identify with the state's national anthem, its Independence Day, its symbols of statehood — all of which aren't Israeli, but Jewish."

"I don't understand — do you prefer a non-Jewish state?" asked Noa.

"I prefer a state that on its Independence Day does not forget that it has half a million Arab citizens. I don't want the chief rabbi making a speech to the nation on Independence Day on all radio and TV networks. In this state there are fewer religiously observant Jews than there are religiously observant Muslims. So let the esteemed chief rabbi stay at home, or let's have blessings from the khadis and the bishops, too. This is not the state of the Jewish religion. This is the state of the Jewish nation.

"Our national revival has not occurred in a vacuum. Our historical territory became, in our absence, the homeland of another people. Now they still live here, but as subtenants. I think that all our discomfort about the Arab citizens stems from the fact that the State of Israel is actually a binational state, though it refuses to admit this. There's a national minority here that, even it it doesn't seek political self-determination, is entitled to freedom of self-expression. The wrongs that I, as a Jew, am fighting against in the State of Israel, the wrongs that prevent me from being proud of the quality of life in this state, are the very injustices that keep Walid from identifying himself wholly with the state. So, not only are we not like the heroes of a Greek tragedy, whose fate destined them to destroy each other, but the very contrary is the case: we definitely share a common goal. When Walid is able to declare himself an Israeli without anyone doubting his sincerity, then I'll be able to feel unreservedly proud of my state. Only then will Israel have realized its vision of itself."

Boaz, who had not spoken in a long time, said, "In principle, I agree with you. I too would like to see such a state. I'd feel better in it. But Israel isn't like any other state, and we have to face things the way they are. This is a state of refuge, a state that has to let in and absorb Jews who have nowhere to go. My parents are survivors of the Holocaust, and that's something I can't forget. Though I'm not religious, I can't deny the Jewishness of this state. If the state doesn't remain Jewish, the Jews won't have a home."

Maya rubbed her eyes with her fists, like a little girl trying to get the sleep out of her eyes. "Remind me to talk with you about the Holocaust some other time, Boaz. I think it's a subject best left aside when we're talking about the quality of life in Israel. No, that wasn't what I meant. We need to be careful, to avoid abuse of the Holocaust. We mustn't use it as a scarecrow we're being threatened with, or something we're threatening ourselves with whenever someone tries to break the ghetto walls we've built around the state. The Holocaust must not be allowed to become the supreme justification for the existence of the state. Nor used as license to do what is in itself unjust.

"If we can be threatened with another Holocaust here, in Israel, then the whole thing has been a failure. It isn't true that Israel is a state of refuge. Whom are we deceiving? Why do we go on deceiving ourselves? When the doors are open to Soviet Jews, do they relocate here? For every Russian immigrant Israel gets, two others prefer to seek their fortune in America. When Jews fled from South Africa and Rhodesia, did they rush here? Only a very few. They went to America, Australia, Canada. No, Israel isn't the chosen land for those with other alternatives. But if we want Jews to come here, this has to become the chosen land in the true sense of the phrase. And that's how I'd like Israel to be — attracting people, not compelling them. A land of challenge. But that's not feasible if what we set up here is a nature reserve of a medieval Jewish ghetto from Eastern Europe. After all, not only the physical existence of Jews as individuals is assured today in the Western world. Their religious freedom is safe too. The Lubavitcher Rabbi is happy living in New York."

Boaz asked, "Do you want him to enjoy himself in New York and not in Tel Aviv?"

Maya replied, "God forbid! I'll fight for his right to feel as at home here as he does in New York. But no more than that. I demand from him the same degree of respect toward me as he has toward the non-Jewish citizens of America. He doesn't try to dictate to the Americans how to live, and he respects their right to live in their own way. I demand the same; I don't want him trying to dictate to me how to live. Understand me, Boaz, Hitler stamped the word 'Jew' in the Jews' identity papers, and by this he intended the word to determine my fate and the way I could live. That because I'm a Jew I'm not free to determine how to live my life. I'm not willing to relinquish that right to anybody. Not even to a Jew. Yet that's precisely what the religious bloc is trying to do here in Israel. They've decided that my Jewishness deprives me of my freedom, and, not satisfied with that, they've also determined what this Jewishness is."

NOA: You mean that for the Jewish state to be an ideal state it has to stop being Jewish?

MAYA: No. It has to stop being Jewish according to the religious definition of Jewishness. My national definition is no less valid. I'd put it this way: the Jewish state will be faithful to Jewish values as I understand them if its Jewish citizens do not have a preferred status over its non-Jewish citizens.

RAFI: That sounds reasonable. I must mull that over — I might even find myself convinced. But if we start the count-down, back from your millennial vision, we'll get back to Walid's appropriated lands. How will we handle that issue?

MAYA: I can't answer that; you'll have to ask Walid.

Walid had been concentrating so hard that it took a few seconds for him to speak. "I'll answer you. Now that Maya's spoken, it's easier for me to answer. I wanted to respond earlier, but I didn't want you to suspect me of self-righteousness. The question you ask has been put to my father many times. My father is no lawyer or politician. He lives according to the dictates of his heart. Not only Jews have asked him the question. We, his sons, have asked him, too. Some of the lands that have been appropriated my father has never given up fighting for, refusing to this day to accept compensation for them. These are our lands, inside the village, which the administration wanted to lease to someone else from our own village. My father threatened that he'd shoot the man if he tried to take over this land.

"This was during the period of the military administration. That man complained to the military governor. My father was summoned, and the governor asked him if it was true that he had threatened to shoot this man. 'Yes,' said my father. The governor, who had grown up in one of the settlements in the area, said, 'Abu-Hana, you've lost a lot of land. Why are you being so stubborn this time?' And my father answered, 'Everyone has to give up a little to make it possible for Jews and Arabs to live in peace in this country. But when they appropriate my land to lease it to an Arab neighbor of mine, then they're denying me my right to any land whatsoever. They want to turn me into a serf on my own land. That isn't compromise anymore; that's plain robbery.'

"My father doesn't believe that reality is either black or white. There are people in this country who think that because you can't give Arabs everything due them, you can inflict whatever injustice you like on them. Now after Maya has showed the way to solve the basic dilemma I feel like someone wandering in the desert, almost at the end of his strength, who suddenly arrives at an oasis. Since Land Day, it's looked as if everyone has been conspiring, left and right, doves and hawks, to undermine our hope that some day we'll be able to say proudly 'I'm an Arab and I'm an Israeli.'

"I haven't spoken about this even with Maya. We've always discussed specific cases — a particular injustice, a Supreme Court hearing, a case of a student being injured — as if I were afraid that if we tackled the basics we'd reach a hopeless conclusion. But Maya's right. Anyone who thinks that to be a Jew means to be a Jew according to the religious code won't be able to agree with her. But, then, his own reasoning should lead him to a rejection of the State of Israel. He would have to wait for the Messiah, or decide that Rabbi Levinger or Rabbi Kahana is his prophet. Anyone who's frightened by the natural increase of the Arab population, or who talks about 'Judaizing' the Galilee, is still living in the ghetto.

"In my opinion, those people who identify Jewishness with the Jewish religion are leading Israel toward a future in which there will exist an autonomous Jewish religious ghetto within a Muslim empire or federation. If Noa wouldn't think that it's something to boast of that I have civil rights, and if people wouldn't need to take pride in an Arab having been given the post of a deputy minister in the sphere of public services, and when it seems acceptable for Israel to have an Arab foreign minister — the same way it's acceptable for Kissinger or Andrew Young to represent America — I think only then will Israel be able to break through her territorial boundaries and develop all her human resources.

"Enough, let's leave the purple phrases to the Knesset members. I'll rest content that Maya and I won't have to point rifles at each other."

Temple Israel
Minneapolis, Minnesota

IN MEMORY OF
SYLVIA ROSTON
FROM
J. D. ROSTON